THE PILLAR NEW TESTAMENT COMMENTARY

General Editor

D. A. CARSON

The Letters
of
JOHN

COLIN G. KRUSE

WILLIAM B. EERDMANS PUBLISHING COMPANY
GRAND RAPIDS, MICHIGAN / CAMBRIDGE, U.K.

© 2000 Colin G. Kruse
255 Jefferson Ave. S.E., Grand Rapids, Michigan 49503 /
P.O. Box 163, Cambridge CB3 9PU U.K.

First published 2000
in the United States of America by
Wm. B. Eerdmans Publishing Co.

and in the United Kingdom by
APOLLOS
38 De Montfort Street, Leicester, England LE1 7GP

Printed in the United States of America

09 08 07 06 05 04   7 6 5 4 3 2

Library of Congress Cataloging-in-Publication Data

Kruse, Colin G.
The letter of John/Colin G. Kruse.
p.   cm. — (The Pillar New Testament commentary)
Includes bibliographical references and index.
ISBN 0-8028-3728-X (alk. paper)
1. Bible. N.T. Epistles of John — Commentaries.
I. Title.   II. Series.

BS2805.3 .K78 2000
227′.94077 — dc21

00-020305

British Library Cataloguing in Publication Data

A catalogue record for this book is available from the British Library.
ISBN 0-85111-776-7

Affectionately dedicated to my grandchildren
and their wonderful parents

Contents

CONTENTS

CONTENTS

Series Preface

Commentaries have specific aims, and this series is no exception. Designed for serious pastors and teachers of the Bible, the Pillar commentaries seek above all to make clear the text of Scripture as we have it. The scholars writing these volumes interact with the most important, informed contemporary debate, but avoid getting mired in undue technical detail. Their ideal is a blend of rigorous exegesis and exposition, with an eye alert both to biblical theology and the contemporary relevance of the Bible, without confusing the commentary and the sermon.

The rationale for this approach is that the vision of "objective scholarship" (a vain chimera) may actually be profane. God stands over against us; we do not stand in judgment of him. When God speaks to us through his Word, those who profess to know him must respond in an appropriate way, and that is certainly different from a stance in which the scholar projects an image of autonomous distance. Yet this is no surreptitious appeal for uncontrolled subjectivity. The writers of this series aim for an evenhanded openness to the text that is the best kind of "objectivity" of all.

If the text is God's Word, it is appropriate that we respond with reverence, a certain fear, a holy joy, a questing obedience. These values should be reflected in the way Christians write. With these values in place, the Pillar commentaries will be warmly welcomed not only by pastors, teachers, and students, but by general readers as well.

*   *   *   *   *

This commentary on the Letters of John admirably meets the series' goals. In several discerning books, Colin Kruse has displayed an enviable ability to assimilate complex debates and evenhandedly evaluate them, always taking people back to the text. These skills are on display in this commentary. The Letters of John, superficially simple, are in reality a minefield of complexities that have generated difficult debates among Christians who have studied them. Dr. Kruse is sure-footed and reasoned, clear and remarkably concise without being simplistic or condescending. His use of both primary and secondary sources is always pertinent and restrained, and he never lets the reader lose sight of the text he is studying. I hope Dr. Kruse's commentary achieves the wide circulation it deserves.

D. A. CARSON

Author's Preface

Some years ago I wrote a manuscript for a small book on the major themes of the Letters of John. However, it never saw the light of day because the series for which it was intended was cancelled by the publishers. Some time afterwards I wrote to Wm. B. Eerdmans Jr. to ask whether he might be interested in publishing the material. In reply he said Eerdmans would be happy to look at the manuscript, but also asked whether I would like to write a full commentary on the Letters of John instead. So it was that I began work on this commentary, work to which I devoted most of my discretionary time over the last four years.

I am grateful to Eerdmans Publishing Company for including my work in their Pillar New Testament Commentary series. I am particularly grateful to Professor Don Carson, the General Editor of the series, for his encouragement and for his helpful and very prompt comments on the manuscript. I also want to thank Milton Essenburg for his specialised editorial work on the manuscript.

The Council of the Bible College of Victoria gave me study leave in the first half of 1996, during which time I began serious work on the preparation of the commentary. I want to express my gratitude to members of the Council for releasing me from my normal duties for that time. Several months of my study leave were spent in Tyndale House, Cambridge, where once again my wife, Rosemary, and I enjoyed the friendship and encouragement of the Warden, Bruce Winter, and his wife, Lyn Winter, as well as that of other researchers resident in Tyndale House at that time.

The writing of this commentary on the Letters of John has given me a greater understanding of the crisis of secession which formed the historical context of the letters. I have also been encouraged by the reassurance offered to the readers, and reminded of the importance of holding on to the gospel of Christ which has come down to us from the beginning. In addition, I have been challenged to implement in my own life the commandment of Christ that we love one another, the commandment which was handed down from the beginning alongside the gospel itself. My hope is that, by the grace of God, this commentary might help others to benefit in similar ways.

COLIN G. KRUSE

Abbreviations

PERIODICALS, REFERENCE WORKS, AND SERIALS

AB	Anchor Bible
AUSS	*Andrews University Seminary Studies*
BAG	W. Bauer, W. F. Arndt, and F. W. Gingrich, *Greek-English Lexicon of the New Testament*
Bib	*Biblica*
BibNotiz	*Biblische Notizen*
BJRL	*Bulletin of the John Rylands University Library of Manchester*
BSac	*Bibliotheca Sacra*
BT	*The Bible Translator*
BTB	*Biblical Theology Bulletin*
BZ	*Biblische Zeitschrift*
CBQ	*Catholic Biblical Quarterly*
EKKNT	Evangelisch-katholischer Kommentar zum Neuen Testament
EvQ	*Evangelical Quarterly*
ExpTim	*Expository Times*
Int	*Interpretation*
JBL	*Journal of Biblical Literature*
JSNT	*Journal for the Study of the New Testament*
JSNTSup	JSNT Supplement Series
JTS	*Journal of Theological Studies*
Jub.	*Jubilees*
MM	J. H. Moulton and G. Milligan, *The Vocabulary of the Greek Testament*
Neot	*Neotestamentica*

ABBREVIATIONS

NICNT	New International Commentary on the New Testament
NIV	New International Version
NotesTrans	*Notes on Translation*
NovT	*Novum Testamentum*
NRSV	New Revised Standard Version
NTS	*New Testament Studies*
OTP	J. H. Charlesworth (ed.), *Old Testament Pseudepigrapha*
RB	*Revue biblique*
REB	Revised English Bible
ResQ	*Restoration Quarterly*
RevExp	*Review and Expositor*
RevScRel	*Revue des sciences religieuses*
SBL	Society of Biblical Literature
SBLDS	SBL Dissertation Series
SJT	*Scottish Journal of Theology*
SNTSMS	Society for New Testament Studies Monograph Series
TU	Texte und Untersuchungen
TynBul	*Tyndale Bulletin*
TZ	*Theologische Zeitschrift*
WBC	Word Biblical Commentary
WTJ	*Westminster Theological Journal*
ZNW	*Zeitschrift für die neutestamentliche Wissenschaft*
ZTK	*Zeitschrift für Theologie und Kirche*

DEAD SEA SCROLLS, AND PSEUDEPIGRAPHICAL AND EARLY PATRISTIC WORKS

1QH	*Thanksgiving Hymns*
1QS	*Rule of the Community*
As. Mos.	*Assumption of Moses*
Did.	*Didache*
Hist. Eccl.	Eusebius, *Historia Ecclesiastica*
Ign. *Eph.*	Ignatius, *Letter to the Ephesians*
Ign. *Magn.*	Ignatius, *Letter to the Magnesians*
Ign. *Smyrn.*	Ignatius, *Letter to the Smyrnaeans*
Ign. *Trall.*	Ignatius, *Letter to the Trallians*
Pol. *Phil.*	Polycarp, *Letter to the Philippians*
T. Dan	*Testament of Dan*
T. Gad	*Testament of Gad*
T. Naph.	*Testament of Naphtali*

Bibliography

Bauckham, Richard, ed., *The Gospels for All Christians: Rethinking the Gospel Audiences*. Edinburgh: T & T Clark, 1998.

Bauer, Walter, *Orthodoxy and Heresy in Earliest Christianity*. Philadelphia: Fortress, 1971.

Baylis, Charles P., 'The Meaning of Walking "in the Darkness" (1 John 1:6)', *BSac* 149 (1992) 214-22.

Berger, Klaus, 'Die Bedeutung der wiederentdeckten Weisheitsschrift aus der kairoer Geniza für das neue Testament', *NTS* 36 (1990) 415-30.

Black, David Alan, 'An Overlooked Stylistic Argument in Favor of *panta* in 1 John 2:20', *Filologia Neotestamentaria* 5 (1992) 205-8.

Bogart, John, *Orthodox and Heretical Perfectionism in the Johannine Community as Evident in the First Epistle of John*. SBLDS 33, Missoula, MT: Scholars Press, 1977.

Boismard, M.-E., 'Une liturgie baptismale dans la prima Petri', *RB* 63 (1956) 182-208.

Bonsack, Bernhard, 'Der Presbyteros des dritten Briefs und der geliebte Jünger des Evangeliums nach Johannes', *ZNW* 79 (1988) 45-62.

Breck, John, 'The Function of *PAS* in 1 John 2:20', *St. Vladimir's Theological Quarterly* 35 (1991) 187-206.

Brown, Raymond E., *The Community of the Beloved Disciple*. New York: Paulist, 1979.

Brown, Raymond E., *The Epistles of John*. AB 30, New York: Doubleday, 1982.

Bruns, J. Edgar, 'A Note on John 16 33 and I John 2 13-14', *JBL* 86 (1967) 451-53.

Bultmann, Rudolf, *The Johannine Epistles*. Hermeneia, Philadelphia: Fortress, 1973.

Burge, Gary M., *The Anointed Community: The Holy Spirit in the Johannine Tradition*. Grand Rapids: Eerdmans, 1987.

xvii

BIBLIOGRAPHY

Burge, Gary M., *The Letters of John*. NIV Application Commentary, Grand Rapids: Zondervan, 1996.

Clavier, Henri, 'Notes sur un mot-clef du Johannisme et de las soteriologie biblique: *hilasmos*', *NovT* 10 (1968) 287-304.

Coetzee, J. C., 'The Holy Spirit in 1 John', *Neot* 13 (1979) 43-67.

Court, J. M., 'Blessed Assurance?' *JTS* 33 (1982) 508-17.

De Boer, Martinus C., 'The Death of Jesus Christ and His Coming in the Flesh (1 John 4:2)', *NovT* 33 (1991) 326-46.

De Boer, Martinus C., 'Jesus the Baptizer: 1 John 5:5-8 and the Gospel of John', *JBL* 107 (1988) 87-106.

De la Potterie, Ignace, 'Anointing of the Christian by Faith', in Ignace de la Potterie and Stanislaus Lyonnet, *The Christian Lives by the Spirit*. New York: Alba House, 1971, 79-143.

De la Potterie, Ignace, '"Sin Is Iniquity" (I Jn 3, 4)', in Ignace de la Potterie and Stanislaus Lyonnet, *The Christian Lives by the Spirit*. New York: Alba House, 1971, 36-55.

De la Potterie, Ignace, 'The Truth in Saint John', in *The Interpretation of John*, ed. John Ashton. Philadelphia/London: Fortress/SPCK, 1986, 53-66.

Deissmann, Adolph, *Light from the Ancient East: The New Testament Illustrated by Recently Discovered Texts of the Graeco-Roman World*. London: Hodder and Stoughton, 1927.

Dodd, C. H., 'HILASKESTHAI, Its Cognates, Derivatives, and Synonyms, in the Septuagint', *JTS* 32 (1931) 82-95.

Dodd, C. H., *The Johannine Epistles*. London: Hodder and Stoughton, 1946.

Du Preez, J., '"Sperma autou" in 1 John 3:9', *Neot* 9 (1975) 105-10.

Du Toit, B. A., 'The Role and Meaning of Statements of "Certainty" in the Structural Composition of 1 John', *Neot* 13 (1979) 84-100.

Edwards, M. J., 'Martyrdom and the *First Epistle* of John', *NovT* 31 (1989) 164-71.

Ehrman, Bart E., '1 Joh 4 3 and the Orthodox Corruption of Scripture', *ZNW* 79 (1988) 221-43.

Grayston, Kenneth, '"Logos" in 1 Jn1¹', *ExpTim* 86 (1974-75) 279.

Grayston, Kenneth, 'The Meaning of *Paraklētos*', *JSNT* 13 (1981) 67-82.

Griffith, Terry, 'A Non-Polemical Reading of 1 John: Sin, Christology and the Limits of Johannine Christianity', *TynBul* 49 (1998) 253-76.

Hill, David, *Greek Words and Hebrew Meanings: Studies in the Semantics of Soteriological Terms*. Cambridge: Cambridge University Press, 1967.

Hills, Julian, '"Little children, keep yourselves from idols": 1 John 5:21 Reconsidered', *CBQ* 51 (1989) 285-310.

Hoffman, Thomas A., '1 John and the Qumran Scrolls', *BTB* 8 (1978) 117-25.

Horvath, Tibor, '3 Jn 11b: An Early Ecumenical Creed?', *ExpTim* 85 (1973-74) 339-40.

Inman, Kerry, 'Distinctive Johannine Vocabulary and the Interpretation of I John 3:9', *WTJ* 40 (1977-78) 136-44.

Käsemann, Ernst, 'Ketzer und Zeuge. Zum johanneischen Verfasserproblem', *ZTK* 48 (1951) 292-311.

Klauck, Hans-Josef, 'Bekenntnis zu Jesus und Zeugnis Gottes: Die christologische Linienführung im Ersten Johannesbrief', in *Anfänge der Christologie. Festschrift für Ferdinand Hahn zum 65. Geburtstag*, ed. Cilliers Breytenbach and Henning Paulsen. Göttingen: Vandenhoeck & Ruprecht, 1991, 293-306.

Klauck, Hans-Josef, *Der erste Johannesbrief*. EKKNT, Zürich & Braunschweig: Benziger, 1991.

Klauck, Hans-Josef, 'Internal Opponents: The Treatment of the Secessionists in the First Epistle of John', *Concilium* 200 (1988) 55-65.

Klauck, Hans-Josef, '*Kyria ekklēsia* in Bauers Wörterbuch und die Exegese des zweiten Johannesbriefes', *ZNW* 81 (1990) 135-38.

Klauck, Hans-Josef, 'Zur rhetorischen Analyse der Johannesbriefe', *ZNW* 81 (1990) 205-24.

Kotzé, P. P. A., 'The Meaning of 1 John 3:9 with Reference to 1 John 1:8 and 10', *Neot* 13 (1979) 68-83.

Kubo, Sakae, 'I John 3:9: Absolute or Habitual', *AUSS* 7 (1969) 47-56.

Kügler, Joachim, 'Die Belehrung der Unbelehrbaren: Zur Funktion des Traditionsarguments in 1 Joh', *BZ* n.s. 32 (1988) 249-54.

Kügler, Joachim, '"Wenn das Herz uns auch verurteilt . . .". Ägyptische Anthropologie in 1 Joh 3,19-21?', *BibNotiz* 66 (1993) 10-14.

Law, Robert, *The Tests of Life: A Study of the First Epistle of St. John*. Grand Rapids: Baker, 1968 (repr. from 3rd ed. Edinburgh: T. & T. Clark, 1913).

Lazure, Noël, 'La convoitise de la chair en I Jean, II,16', *RB* 76 (1969) 161-205.

Lieu, J. M., 'Blindness in the Johannine Tradition', *NTS* 34 (1988) 83-95.

Lieu, Judith, *The Second and Third Epistles of John: History and Background*. Edinburgh: T. & T. Clark, 1986.

Lieu, Judith, *The Theology of the Johannine Epistles*. Cambridge: Cambridge University Press, 1991.

Lieu, Judith M., 'What Was from the Beginning: Scripture and Tradition in the Johannine Epistles', *NTS* 39 (1993) 458-77.

Lyonnet, Stanislaus, 'The Notion of Sin in the Johannine Writings', in Stanislaus Lyonnet and Léopold Sabourin, *Sin, Redemption, and Sacrifice: A Biblical and Patristic Study*. Rome: Biblical Institute Press, 1970, 38-45.

Lyonnet, Stanislaus, 'The Terminology of "Expiation" in the New Testament', in Stanislaus Lyonnet and Léopold Sabourin, *Sin, Redemption, and Sacrifice: A Biblical and Patristic Study*. Rome: Biblical Institute Press, 1970, 147-66.

Malatesta, Edward, '*Tēn agapēn en [sic] echei ho theos en hēmin*: A Note on

1 John 4:16a', in *The New Testament Age: Essays in Honor of Bo Reicke*, vol. 2, ed. William C. Weinrich. Macon, GA: Mercer University Press, 1984, 301-11.

Malherbe, Abraham J., 'Hospitality and Inhospitality in the Church', in *Social Aspects of the Early Church*. 2nd enl. ed., Philadelphia: Fortress, 1983, 92-112.

Malina, Bruce J., 'The Received View and What It Cannot Do: III John and Hospitality', *Semeia* 35 (1986) 171-94.

Manns, Frédéric, '"le péché, c'est Bélial" 1 Jn: 3,4 a la lumière du Judaïsme', *RevScRel* 62 (1988) 1-9.

Marshall, I. Howard, *The Epistles of John*. NICNT, Grand Rapids: Eerdmans, 1978.

Metzger, Bruce M., *A Textual Commentary on the Greek New Testament*. 2nd ed., Stuttgart: German Bible Society, 1994.

Meye Thompson, Marianne, 'Intercession in the Johannine Community: 1 John 5.16 in the Context of the Gospel and Epistles of John', in *Worship, Theology and Ministry in the Early Church: Essays in Honor of Ralph P. Martin*, ed. Michael J. Wilkins and Terence Paige. JSNTSup 87, Sheffield: Sheffield Academic Press, 1992, 225-45.

Meye Thompson, Marianne, *1-3 John*. Downers Grove: InterVarsity Press, 1992.

Michl, Johann, 'Der Geist als Garant des rechten Glaubens', in *Vom Wort des Lebens*, Festschrift für Max Meinertz, ed. Nikolaus Adler. Münster: Aschendorffsche Verlagsbuchhandlung, 1951, 142-51.

Minear, Paul S. 'The Idea of Incarnation in First John', *Int* 24 (1970) 291-302.

Mitchell, Margaret M., '"Diotrephes does not receive us": The Lexicographical and Social Context of 3 John 9-10', *JBL* 117 (1998) 299-320.

Morris, Leon, *The Apostolic Preaching of the Cross*. 3rd ed., London: Tyndale, 1965.

Noack, B., 'On I John II.12-14', *NTS* 6 (1959-60) 236-241.

Olssen, Birger, 'Structural Analyses in Handbooks for Translators', *BT* 37 (1986) 117-27.

Padilla, C. René, 'A Reflection on 1 John 3:16-18', *Transformation* 6 (1989) 15-18.

Painter, John, *John: Witness and Theologian*. London: SPCK, 1975.

Painter, John, 'The "Opponents" in 1 John', *NTS* 32 (1986) 48-71.

Perkins, Pheme, '*Koinōnia* in 1 John 1:3-7: The Social Context of Division in the Johannine Letters', *CBQ* 45 (1983) 631-41.

Persson, Andrew, 'Some Exegetical Problems in 1 John', *NotesTrans* 4 (1990) 18-26.

Porter, Stanley E., *Idioms of the Greek New Testament*. 2nd ed., Sheffield: Sheffield Academic Press, 1995.

Price, Robert M., 'The Sitz-im-Leben of Third John: A New Reconstruction', *EvQ* 61 (1989) 109-19.

Rese, Martin, 'Das Gebot der Bruderliebe in den Johannesbriefen', *TZ* 41 (1985) 44-58.

Schnackenburg, Rudolf, *The Johannine Epistles*. Tunbridge Wells, Kent: Burns & Oates, 1992.

Scholer, David M., '1 John 4:7-21', *RevExp* 87 (1990) 309-14.

Scholer, David M., 'Sins Within and Sins Without: An Interpretation of 1 John 5:16-17', in *Current Issues in Biblical and Patristic Interpretation: Studies in Honor of Merrill C. Tenney Presented by His Former Students*, ed. Gerald F. Hawthorne. Grand Rapids: Eerdmans, 1975, 230-46.

Schweizer, Eduard, 'Zum religionsgeschichtlichen Hintergrund der "Sendungsformel" Gal 4 4f. Rm 8 3f. Joh 3 16f. I John 4 9', *ZNW* 57 (1966) 199-210.

Smalley, Stephen S., *1, 2, 3 John*. WBC 51, Waco, TX: Word, 1984.

Spicq, C., 'Notes d'exégèse johannique: la charité est amour manifeste', *RB* 65 (1958) 358-70.

Spicq, C., 'La place ou le rôle des jeunes dans certaines communautés néotestamentaires', *RB* 76 (1969) 509-27.

Sproston, Wendy E., 'Witness to What Was *ap' archēs:* 1 John's Contribution to Our Knowledge of Tradition in the Fourth Gospel', *JSNT* 48 (1992) 43-65.

Stegemann, Ekkehard, '"Kindlein, hütet vor den Götterbildern!" Erwägungen zum Schluss des 1. Johannesbriefes', *TZ* 41 (1985) 284-94.

Storm, Melvin R., 'Diotrephes: A Study of Rivalry in the Apostolic Church', *ResQ* 35 (1993) 193-202.

Stowers, Stanley K., *Letter Writing in Greco-Roman Antiquity*. Philadelphia: Westminster, 1986.

Strecker, Georg, 'Die Anfänge der johanneischen Schule', *NTS* 32 (1986) 31-47.

Strecker, Georg, *The Johannine Letters*. Hermeneia, Philadelphia: Fortress, 1996.

Strecker, Georg, 'Der religionsgeschichtlichen Hintergrund von 1 Joh 2,18.22; 4,3 und 2 Joh 7', in *Text and Testimony: Essays on New Testament and Apocryphal Literature in Honour of A. F. J. Klijn*, ed. T. Baarda, A. Hilhorst, G. P. Luttikhuizen, and A. S. van der Woude. Kampen: J. H. Kok, 1988, 247-54.

Sugit, J. N., 'I John 5:21: ΤΕΚΝΙΑ, ΦΥΛΑΞΑΤΕ ΕΑΥΤΑ ΑΠΟ ΤΩΝ ΕΙΔΩΛΩΝ', *JTS* 36 (1985) 386-90.

Swadling, Harry C., 'Sin and Sinlessness in I John', *SJT* 35 (1982) 205-11.

Synge, F. C., '1 John 3,2', *JTS* 3 (1952) 79.

Taeger, Jens-W., 'Der konservative Rebell: Zum Widerstand des Diotrephes gegen den Presbyter', *ZNW* 78 (1987) 267-87.

BIBLIOGRAPHY

Thornton, T. C. G., 'Propitiation or Expiation?' *ExpTim* 80 (1968-69) 53-55.
Trites, Allison A., *The New Testament Concept of Witness*. SNTSMS 31, Cambridge: Cambridge University Press, 1977.
Van der Horst, P. W., 'A Wordplay in 1 Joh 4 12?' *ZNW* 63 (1972) 280-82.
Van Unnik, W. C., 'The Christian's Freedom of Speech in the New Testament', *BJRL* 44 (1961-62) 466-88.
Venetz, Hermann-Josef, '"Durch Wasser und Blut gekommen": Exegetische Überlegungen zu 1 Joh 5,6', in *Die Mitte des Neuen Testaments: Einheit und vielfalt neutestamentlicher Theologie. Festschrift für Eduard Schweizer zum siebsigsten Geburtstag*, ed. Ulrich Luz and Hans Weder. Göttingen: Vandenhoeck & Ruprecht, 1983, 345-61.
Von Wahlde, Urban C., 'The Theological Foundation of the Presbyter's Argument in 2 Jn (2 Jn 4-6)', *ZNW* 76 (1985) 209-24.
Vouga, François, 'The Johannine School: A Gnostic Tradition in Primitive Christianity?' *Bib* 69 (1988) 371-85.
Ward, Tim, 'Sin "Not unto Death" and Sin "unto Death" in 1 John 5:16', *Churchman* 109 (1995) 226-37.
Watson, Duane F., 'Amplification Techniques in 1 John: The Interaction of Rhetorical Style and Invention', *JSNT* 51 (1993) 99-123.
Watson, Duane F., '1 John 2.12-14 as *Distributio, Conduplicatio,* and *Expolitio*: A Rhetorical Understanding', *JSNT* 35 (1989) 97-110.
Watson, Duane F., 'A Rhetorical Analysis of 2 John according to Greco-Roman Convention', *NTS* 35 (1989) 104-30.
Watson, Duane F., 'A Rhetorical Analysis of 3 John: A Study in Epistolary Rhetoric,' *CBQ* 51 (1989) 479-501.
Weir, J. Emmette, 'The Identity of the Logos in the First Epistle of John', *ExpTim* 86 (1974-75) 118-20.
Wendland, E. R., 'What Is Truth? Semantic Density and the Language of the Johannine Epistles (with Special Reference to 2 John)', *Neot* 24 (1990) 301-33.
Westcott, Brooke Foss, *The Epistles of St John*. Cambridge and London: Macmillan, 1886.
Whitacre, Rodney A., *Johannine Polemic: The Role of Tradition and Theology*. SBLDS 67, Chico, CA: Scholars Press, 1982.
Witherington, Ben III, 'The Waters of Birth: John 3.5 and 1 John 5.6-8', *NTS* 35 (1989) 155-60.
Yates, Roy, 'The Antichrist', *EvQ* 46 (1974) 42-50.
Zahn, Theodore, *Introduction to the New Testament*, 3 vols. Repr., Minneapolis, MN: Klock & Klock, 1953.

Introduction

INTRODUCTORY MATTERS RELATED TO 1, 2, AND 3 JOHN

The Letters of John provide readers with a cameo of life in one part of the early church. They represent an unhappy time in the life of the Christian communities involved; a time of dispute between believers involving both theological and behavioural concerns. The letters reflect only one side of this dispute, but the side which represented the truth of the matter as far as the later church was concerned.

The three letters appear to be interrelated, all dealing with one aspect or another of this dispute, and a suggested scenario depicting its progress is provided below. In the response these letters make to the dispute they also provide significant input on a number of key theological themes. These include such matters as the bases of Christian assurance, the role of the Spirit in the Christian community, Christian perfection, the meaning of *koinōnia,* the atonement, and Christology. These letters will repay readers for their careful study with a greater appreciation of these matters.

A Scenario

Anyone seeking to make sense of the Letters of John really needs to have a working hypothesis concerning the events which lie behind them. Such a hypothesis involves historical reconstruction, and this in turn will have to be based on certain assumptions about literary matters. However, to some extent the literary assumptions depend on decisions made in the historical reconstruction. The interpreter has no alternative but to work in a circle, while continually checking historical decisions against the literary assumptions and vice versa. What is offered below is one reconstruction of events, which depends on a number of literary assumptions and is only as good as they are.

The following scenario proceeds on the assumption that there is a very close relationship between the Fourth Gospel and the three letters of John. If they are not all written by the same person, then the person(s) who wrote the letters had been deeply immersed in the thought of the Gospel and used its language. The following reconstruction of events assumes that an early form of the Fourth Gospel had been completed before the writing of the letters, and that the Beloved Disciple, an eyewitness of most of the events described in the Gospel, was responsible for producing that early form. The Gospel deals primarily with the ministry of Jesus and reflects the conflict between Jesus and some of his Jewish contemporaries. At a secondary level, the way the story of Jesus is written may reflect something of the experience of the Christian community of which the Beloved Disciple was a member when he wrote his Gospel. This community consisted of a number of churches, probably located in and around Ephesus in the Roman province of Asia.

Sometime after the writing of this early form of the Gospel, difficulties arose within this community. Some of the members had taken on board certain beliefs about the person and work of Christ that were unacceptable to the author[1] of the letters and those associated with him. These new beliefs involved a denial that Jesus was the Christ, the Son of God, come in the flesh (1 John 4:2-3), and that his death was necessary for the forgiveness of sins (1 John 5:6-7). A sharp disagreement arose which resulted in the secession of those who embraced these new views (1 John 2:19).

The secessionists (as we shall call them hereafter) were not content to keep their new beliefs to themselves. Instead they organised a group of itinerant preachers who circulated among the churches and propagated their beliefs with a view to winning people over to their understanding of things (1 John 2:26; 4:1-3; 2 John 7). This created confusion among the believers who remained loyal to the gospel as it had been proclaimed at the beginning, the gospel that had come down from the eyewitnesses. As a result of the confusion, these believers began to question whether they really knew God, whether they really were experiencing eternal life, and

---

1. The singular expression 'author' is used here without prejudging the question whether all three letters were written by the same person. This is done to avoid what would otherwise be rather cumbersome expressions. The question of the authorship of the letters is discussed below.

2

whether they were really in the truth. The author of 1 John wrote to bolster the assurance of such people by providing them with criteria they could use to evaluate the claims being made by the secessionists and with which they could reassure themselves that they were in the truth (1 John 1:5–2:2; 2:3-11; 3:7-10, 14-15; 4:4-6, 7-8, 13-15; 5:13, 18-20). This letter appears to have been sent as a circular letter to the churches affected by the mission of the secessionists.

As a follow-up to this circular letter two other letters were written. The first, 2 John, was sent to one of the churches involved (to the 'chosen lady and her children') to warn the members about the itinerant teachers who represented the secessionists and were peddling their new and heretical teaching, trying to deceive people (2 John 7-8). The elder, who wrote 2 John, urged his readers not to aid and abet these teachers by providing them with hospitality. To do so would be to participate in their 'wicked work' (2 John 10-11).

However, it was not just those who represented the secessionist teaching who were itinerating among these churches. There were also people of good standing who had gone from the elder's church 'for the sake of the Name' (3 John 7). These people needed to receive hospitality in Christian homes as they travelled about. The second of the follow-up letters, 3 John, was written by the elder to an individual named Gaius. He was commended for providing hospitality to travelling preachers of good standing (3 John 5-6), and informed of the actions of another person, named Diotrephes, who lived in the same town but refused to provide this hospitality, and who was at loggerheads with the elder (3 John 9-10). It is not absolutely clear whether his refusal was based on doctrinal reasons (e.g., he agreed with the secessionists against the elder) or personal conflict (e.g., a rejection of the elder's authority).

Sometime during or after the writing of the Letters of John, the Beloved Disciple died (John 21:23). It was then that later editors revised and added to the Fourth Gospel, and issued it in the form we know it today, complete with assurances about the trustworthiness of the testimony of the Beloved Disciple (John 19:35; 21:24).

We do not know what happened to the secessionist movement — whether it developed into the sort of second-century Gnosticism we know through the writings of Irenaeus, or whether it simply died out. We do know that the position adopted by the writer(s) of the Letters of John won the day insofar as it was these letters which found their way into the NT canon.

This scenario involves a number of assumptions about the relationship between the Fourth Gospel and the Letters of John, and about the interrelationship between the three letters of John themselves. We will discuss these matters below, but before we do so we need to make some comments about the Johannine community.

The Johannine Community

When we study any book of the NT, it is helpful to be able to place it somewhere along the trajectory of the development of early Christianity. Early Christianity was anything but a homogeneous entity. It developed in different ways in different places under the influence and guidance of different personalities. The most obvious examples of this diversity is to be found in the distinctions between the Jerusalem/ Judean churches and the churches created through the Pauline mission. Scholars talk about a third major stream within early Christianity, namely Johannine Christianity. The existence and characteristics of this stream are deduced from those writings within the NT that are associated with it, namely the Fourth Gospel, the three letters of John, and (less clearly) Revelation.

When we read the Letters of John, it becomes clear that a number of loosely related churches were operating in fellowship with the author(s) of these letters. 1 John itself appears to be a circular letter (because it lacks any specific address or greetings) sent to a number of churches to warn them of the danger represented by the secessionists. 2 John is addressed to 'the chosen lady and her children', almost certainly a designation for a church and its members, a church different from the one of which the elder who wrote this letter was a member. 3 John is addressed to Gaius, who is informed that the elder wrote to the church (in the town where Gaius lived) but that a certain Diotrephes, a leading figure in that church, had rejected the elder's requests. From this information we may deduce that there were a number of churches, which were in communication with one another. We may, then, justifiably speak of a Johannine community, by which we mean a group of churches in fellowship with the author(s) of 1, 2, and 3 John. However, in recent times the expression 'the Johannine community' has come to be imbued with much more clearly defined and particular connotations.

Based on the contents of the three letters, the way the readers are addressed, the language used, and the concepts involved, many scholars have concluded that these churches shared a common adherence to the sort of Christianity which is reflected in the Fourth Gospel. Such churches are believed to make up what is referred to as the Johannine community. This general approach has given rise to some highly sophisticated theories, including the idea that the Fourth Gospel reflects the ex-

4

periences of this community, and the widely held view that the Fourth Gospel was written specifically for this community.

However, the assumptions upon which these theories rest have been questioned in recent times, in particular the assumption that Gospels were written for particular communities. The Gospels, it is argued, were not written with particular communities in mind, especially not the community of which their authors were members, but were intended for a much wider readership.[2] This is not the place to go into a detailed discussion of these things. Suffice it to say that the case made against the view that the Gospels were written for specific communities is quite compelling. It remains to be seen whether this challenge to the scholarly consensus wins the day. In the meantime it is unwise simply to assume that the Fourth Gospel was written just for the Johannine community, or that the group of churches to which 1, 2, and 3 John were written formed a 'hermetically sealed' group quite distinct from other early Christian communities. In the commentary which follows, where reference is made to the Johannine community, the author's community, or the like, what is meant is simply that group of loosely related churches operating in fellowship with one another and with the author(s) of 1, 2, and 3 John.

1, 2, and 3 John and the Fourth Gospel

Anyone reading the Gospel of John and the Letters of John can hardly help recognising the similarities of language and concepts that exist between them. When one seeks parallels in the NT to words and ideas found in the letters, these are nearly always found in the Gospel. There are many examples of this,[3] but most striking of all are the similarities between the prologue of the Fourth Gospel and the opening section of 1 John. Also, the purpose of both the Fourth Gospel and 1 John has to do with faith in Christ and receiving eternal life (John 20:31/1 John 5:13).

---

2. See Richard Bauckham, ed., *The Gospels for All Christians: Rethinking the Gospel Audiences* (Edinburgh: T & T Clark, 1998).

3. Compare, e.g., the following: the word of life from the beginning — 1 John 1:1-2/John 1:1-4; the light — 1 John 1:5-7/John 1:6-9; the Paraclete — 1 John 2:1/John 14:16, 26; 15:26; 16:7; the new commandment — 1 John 2:7/John 13:34; the love of fellow believers and the world's hatred — 1 John 3:13/John 15:9-25; passing from death to life — 1 John 3:14/John 5:24; Jesus lays down his life for us — 1 John 3:16/John 10:11, 15, 17, 18; 15:12-14; God's command to believe in Jesus Christ — 1 John 3:23/John 6:29; no one has ever seen God — 1 John 4:12/John 1:18; the 'Saviour of the world' — 1 John 4:14/John 4:42; being born of God — 1 John 5:1/John 1:12-13; water and blood — 1 John 5:6/John 19:34; eternal life — 1 John 5:13/John 3:16; the love commandment — 2 John 5-6/John 13:34.

These many similarities have led several recent scholars to conclude that the one who wrote the Gospel in its original form is also responsible for the writing of 1 John, and perhaps 2 John and 3 John,[4] though some scholars deny this,[5] and others leave the question open.[6]

Even though there is a close relationship between the Gospel and the letters in respect to language and ideas, their historical backgrounds differ substantially. As noted above, the background to the Gospel is the conflict between Jesus and some of his unbelieving Jewish contemporaries (recorded possibly for its significance for Christians who now found themselves in conflict with members of local synagogues). The background to the letters, however, is a conflict in the Christian community, a conflict between continuing members of the author's community and the secessionists. It is not surprising, then, that when the language and concepts of the Fourth Gospel are taken up and used in the letters they are given a different spin in order to serve the purposes of the letters. One notable example of this is the way in which the word *paraklētos* is used. In the NT it is found only in the Gospel and Letters of John, but it is applied differently in each case. In the Gospel *paraklētos* denotes the Holy Spirit about whom Jesus gives teaching to prepare his disciples for their encounter with a hostile world after his departure. The *paraklētos* replaces Jesus and has a role vis-à-vis the world (which he convinces of sin, righteousness, and judgement) in the one case, and vis-à-vis believers (whom he guides and teaches) in the other. In the letters *paraklētos* denotes, not the Holy Spirit, but Jesus himself.[7] In the letters the *paraklētos* has a role, not vis-à-vis the world and believers, but vis-à-vis the Father on behalf of believers (if believers sin, he acts as their sponsor/advocate [*paraklētos*] in the presence of the Father). The author introduces this teaching in order to distinguish his views about sin from those of the secessionists.

---

4. So, e.g., Brooke Foss Westcott, *The Epistles of St John* (Cambridge and London: Macmillan, 1886) xxx-xxxii, xliii-xlvi; I. Howard Marshall, *The Epistles of John* (NICNT, Grand Rapids: Eerdmans, 1978) 42-48; and Gary M. Burge, *The Letters of John* (NIV Application Commentary, Grand Rapids: Zondervan, 1996) 38-40.

5. So, e.g., Raymond E. Brown, *The Epistles of John* (AB 30, New York: Doubleday, 1982) 30; Rudolf Bultmann, *The Johannine Epistles* (Hermeneia, Philadelphia: Fortress, 1973) 1; Rudolf Schnackenburg, *The Johannine Epistles* (Tunbridge Wells, Kent: Burns & Oates, 1992) 40-41.

6. So, e.g., Burge, *The Letters of John*, 38-40; Marianne Meye Thompson, *1-3 John* (Downers Grove: InterVarsity Press, 1992) 20-21.

7. I am grateful to Don Carson, who pointed out to me that the Fourth Gospel includes a hint that Jesus himself is a *paraklētos*, insofar as it describes the Holy Spirit as 'another *paraklētos*'. Therefore, those who had read the Fourth Gospel would not be surprised to find Jesus described as *paraklētos* in 1 John 2:1.

What all this means for interpreters of the letters is that they find themselves referring again and again to the Gospel to seek elucidation concerning words and ideas found in the letters; but when they do so they must be careful, for often there is not a one-to-one equivalence of usage. Nevertheless, the Gospel remains a most important source of comparison for the exegesis of the letters.

The Interrelationship of 1, 2, and 3 John

There are many similarities between 1 John and 2 John. First, in 1 John the author deals with the same historical situation as that reflected in 2 John. He speaks of those who 'went out from us' and do not acknowledge 'Jesus Christ as coming in the flesh' (1 John 2:19, 22-23; cf. 2 John 7). Second, he brands these false teachers as antichrists, as does the elder in 2 John (1 John 2:18, 22; cf. 2 John 7). Third, he stresses the great importance of the love command, which was received at the beginning along with the gospel, just as the elder does in 2 John (1 John 3:11, 23; 4:7, 21; 5:1-4a; cf. 2 John 4-6). Fourth, the author of 1 John, like the elder, finds his joy in seeing his children walking in the truth of the gospel (1 John 1:3-4; cf. 2 John 4).

There are also striking similarities of language, content, and style between 2 John and 3 John, and these indicate that the same elder was responsible for writing both letters: in both of them he expresses joy that the 'children' are 'walking in the truth' (2 John 4; 3 John 4); in both the addressees (the 'chosen lady' and Gaius respectively) are described as those whom the elder loves 'in the truth' (2 John 1; 3 John 1); and both conclude with virtually identical statements (2 John 12: 'I have much to write to you, but I do not want to use paper and ink. Instead, I hope to visit you and talk with you face to face'; 3 John 13-14a: 'I have much to write you, but I do not want to do so with pen and ink. I hope to see you soon, and we will talk face to face').

Because of the close connections between 1 John and 2 John, and between 2 John and 3 John, there is a prima facie case for saying that the three letters were written by the same person, at about the same time, and in response to various aspects of the same crisis. But there are also a number of dissimilarities between the letters, which have caused some scholars to conclude that different authors were responsible for the writing of the first and last two letters. It is possible, however, to account for these in terms of variations in style adopted by the same author in different letters. The working hypothesis adopted in this commentary is that the three letters were written by the same author. He did not append his name to 1 John, and called himself simply the elder in 2 and 3 John.[8] In this commentary the writer of 1 John will be denoted simply as 'the author', and the writer of 2 John and 3 John will be referred to as 'the elder'. This is in line with the desire for anonymity on the part of the author of 1 John, and the chosen self-designation of the author in 2 John and 3 John.

It is very difficult, perhaps even impossible, to determine the order of writing of the three letters. As indicated in the scenario above, the hypothesis adopted in this commentary is that 1 John was written first as a circular letter to address theological issues that were causing problems in various local churches, and was followed by the writing of 2 John and 3 John to one of these churches and an individual respectively.

1, 2, and 3 John and the NT Canon

Brown provides a full discussion of this matter,[9] which does not need repeating here; only a brief summary is necessary. He points out that no unambiguous citations from the letters of John are found before A.D. 175. Brown lists the possible echoes from the early period, and concludes:

> By the mid-second century ideas, themes, and even slogans of the Johannine Epistles (or, at least, of I John) were being cited in other Christian works. But no one of the proposed similarities consists of a verbatim citation, so that it is still very difficult to be certain that any of the mentioned authors had the text of a Johannine Epistle before him. Nevertheless, the likelihood that I John was available to Polycarp is increased by the information of Eusebius (*Hist.* 3.39.17) that Papias, who was a contemporary of Polycarp (3.36.1-2), "made use of testimonies from the First Epistle of John."[10]

It is only late in the second century that undeniable citations from the letters of John appear in Christian writings. The earliest of these are found in the works of Irenaeus (cf. *Against Heresies* 1.16.3; 3.16.5, 8), which cite 1 and 2 John. Among other writings including citations are

---

8. Other reconstructions are possible. Georg Strecker, 'Die Anfänge der johanneischen Schule', *NTS* 32 (1986) 31-47, e.g., suggests that 2 John was the first of the three letters to be written, and it was sent by the elder to deal with the threat to one of the Johannine churches posed by the coming of the secessionists, and 3 John documents reactions to missionaries whom the elder himself sent out to propagate the truth. 1 John and the Fourth Gospel were written later by other members of what he calls the Johannine school.

9. Brown, *The Epistles of John*, 5-13.

10. Brown, *The Epistles of John*, 9.

the Muratorian Fragment, which cites from 1 John and mentions two letters of John, most likely 1 and 2 John. Tertullian (d. A.D. 215) cites 1 John many times, and Clement of Alexandria (d. ca. A.D. 220) refers to 1 John and calls it 'the greater epistle', indicating that he knew of at least one other. However, it is not until the mid-third century that the first attestation of 3 John is found. Eusebius (*Hist. Eccl.* 6.25.10) says that Origen (d. A.D. 253) knew both 2 and 3 John, adding that 'all do not consider them genuine'. Early in the fourth century Eusebius of Caesarea included 1 John among the 'acknowledged books', but notes that 2 and 3 John, while accepted by most, were still listed as disputed books. It was not until late in the fourth century that all three letters of John came to be accepted, and that was on the assumption that all three were written by the apostle John. Brown suggests that 1 John gained acceptance earlier because it was associated with the Fourth Gospel and believed to have been written by the apostle John. Later 2 and 3 John were accepted because the author's self-designation as the elder was regarded as evidence of modesty on the part of the author, who was really the apostle John.[11]

INTRODUCTORY MATTERS RELATED TO 1 JOHN

Authorship

Internal Evidence. While 1 John lacks the usual opening A to B greeting formula, and accordingly there is no clear indication as to who wrote it, nevertheless we can say certain things about the author: (i) he writes as an individual, something which his repeated self-references in the first person singular indicate (2:1, 7, 8, 12, 13, 14, 21, 26; 5:13); (ii) his language and thought bear very striking resemblance to that of the Fourth Gospel, suggesting that he either wrote the Gospel as well or was deeply influenced by its language and concepts; (iii) he writes as an eyewitness of Jesus Christ, introducing himself, along with others, as one who has heard, seen with his eyes, looked at, and touched with his hands the incarnate Word of life (1:1-5).

Most scholars recognise, rightly, that the language used by the author in his claim to have seen, heard, and touched the Word of life is the language of sense perception. However, this is not always the case. Bultmann, for example, says: 'The question of the we' can be answered

11. Brown, *The Epistles of John*, 9-13.

'by recognising the paradox that an historical event can be, or in this case really is, at the same time an eschatological event. The "we" therefore are the "eschatological" contemporaries of Jesus'.[12] But, as Kügler points out, the strength of the expressions used in the claim to be an actual eyewitness is such that any such 'spiritual' interpretation as that suggested by Bultmann is ruled out.[13]

Schnackenburg takes a different approach, suggesting that, if the author is not himself an eyewitness, he was a pupil of the fourth evangelist, or at least a member of the circle of people who gathered around him.[14] Brown believes that the author speaks as a representative of a 'Johannine School' who shares a 'vicarious participation in the contact of the Beloved Disciple with Jesus'.[15] These suggestions, like Bultmann's, are susceptible to the same criticism that they do not take sufficient account of the strength of the author's claim to testify as an eyewitness; to say he was a pupil of an eyewitness or a member of a 'Johannine School' does not do justice to the language.[16]

Kügler argues that the way forward is to recognise in 1 John both an actual and an implied author and actual and implied readers. The actual author is not an eyewitness, but the implied author is. The implied readers have all knowledge and have no need to be taught anything. The actual readers, however, need instruction to prevent them from being taken in by the antichrists. The actual author employs literary fiction in order to gain a hearing from his actual readers, which he could not expect to receive otherwise.[17] Kügler's approach does take full cognisance of the strength of the eyewitness language, but the question remains whether 1 John displays solid evidence that the author has adopted such a literary fictional approach, and whether there were any contemporary precedents for this sort of literary communication in the ancient world. Early Christians appear to have been unwilling to accept pseudepigraphical writings into the New Testament canon.[18]

Klauck contends that, while there is sufficient proof for a metaphorical use of the verb 'to touch' (psēlaphaō) in 1 John 1:1, nevertheless the de-

---

12. Bultmann, *The Johannine Epistles*, 10.

13. Joachim Kügler, 'Die Belehrung der Unbelehrbaren: Zur Funktion des Traditionsarguments in 1 Joh', *BZ* n.s. 32 (1988) 249.

14. Schnackenburg, *The Johannine Epistles*, 38, 41.

15. Brown, *The Epistles of John*, 163; cf. Georg Strecker, *The Johannine Letters* (Hermeneia, Philadelphia: Fortress, 1996) xxxv-xlii.

16. So Kügler, 'Belehrung', 249-50.

17. Kügler, 'Belehrung', 250-54.

18. Cf. D. A. Carson, 'Pseudonymity and Pseudepigraphy', in *Dictionary of New Testament Background*, ed. Craig A. Evans and Stanley E. Porter (forthcoming).

ciding factor in interpretation must always be the immediate context, and in this case that speaks against any metaphorical interpretation and demands a literal one.[19] However, Klauck rejects the idea that this must lead to the adoption of a conservative solution to the question of authorship, one which would ascribe it to a genuine disciple of Jesus.[20] Instead, he argues that the author is the voice of the 'Johannine tradition', which is grounded on the witness of the beloved disciple.[21] However, the claim to be the voice of 'Johannine tradition' is a far cry from the claim to be an actual eyewitness, which is what the text taken at face value implies.

In the end, it seems better to take with the utmost seriousness the claims of the author to be one of a number of the original eyewitnesses of the incarnate Christ, despite the problems that raises — for example, trying to account for a number of elderly people, all of whom had been with Jesus during his earthly ministry, who were still alive when the author wrote this letter. But this is not an insurmountable problem because we could say that the author identified himself with others who had been eyewitnesses at the beginning of his letter, even though they were no longer living. It is clear from later self-references in the singular that they are not associated with him in the writing of the letter itself (see 'A Note on the Use of First Person Forms', p. 61). If we are prepared to accept that the author was an eyewitness, then there exists a prima facie case for identifying the author of 1 John with the author of (the original version of) the Fourth Gospel, because of the striking similarities of language and concepts, which were noted above.[22]

External Evidence. Early Christian tradition ascribes 1 John to the apostle John. A number of the relevant texts are reproduced below. Irenaeus (d. A.D. 202), Dionysius of Alexandria (d. ca. A.D. 265), and Tertullian (d. after A.D. 220) all ascribe the authorship of the Fourth Gospel and 1 John unequivocally to John the disciple and apostle of the Lord:

> The Gospel, therefore, knew no other son of man but Him who was of Mary, who also suffered; and no Christ who flew away from Jesus before the passion; but Him who was born it knew as Jesus Christ the Son of God, and that this same suffered and rose again, as John, the disciple of the Lord, verifies, saying: "But these are written, that ye might believe that Jesus is the Christ, the Son of God, and believing ye might

---

19. Hans-Josef Klauck, *Der erste Johannesbrief* (EKKNT, Zürich and Braunschweig: Benziger, 1991) 63.

20. Klauck, *Der erste Johannesbrief,* 75.

21. Klauck, *Der erste Johannesbrief,* 75-77.

22. See pp. 5-6.

have eternal life in His name," — foreseeing these blasphemous systems which divide the Lord, as far as lies in their power, saying that He was formed of two different substances. For this reason also he has thus testified to us in his Epistle: "Little children, it is the last time; and as ye have heard that Antichrist doth come, now have many antichrists appeared; whereby we know that it is the last time. They went out from us, but they were not of us; for if they had been of us, they would have continued with us: but [they departed], that it might be made manifest that they are not of us. Know ye, therefore, that every lie is from without, and is not of the truth. Who is a liar, but he that denieth that Jesus is the Christ? This is Antichrist". (Irenaeus, *Against Heresies* 3.16.5)

These are they against whom the Lord has cautioned us beforehand; and His disciple, in his Epistle already mentioned, commands us to avoid them, when he says: "For many deceivers are entered into the world, who confess not that Jesus Christ is come in the flesh. This is a deceiver and an antichrist. Take heed to them, that ye lose not what ye have wrought". (Irenaeus, *Against Heresies* 3.16.8)

I do not, therefore, deny that he [the author of Revelation] was called John and that this was the writing of one John, and I agree that it was the work, also, of some holy and inspired man. But I would not easily agree that this was the apostle, the son of Zebedee, the brother of James, who is the author of the gospel, and the general (catholic) epistle that bears his name. But I conjecture, both from the general tenor of both, and the form and complexion of the composition, and the execution of the whole book, that it is not from him. For the evangelist never prefixed his name, never proclaims himself, either in the gospel or in his epistle. (Dionysius of Alexandria, cited in Eusebius, *Hist. Eccl.* 7.25.6ff.)

There is a certain emphatic saying by John: "No man hath seen God at any time"; meaning, of course, at any previous time. . . . But the very same apostles testify that they had both seen and "handled" Christ. . . . Let us, in short, examine who it is whom the apostles saw. "That," says John, "which we have seen with our eyes, which we have looked upon, and our hands have handled, of the Word of Life". (Tertullian, *Adversus Praxeas* 15).

To whom would He [Christ] have rather made known the veiled import of His own language, than to him to whom He disclosed the likeness of His own glory — Peter, John, and James, and afterwards to Paul, to whom He granted participation in (the joys of) Paradise too, prior to his martyrdom? Or do they write differently from what they think — teachers using deceit, not truth? . . . John, in fact, exhorts us to lay down

12

our lives even for our brethren, affirming that there is no fear in love: "For perfect love casteth out fear, since fear has punishment; and he who fears is not perfect in love." . . . And if he teaches that we must die for the brethren how much more for the Lord, — he being sufficiently prepared, by his own Revelation too, for giving such advise! For indeed the Spirit had sent the injunction to the angel of the church in Smyrna: "Behold, the devil shall cast some of you into prison, that ye may be tried ten days. . . . "But the fearful," says John — and then come the others — "will have their part in the lake of fire and brimstone." Thus fear, which, as stated in his epistle, love drives out, has punishment. (Tertullian, *Scorpiace* 12)

Also relevant are the fragments of Papias (born probably between A.D. 60-70, and who published his *Exposition of Oracles of the Lord* late in life, ca. A.D. 130-40), cited by Eusebius. In these, reference is made to the apostle John as one of the 'elders', but also to what appears to be another 'elder John'. In Eusebius's own comments about Papias's statement, he says that this other 'elder John' was probably the author of Revelation. From this we might infer that he thought that the apostle John was the author of 1 John:

But I will not scruple also to give a place for you along with my interpretations to everything that I learnt carefully and remembered carefully in time past from the Elders, guaranteeing its truth. For, unlike the many, I did not take pleasure in those who have very much to say, but in those who teach the truth; nor in those who relate foreign commandments, but in those (who record) such as were given from the Lord to the Faith, and are derived from the Truth itself. And again, on any occasion when a person came (in my way) who had been a follower of the Elders, I would inquire about the discourses of the Elders — what was said by Andrew, or by Peter, or by Philip, or by Thomas or James, or by John or Matthew or any other of the Lord's disciples, and what Aristion and the Elder John, the disciples of the Lord, say. For I did not think that I could get so much profit from the contents of books as from the utterances of a living and abiding voice. (Papias, cited by Eusebius, *Hist. Eccl.* 3.39).

Here it is worth while to observe that he twice enumerates the name of John. The first he mentions in connexion with Peter and James and Matthew and the rest of the Apostles, evidently meaning the Evangelist, but the other John he mentions after an interval and classes with others outside the number of the Apostles, placing Aristion before him, and he distinctly calls him an Elder. So that he hereby makes it quite evident that their statement is true who say that there were two persons of that name in Asia, and that there are two tombs in Ephesus, each of which even now is called (the tomb) of John. And it is important to notice this; for it is probable that it was the second, if one will not admit that it was the first, who saw the Revelation which is ascribed by name to John. . . . (Eusebius, *Hist. Eccl.* 3.39)

The same Papias fragment is also cited by Jerome:

Papias, the pupil of John, bishop of Hierapolis in Asia, wrote five volumes which he entitled *Expositions of the words of our Lord,* in which, when he had asserted in his preface that he did not follow various opinions but had the apostles for authority, he said, "I considered what Andrew and Peter said, what Philip, what Thomas, what James, what John, what Matthew or any one else among the disciples of our Lord, what also Aristion and the elder John, disciples of the Lord, had said, not so much that I have their books to read, as that their living voice is heard until the present day in the authors themselves." It appears through this catalogue of names that the John who is placed among the disciples is not the same as the elder John whom he places after Aristion in his enumeration. This we say moreover because of the opinion mentioned above, where we record that it is declared by many that the last two epistles of John are the work not of the apostle but of the presbyter. (Jerome, *Lives of Illustrious Men,* 13).

Here again reference is made to two Johns, the apostle and the elder, and Jerome notes the widespread belief in his time that 2 and 3 John were written by the elder John, and not the apostle. From this it may be inferred that Jerome believed that 1 John was written by the apostle.

What is clear from these citations is that early Christian tradition is unanimous in ascribing 1 John to John, the disciple and apostle of the Lord. This corresponds with the internal evidence, which, taken at face value, indicates that the author was an eyewitness of the Word of life. Although there is, as we have seen above, a reluctance on the part of modern scholars to accept this testimony, it does seem to be the fairest way to read the evidence.

Addressees

Because 1 John lacks the normal opening greeting, it contains no designation of those to whom the letter is addressed. However, a careful reading of the letter does allow us to say something about the readers, and the way the author thought and felt about them. The readers appear to have been members of a number of churches in fellowship with the church of which the author was a member. They were encountering people who had seceded from the author's church and were propagating an aberrant form of the gospel (2:18-27).

The author's precise relationship with his readers is not easy to determine. His concern, he says, is 'that you also may have fellowship with us' (1:3). On the surface it might appear that the readers are those whom the author regards as not yet in fellowship with him. However, in the light of later statements in the letter, it is better to say that he regards them as those whose fellowship with him is under threat. The readers have already heard the message of the gospel, including its fundamental demand to love their brothers and sisters in Christ (2:7, 24; 3:11). This message has already impacted their lives (2:8). They already know the truth of the gospel (2:21), that Christ appeared to take away sins (3:5), and they have already received an anointing from God (2:20).

The author has an affectionate regard for his readers, addressing them repeatedly as his 'dear friends' (agapētoi, 2:7; 3:2, 21; 4:1, 7, 11). On one occasion he addresses them as 'brothers' (adelphoi, 3:13). More often calls them his 'children' (teknia or paidia, 2:1, 12, 18, 28; 3:7, 18; 4:4; 5:21), indicating that he relates to them as their senior in the Lord. In one place he addresses them all as 'children', then variously as 'fathers' and 'young men' (2:12-14), indicating the various levels of Christian maturity that existed among his readers. Both the author and his readers live as aliens in the world of unbelieving humanity, a world under the control of the evil one (5:19). The world does not 'know' them just as it did not 'know' Christ (3:1), and it is hostile towards them (3:13). The world and its values are opposed to God, and the author urges his readers to resist its vain attractions (2:15-17).

Opponents

Our working hypothesis, based upon what I hope is responsible mirror reading of 1 John, is that certain people had seceded from the author's community (2:19) because they held different views concerning the person and work of Christ (4:1-3) and Christians' obligations to keep God's commands (2:4), namely to believe in his Son, Jesus Christ, and love one another (3:23). Though they had seceded, they nevertheless continued to try to influence those remaining in the author's community to accept their heretical teachings (2:26). Some of the secessionists appear to have undertaken an itinerant ministry among the churches (2:18-19, 26). The effect of their teaching upon the members of these churches was to undermine confidence in the message of the gospel as originally received, so that the author found it necessary to bolster their assurance (5:13). The secessionists' insistence that they had a special anointing of the Spirit (which had led them to go beyond the primitive Christian gospel) made those remaining in the author's community wonder whether they lacked that anointing (2:20, 27) and therefore also lacked the spiritual insight which the secessionists claimed to have.[23]

The Teaching of the Secessionists. The actual teaching of the secessionists can be inferred from the Letters of John by a judicious mirror reading of the text. In the first place, the author responds to the secessionists' claims to know God when he says, 'If we claim to have fellowship with him yet walk in the darkness, we lie and do not live by the truth' (1:6); 'The man who says, "I know him," but does not do what he commands is a liar, and the truth is not in him' (2:4); 'Whoever claims to live in him must walk as Jesus did' (2:6); 'Anyone who claims to be in the light but hates his brother is still in the darkness' (2:9). It is clear that the author regarded these claims as spurious because the behaviour of the secessionists belied their claims.

In the second place, the author refers to claims to sinlessness made by the secessionists when he writes: 'If we claim to be without sin, we deceive ourselves and the truth is not in us' (1:8); 'If we claim we have not sinned, we make him out to be a liar and his word has no place in our lives' (1:10).

In the third place, the author deals with the secessionists' teaching when he speaks of errors relating to the person of Christ: 'Who is the liar? It is the man who denies that Jesus is the Christ. Such a man is the antichrist — he denies the Father and the Son. No one who denies the Son

---

23. In recent times some scholars have argued that the interpretation of 1 John with the secessionist challenge in mind is unnecessary. Judith Lieu, *The Theology of the Johannine Epistles* (Cambridge: Cambridge University Press, 1991) 16, while recognising that a schism has occurred, argues that the purpose of the letter is not so much to deal with the effects of the schism as 'to engender a debate within the framework of the author's or community's theology'. Terry Griffith, 'A Non-polemical Reading of 1 John: Sin, Christology and the Limits of Johannine Christianity', *TynBul* 49 (1998) 275, believes that a return of some Jewish Christians to Judaism is sufficient to account for the rhetoric of 1 John, and that the author's aim is pastoral, i.e., 'to secure the boundaries of the community against further losses'. However, the author's reference to those 'who went out from us' (2:19) and his view that they are antichrists (2:18), together with his reference to false prophets who 'have gone out into the world' (4:1) and his identifying them with the spirit of antichrist (4:3), do seem to indicate that the author had a polemic purpose in writing.

has the Father; whoever acknowledges the Son has the Father also' (2:22-23); 'Dear friends, do not believe every spirit, but test the spirits to see whether they are from God, because many false prophets have gone out into the world. This is how you can recognise the Spirit of God: Every spirit that acknowledges that Jesus Christ has come in the flesh is from God, but every spirit that does not acknowledge Jesus is not from God. This is the spirit of the antichrist, which you have heard is coming and even now is already in the world' (4:1-3); 'We accept man's testimony, but God's testimony is greater because it is the testimony of God, which he has given about his Son. Anyone who believes in the Son of God has this testimony in his heart. Anyone who does not believe God has made him out to be a liar, because he has not believed the testimony God has given about his Son' (5:9-10). From these texts it is apparent that the secessionists denied that Jesus is the Christ, the Son of God, come in the flesh.

In the fourth place, the author appears to be refuting secessionist teaching when he says, 'This is the one who came by water and blood — Jesus Christ. He did not come by water only, but by water and blood. And it is the Spirit who testifies, because the Spirit is the truth' (5:6). The secessionists denied that Jesus came by blood, that is, the importance of Jesus' atoning death (see commentary *ad loc.*).

In the fifth place, the author refers to the secessionists' behaviour when he speaks of those who do not show love to fellow believers: 'But whoever hates his brother is in the darkness and walks around in the darkness; he does not know where he is going, because the darkness has blinded him' (2:11); 'Anyone who hates his brother is a murderer, and you know that no murderer has eternal life in him' (3:15); 'Whoever does not love does not know God, because God is love' (4:8); 'If anyone says, "I love God," yet hates his brother, he is a liar. For anyone who does not love his brother, whom he has seen, cannot love God, whom he has not seen' (4:20). The secessionists' relationship with the believers remaining in the author's community was not marked by the love which Christ himself enjoined upon his disciples.

Finally, the author also seems to be referring to the secessionists' behaviour when he speaks of those who go on sinning and do not 'do right': 'No one who lives in him keeps on sinning. No one who continues to sin has either seen him or known him' (3:6); 'He who does what is sinful is of the devil, because the devil has been sinning from the beginning. The reason the Son of God appeared was to destroy the devil's work' (3:8); 'This is how we know who the children of God are and who the children of the devil are: Anyone who does not do what is right is not a child of God; nor is anyone who does not love his brother' (3:10). While the secessionists claimed 'to have no sin', the author clearly implies that their behaviour was marked by wrongdoing. He implies that they continued in sin and did not do what is right.

If what has been outlined above is a responsible reading of the text of 1 John, and does represent what the secessionists stood for, the next question is how the secessionists came to adopt such aberrant teaching and behaviour. One possibility is that this teaching was self-generating within the Christian community, and the other that the secessionists embraced the teaching of other early Christian heretics. We will now deal with each of these possibilities in turn.

The Secessionists and the Author's Community. A number of scholars have sought to explain the teaching of the secessionists in terms of the experiences of the author's community itself, or the ways different members of the community interpreted the Fourth Gospel, or a combination of the two.

Painter suggests that the author's community was originally made up of two distinct groups: 'those who had been through the struggle with the synagogue and those who had entered the community after the breach with Judaism'. The latter did not understand the Gospel of John tradition against the background of the struggle with Judaism but rather against their own Gentile background, which included the mystery religions and their initiatory rites. They believed that the divine *sperma* had descended upon the human Jesus at his baptism, but in such a way that the human Jesus was to be distinguished from the divine Christ. Hence they could deny that Jesus was the Christ come in the flesh. They believed that through their baptismal initiation they, too, had received the divine *sperma* and been born of God, thus sharing the divine nature and enjoying immunity from sin. What was important for them was their own experience of God, or their *koinōnia* with him, and human relationships were deemed less significant. 'Love' for God, not love for one another, was the crucial matter.[24] It was these people who in the end seceded from the author's community.

Brown argues that the division between the secessionists and the author's community resulted from different readings of the Fourth Gospel. From the secessionists' point of view those remaining with the author of 1 John were revisionists. They were harking back to a primitive form of Christology instead of embracing the christological implications of the Fourth Gospel. For his part the author of 1 John regarded the secessionists as innovators, people who had distorted the tradition that had been handed down from the beginning and enshrined in the Fourth Gos-

24. John Painter, 'The "Opponents" in 1 John', *NTS* 32 (1986) 48-49, 66-67.

pel. Ironically, both groups appealed to the Fourth Gospel in support of their respective positions. According to Brown, the secessionists did not deny the incarnation but rather that Christ's being in the flesh was salvific.[25]

Smalley argues that three different groupings of Christians may be distinguished within the author's community. First, there were those who were committed to the apostolic teaching as it had come down from the beginning. These gathered around the author of 1 John. Second, there were those from a Jewish background who had made some sort of commitment to Jesus but were not prepared to regard him as the Messiah. These people held the law in high regard and probably developed into Ebionites. Third, there were those of a pagan Hellenistic background (possibly some Hellenistic Jews were also associated with this group) who had been influenced by dualistic (Gnostic) ideas. These people found it difficult to accept the full humanity of Christ and probably developed into Docetics. All of these groups continued in the author's community, despite the inner tensions that resulted from their different emphases. However, for some this tension became too great, and they eventually seceded from the community. These secessionists, Smalley says, were probably spearheaded by those of a docetic frame of mind.[26]

Klauck argues, in the light of such texts as 2:15-17 (the reference to boasting of what one has) and 3:17 (the reference to having material possessions and closing one's heart to those in need), that the secessionists were much better off financially and materially than those believers who remained in the author's community. The secessionists were the ones who provided meeting places for the church and hospitality for itinerant missionaries.[27] They were people for whom the experience of the Spirit received through baptism was of great importance, and through this experience they achieved sinlessness. For these people the most important christological event was Jesus' baptism, when the Spirit descended and remained upon him. Accordingly, they deemphasised Jesus' incarnation and death on the cross. These beliefs, both about their own experience and the significance of Christ, they derived from their reading of the Fourth Gospel.[28]

The exact influences which led the secessionists to formulate their understanding of Christianity, whether it was the influence of their background in mystery religions (Painter), their particular interpretation of

25. Brown, *The Epistles of John*, 67-68, 505.

26. Stephen S. Smalley, *1, 2, 3 John* (WBC 51, Waco, TX: Word, 1984) xxiii-xxv.

27. Hans-Josef Klauck, 'Internal Opponents: The Treatment of the Secessionists in the First Epistle of John', *Concilium* 200 (1988) 56-57.

28. Klauck, 'Internal Opponents', 57-58.

the Fourth Gospel (Brown), a pagan Hellenistic background involving dualistic ideas, or their experience of the Spirit (Klauck), will continue to be debated. But it does seem clear that, whatever the influences that affected them were, they all led to a deemphasising of the incarnation and vicarious death of Christ and a concomitant deemphasising of the commands of Christ, especially the command to love one another.

The Secessionists and Early Christian Heretics. It would be very helpful to know whether the opponents reflected in 1 John can be identified with, or had been influenced by, any of the early heretical teachers mentioned by extracanonical writers. The relevant texts are reproduced below, so that readers can make their own judgements. Irenaeus (A.D. 120-202), bishop of Lyons, in his magnum opus *Against Heresies,* provides firsthand information concerning several heretical teachings which assailed the church in the second century. Among other things, he recounts Polycarp's story about John the disciple of the Lord meeting Cerinthus in the bath-house in Ephesus, and provides a description of Cerinthus's teaching:

> There are also those who heard from him [Polycarp] that John, the disciple of the Lord, going to bathe at Ephesus, and perceiving Cerinthus within, rushed out of the bath-house without bathing, exclaiming, "Let us fly, lest even the bath-house fall down, because Cerinthus, the enemy of the truth, is within." (*Against Heresies* 3.3.4)

> Cerinthus, again, a man who was educated in the wisdom of the Egyptians, taught that the world was not made by the primary God, but by a certain Power far separated from him, and at a distance from that Principality who is supreme over the universe, and ignorant of him who is above all. He represented Jesus as having not been born of a virgin, but as being the son of Joseph and Mary according to the ordinary course of human generation, while he nevertheless was more righteous, prudent, and wise than other men. Moreover, after his baptism, Christ descended upon him in the form of a dove from the Supreme Ruler, and that then he proclaimed the unknown Father, and performed miracles. But at last Christ departed from Jesus, and that then Jesus suffered and rose again, while Christ remained impassible, inasmuch as he was a spiritual being. (*Against Heresies* 1.26.1)

> John, the disciple of the Lord, preaches this faith, and seeks by the proclamation of the Gospel, to remove that error which by Cerinthus had been disseminated among men, and a long time previously by those termed Nicolaitans, who are an offset of that "knowledge" falsely so called, that he might confound them, and persuade them that there is

but one God, who made all things by His Word; and not, as they allege, that the Creator was one, but the Father of the Lord another; and that the Son of the Creator was, forsooth, one, but the Christ from above another, who also continued impassible, descending upon Jesus, the Son of the Creator, and flew back again into His Pleroma; and that Monogenes was the beginning, but Logos was the true son of Monogenes; and that this creation to which we belong was not made by the primary God, but by some power lying far below Him, and shut off from communion with the things invisible and ineffable. The disciple of the Lord therefore desiring to put an end to all such doctrines, and to establish the rule of truth in the Church, that there is one Almighty God, who made all things by His Word, both visible and invisible; showing at the same time, that by the Word, through whom God made the creation, He also bestowed salvation on men included in the creation; thus commended His teaching in the Gospel: "In the beginning was the Word, and the Word was with God, and the Word was God. The same was in the beginning with God. All things were made by Him, and without Him was nothing made. What was made was life in Him, and the life was the light of men. And the light shineth in darkness, and the darkness comprehended it not." "All things," he says, "were made by Him"; therefore in "all things" this creation of ours is [included], for we cannot concede to these men that [the words] "all things" are spoken in reference to those within their Pleroma. For if their Pleroma do indeed contain these, this creation, as being such, is not outside, as I have demonstrated in the preceding book; but if they are outside the Pleroma, which indeed appeared impossible, it follows, in that case, that their Pleroma cannot be "all things": therefore this vast creation is not outside [the Pleroma]. (*Against Heresies* 3.11.1)

While it might be attractive to identify the opponents of 1 John with Cerinthus and his followers, seeing that there is evidence that the disciple of the Lord did know of him and repudiate his teaching, nevertheless this identification is highly unlikely. There is no evidence that Cerinthus and his followers were ever members of the community to which the author of 1 John belonged. Also, there is much in the description of the error of Cerinthus provided by Irenaeus that is not reflected in the author's rebuttal of the teaching of the secessionists in 1 John (e.g., distinguishing the Creator from the Father of the Lord, the Son of the Creator from the Christ, etc.).

When we turn to the writings of Ignatius, and references there to his docetic opponents, we find something much closer to the teaching rejected in 1 John.

Ignatius, bishop of Antioch (d. A.D. 107), wrote a number of letters while on his way from Antioch to martyrdom in Rome in the very early part of the second century. These letters, therefore, were written at a time shortly after the writing of 1 John. The salient references in the epistles of Ignatius are reproduced below. Ignatius insists upon the real humanity of Jesus Christ, that he truly suffered death upon the cross, and that he rose bodily from the dead. He warns his readers against those who deny these things and fail in their duty to show love to those in need. The relevant passages are:

> For I have observed that you are established in immoveable faith . . . being fully persuaded as touching our Lord, that he is in truth of the family of David according to the flesh, God's son by the will and power of God, truly born of a virgin, baptized by John that "all righteousness might be fulfilled by Him", truly nailed to a tree in the flesh for our sakes under Pontius Pilate and Herod the tetrarch. (Ign. *Smyrn.* 1:1-2)

> For he suffered all these things for us that we might attain salvation, and he truly suffered, even as he truly raised himself, not, as some unbelievers say, that his Passion was merely in semblance, — but it is they who are merely in semblance, and even according to their opinions it shall be to them, and they shall be without bodies and phantasmal. (Ign. *Smyrn.* 2:1)

> For I know and believe that he was in the flesh even after the resurrection. And when he came to those with Peter He said to them: "Take, handle me and see that I am not a phantom without a body." And they immediately touched him and believed, being mingled both with his flesh and spirit. Therefore they despised even death, and were proved to be above death. And after his Resurrection he ate with them and drank with them as a being of flesh, though he was united in spirit to the Father. (Ign. *Smyrn.* 3:1-3)

> Now I warn you of these things, beloved, knowing that you also are so minded. But I guard you in advance against beasts in the form of men, whom you must not only not receive, but if it is possible not even meet, but only pray for them, if perchance they may repent, difficult though that be, — but Jesus Christ who is our true life has the power over this. For if it is merely in semblance that these things were done by our Lord I am also a prisoner in semblance. And why have I given myself up to death, to fire, to the sword, to wild beasts? (Ign. *Smyrn.* 4:1-2)

> There are some who ignorantly deny him, but rather were denied by him, being advocates of death rather than of the truth. These are they whom neither the prophecies nor the law of Moses persuaded, nor the

gospel even until now, nor our own individual sufferings. For they have the same opinion concerning us. For what does anyone profit me, if he praise me but blaspheme my Lord, and do not confess that he was clothed in flesh? But he who says this has denied him absolutely and is clothed with a corpse. Now I have not thought right to put into writing their unbelieving names; but would that I might not even remember them, until they repent concerning the Passion, which is our resurrection. (Ign. *Smyrn.* 5:1-3)

Let no one be deceived; even things in heaven and the glory of the angels, and the rulers visible and invisible, even for them there is a judgment if they do not believe on the blood of Christ. "He that receiveth let him receive." Let not office exalt anyone, for faith and love is everything, and nothing has been preferred to them. But mark those who have strange opinions concerning the grace of Jesus Christ which has come to us, and see how contrary they are to the mind of God. For love they have no care, none for the widow, none for the orphan, none for the distressed, none for the afflicted, none for the prisoner, or for him released from prison, none for the hungry or thirsty. They abstain from Eucharist and prayer, because they do not confess that the Eucharist is the flesh of our Saviour Jesus Christ who suffered for our sins, which the Father raised up by his goodness. (Ign. *Smyrn.* 6:1–7:1)

Be deaf therefore when anyone speaks to you apart from Jesus Christ, who was of the family of David, and of Mary, who was truly born, both ate and drank, was truly persecuted under Pontius Pilate, was truly crucified and died in the sight of those in heaven and on earth and under the earth; who also was truly raised from the dead, his Father raised him up, as in the same manner his Father shall raise up in Christ Jesus us who believe in him, without whom we have no true life. (Ign. *Trall.* 9:1-2)

But if, as some affirm who are without God, — that is, are unbelievers, — his suffering was only a semblance (but it is they who are merely a semblance), why am I a prisoner, and why also do I even long to fight with the beasts? In that case I am dying in vain. Then indeed am I lying concerning the Lord. (Ign. *Trall.* 10:1)

These letters reflect the heretical teaching of people who deny the real humanity of Jesus Christ, claim that he 'suffered only in semblance', and therefore deny that he suffered for our sins. They do not show practical love for the needy. All these matters have their parallel in the teaching and behaviour of the secessionists as it is reflected in 1 John, and it is therefore very tempting to identify the secessionists with the docetic opponents of Ignatius. Schnackenburg notes the close similarities between the false teaching of the secessionists and that of Ignatius's docetic opponents, but stops short of saying that the secessionists are to be identified with Ignatius's opponents. The differences are too great, he says, to make that identification. Ignatius's heretics were real docetics who reduced the existence of Jesus to mere semblance, and there is no evidence that the secessionists did this. In addition, Ignatius's heretics had strong affinities with Judaism, as the citation which follows indicates,[29] and there is no hint in 1 John that the secessionists had such affinities:

> For this cause let us be his disciples, let us learn to lead Christian lives. For whoever is called by any name other than this is not of God. Put aside then the evil leaven, which has grown old and sour, and turn to the new leaven, which is Jesus Christ. Be salted in him, that none among you may be corrupted, since by your savour you shall be tested. It is monstrous to talk of Jesus Christ and to practise Judaism. For Christianity did not base its faith on Judaism, but Judaism on Christianity, and every tongue believing on God was brought together in it. (Ign. *Magn.* 10:1-3)

A third but less attractive possibility is that the secessionist teaching may be identified with that of the second-century Gnostics, Basilides and Valentinus. Irenaeus provides testimony to their teaching:

> Basilides again, that he may appear to have discovered something more sublime and plausible [than the doctrines of Saturninus], gives an immense development to his doctrines. He sets forth that Nous was first born of the unborn father, that from him, again, was born Logos, from Logos Phronesis, from Phronesis Sophia and Dynamis, and from Dynamis and Sophia the powers, and principalities, and angels, whom he also calls the *first*; and that by them the first heaven was made. Then other powers, being formed by emanation from these, created another heaven similar to the first; and in like manner, when others, again, had been formed by emanation from them, corresponding exactly to those above them, these, too, framed another third heaven; and then from this third, in downward order, there was a fourth succession of descendants; and so on, after the same fashion, they declare that more and more principalities and angels were formed, and three hundred and sixty-five heavens. Wherefore the year contains the same number of days in conformity with the number of the heavens. Those angels who occupy the lowest heaven, that, namely, which is visible to us, formed

---

29. Schnackenburg, *The Johannine Epistles,* 21-23.

all the things which are in the world, and made allotments among themselves of the earth and of those nations which are upon it. The chief of them is he who is thought to be the God of the Jews; and inasmuch as he desired to render the other nations subject to his own people, that is, the Jews, all the other princes resisted and opposed him. Wherefore all other nations were at enmity with his nation. But the father without birth and without name, perceiving that they would be destroyed, sent his own first-begotten Nous (he it is who is called Christ) to bestow deliverance on them that believe in him, from the power of those who made the world. He appeared, then, on earth as a man, to the nations of these powers, and wrought miracles. Wherefore he did not himself suffer death, but Simon, a certain man of Cyrene, being compelled, bore the cross in his stead; so that this latter being transfigured by him, that he might be thought to be Jesus, was crucified, through ignorance and error, while Jesus himself received the form of Simon, and, standing by, laughed at him. For since he was an incorporeal power, and the Nous (mind) of the unborn father, he transfigured himself as he pleased, and thus ascended to him who had sent him, deriding them, inasmuch as he could not be laid hold of, and was invisible to all. Those, then, who know these things have been freed from the principalities who formed the world; so that it is not incumbent on us to confess him who was crucified, but him who came in the form of a man, and was thought to be crucified, and was called Jesus, and was sent by the father, that by this dispensation he might destroy the works of the makers of the world. If any one, therefore, he declares, confesses the crucified, that man is still a slave, and under the power of those who formed our bodies; but he who denies him has been freed from these beings, and is acquainted with the dispensation of the unborn father. (*Against Heresies* 1.24.3-4)

But there are some who say that Jesus was merely a receptacle of Christ, upon whom the Christ, as a dove, descended from above, and that when He had declared the unnameable Father He entered into the Pleroma in an incomprehensible and invisible manner; for that He was not comprehended, not only by men but not even by those powers and virtues which are in heaven, and that Jesus was the Son, but Christ was the Father, and the Father of Christ, God; while others say that He merely suffered in outward appearance, being naturally impassible. The Valentinians, again, maintain that the dispensational Jesus was the same who passed through Mary, upon whom that Saviour from the more exalted [region] descended, who was also termed *Pan,* because He possessed the names *(vocabula)* of all those who had produced Him; but that [this latter] shared with Him, the dispensational one, His power and His name; so that by His means death was abolished, but the Father was made known by that Saviour who had descended from above, whom they do also allege to be Himself the receptacle of Christ and of the entire Pleroma; confessing indeed, in tongue one Christ Jesus, but being divided in [actual] opinion: for, as I have already observed, it is the practice of these men to say that there was one Christ, who was produced by Monogenes, for the confirmation of the Pleroma; but that another, the Saviour, was sent [forth] for the glorification of the Father; and yet another, the dispensational one, and whom they represent as having suffered, who also bore [in himself] Christ, that Saviour who returned into the Pleroma. I judge it necessary therefore to take into account the entire mind of the apostles regarding our Lord Jesus Christ, and to show that not only did they never hold any such opinions regarding Him; but, still further, that they announced through the Holy Spirit, that those who should teach such doctrines were agents of Satan, sent forth for the purpose of overturning the faith of some, and drawing them away from life. (*Against Heresies* 3.16.1)

While there are some points of contact between the teaching of Basilides and Valentinus on the one hand, and the secessionists of 1 John on the other, so much in the former has no parallel in the latter that it is extremely unlikely that these texts will help us in identifying the influences which affected the opponents of 1 John, though it is possible that the seeds of later gnostic teachings are to be found in the teaching of the secessionists.

Of all the candidates for the source of influence affecting the secessionists, the teaching of the opponents of Ignatius comes closest to what we can know of the secessionist views. But as already noted, there are other features which seem to militate against a one-to-one identification, especially the close association of Ignatius's opponents with Judaism.[30] Schnackenburg's conclusion is hard to improve upon:

The heresy which occasioned 1 and 2 John cannot be parallel with any other manifestation of heresy known from that era. Yet it has affinities with more than one such movement. They all play down the historic person of Jesus Christ as the unique and true savior. They all deny the way of salvation through his flesh and blood. In their precise christological interpretation of the figure of Jesus, these dangerous heretics, dissolving as they did the substance of the Christian faith, evidently went off in different directions. This can be seen by comparing the views of Cerinthus with those of the docetists in the letters of Ignatius,

30. Smalley, *1, 2, 3 John*, xxiii–xxiv, uses Ign. *Magn.* 10:3, as evidence for a Jewish-Christian group in the author's community, and this leaves the door open for a Jewish element in the secessionist teaching, but there is little evidence for this in 1 John itself.

whose precise teaching, however, remains obscure. The christology of the antichrists in the Johannine epistles also can no longer be described with certainty or precision. But it is one example of that pseudo-Christian tendency which manifested itself in gnosticism and was such a threat to the church.[31]

Purpose and Time of Writing

As we have already seen, this letter repeatedly sets forth criteria which, when applied to the secessionists' teaching, show that their claims to know God, to have fellowship with him, and to have eternal life are spurious. The author's purpose, however, was not to correct the secessionists (the letter was not written for them), but to show his readers that the secessionist claims were false. By doing this he wanted to prevent them from being deceived by secessionist teachings. Alongside the provision of criteria to show the secessionists are wrong, the author provided other criteria which, if applied by the readers to themselves, would show that they are in the right; they are the ones who know God, who have fellowship with him, and who have eternal life. The author's purpose was to bolster the assurance of his readers by the double strategy of showing the secessionists' claims to be false and showing his readers that they are in the truth. All this accords with the one explicit statement of purpose in the letter: 'I write these things to you who believe in the name of the Son of God so that you may know that you have eternal life' (5:13). The readers needed this reassurance because their confidence had been shaken by the propaganda of the secessionists and their claims to Spirit-inspired teaching, which went beyond what had been received from the beginning. (See 'A Note on the Bases of Assurance', pp. 198-200.)

If, as we have argued, 1 John was written after the (original version of) the Fourth Gospel, and if it is correct to date the Fourth Gospel around A.D. 85-90, then this places the writing of 1 John in the early part of the last decade of the first century. If the early Christian tradition is correct in ascribing this letter to the apostle John who spent his latter days in Ephesus, then 1 John should be regarded as a letter sent from Ephesus to

---

31. Schnackenburg, *The Johannine Epistles*, 23. Brown, *The Epistles of John*, 67-68, essentially agrees, adding that even if we could identify the secessionists with one or other of the early Christian heretical groups it would not be 'particularly enlightening; for granted the little we know about such groups, it would have been tantamount to explaining *ignotum per ignotius*. Yet it remains useful to know that the views attacked in I and II John were not without parallel in Asia Minor at the beginning of the second century'.

a number of associated churches in the region around Ephesus who were being disturbed by the activities of the secessionists.

Genre, Rhetorical Form, and Structure

In seeking to understand 1 John, and in fact any document within the NT, it is important to appreciate the type of literature it is (genre), to understand what sort of communication it is (rhetorical form), and to be able to describe how it hangs together (structure). In the case of 1 John none of these matters is straightforward.

Genre. 1 John does not fit into the category of the typical Greco-Roman letter. It has no opening greeting, no thanksgiving, and no closing salutations. However, it is addressed to specific (groups of) people who face particular problems (as described in 'A Scenario', p. 1 above). To understand the nature of the document it is probably best to determine its function rather than try to match it with some known type of writing in the ancient world.

Some have regarded the letter as a kind of universal tract intended for the church everywhere, but it is difficult to understand how an anonymous letter would carry much weight as a universal tract. Others have suggested that it was a circular letter intended for churches in a specific area, in particular for a number of churches who were facing similar sorts of problems because of the secessionists' work. Those who adopt this view must account for the fact that there is no opening greeting whatsoever, nor any closing greetings, not even of a general nature as one might expect. Another suggestion is that the material in the letter began life as a homily, and was subsequently produced in written form. But the letter itself contains many references to writing, indicating that the material was first fashioned as a letter and not a homily. Brown has suggested that 1 John was produced in part as a commentary on the Fourth Gospel, especially those parts of it which the secessionists had appropriated, so as to refute their teachings, which were based on it.[32] Smalley prefers to regard the letter as a 'paper', whose purpose is to explain the teaching of the Fourth Gospel to members of the author's community who were interpreting the Gospel in what he believed were erroneous ways.[33]

Of these various suggestions, the one which regards 1 John as a circular letter has the most to commend it. It can account for the absence of

32. Brown, *The Epistles of John,* 90-92.
33. Smalley, *1, 2, 3 John,* xxvii.

opening and closing greetings (these were to be provided in each place by the courier); it accounts for the particularity of the problems addressed (all the churches were experiencing similar problems because of the secessionists); and it accounts for the complete lack of references to particular readers (omitted because the letter was intended for a number of different churches). Whether the letter was consciously designed as a commentary on sections of the Fourth Gospel which were interpreted differently by the secessionists and the author is difficult to prove or disprove.

Rhetorical Form. There are essentially three species of rhetoric: (i) Judicial rhetoric, which relates to the question of truth or justice, is intended to persuade people to make a judgement on past events and involves prosecution or defence. (ii) Deliberative rhetoric, which relates to the question of self-interest and future benefits, is intended to persuade people to take some action in the future and involves exhortation or dissuasion. (iii) Epideictic rhetoric, which relates to attitudes and values, is intended to bring about a deepening and reaffirmation of values already held in the present.

Klauck regards 1 John as a deliberative letter of an advisory nature, which urges the readers to remain faithful to Christ (2:28-29).[34] But Watson argues, correctly in my view, that 1 John falls into the category of epideictic rhetoric — that is, the author is not seeking to defend himself or persuade his hearers to take some course of action; rather, he is trying to increase their adherence to the traditional truths of the community. The epideictic intent of the epistle is quite evident in three places: (i) in the introduction (1:3), where the author says that his purpose in writing is to promote and preserve fellowship; (ii) in the opening of the body of the letter in 1:5, where the author speaks of walking in the light (i.e., according to the values and beliefs of the community) as the prerequisite for fellowship with God; and (iii) in the conclusion (5:21), where the author says, 'Keep yourselves from idols', which is an implicit plea to his readers to remain faithful to the values of the community.

Watson also characterises 1 John as a piece of epideictic rhetoric because it exhibits five characteristics of epideictic rhetoric: (i) It is intended to increase the audience's adherence to just and honourable values they already hold. It is primarily an appeal to the faithful to strengthen their faith and resolve. (ii) It has present time referents. In 1 John the audience is exhorted to maintain its original understanding of the tradition. The past may be recalled and the future anticipated, but the main emphasis is

34. Hans-Josef Klauck, 'Zur rhetorischen Analyse der Johannesbriefe', *ZNW* 81 (1990) 210.

upon doing something in the present. (iii) It uses praise and blame in order to increase or decrease the ethos of others. (iv) The stasis, or basis of the case, of epideictic rhetoric is quality; in other words, it stresses the best course of action to take under the circumstances. It inquires into the nature of something, whether it is just, right, and true or their opposites. The nature of the secessionists and their deceptive doctrine is the subject of inquiry in 1 John. (v) Most directly related to the case for seeing 1 John as epideictic rhetoric is the fact that amplification, rather than formal proof, is the content of the *probatio* (body) of epideictic rhetoric.

Watson further argues, again fairly convincingly, that the author uses the technique of amplification, well known in Greco-Roman handbooks of rhetoric, especially Quintilian's *Institutio Oratoria*. The application of the technique of amplification by the author accounts very well for the repetitive and emphatic character of 1 John, which contains many examples of the different forms of amplification: (i) Strong words can be used to amplify. These can be powerful, yet ordinary, synonyms, compounds, exaggerated words, or words used metaphorically (e.g., 1 John 3:15: 'Anyone who hates his brother is a murderer'). The word 'murderer' is a strong word, a metaphor for extreme hatred. (ii) Augmentation. Amplification by augmentation is effected in a number of ways, such as the use of one step or a series increasing in intensity (1 John 2:2: Jesus is not only the atoning sacrifice for the sins of the Christian community but also for the whole world), and by making it clear that there is no greater degree than what is mentioned (1 John 1:10: The secessionist proposition of denying the possibility of sin after conversion makes God a liar — the highest degree of falsehood). (iii) Comparison. Amplification can be effected by comparison. Like augmentation, comparison moves from the lesser to the greater in an effort to emphasise the greater — in 1 John 3:2, for example, the comparison between the audience's present and future status amplifies the future status ('Dear friends, now we are children of God, and what we will be has not yet been made known. But we know that when he appears, we shall be like him, for we shall see him as he is'), and in 1 John 5:9 the comparison between God's testimony and human testimony amplifies the greatness of God's testimony. (iv) Accumulation. Amplification by accumulation is the amassing of words and sentences identical in meaning, all with one referent — for example, in 1 John 1:1-3 all four sensory verbs have the word of life as a referent: heard, seen, looked at, and touched, and in 1 John 2:14 the three positive attributes of being strong, having the word of God abiding within, and overcoming the evil one all have the young people as a referent. (v) *Expolitio* (refining) is a figure of speech which consists in dwelling on the same topic and yet seeming to say something ever new. Watson lists thirty-five examples of *expolitio* in 1 John. It is by far the most frequently used amplification technique employed by the author of 1 John. These uses include repeating something in equivalent terms (1:2: 'the life appeared . . . the eternal life . . . has appeared to us'); repeating something in opposite terms (1:5: 'God is light; and in him is no darkness at all'); repetition with a reason (2:13-14: 'you have overcome the evil one. . . . You are strong, and the word of God lives in you, and you have overcome the evil one'). (vi) *Reflexio* is a figure of speech in which the same word is used with two different meanings (2:7-8: when the author says, 'I am not writing you a new command', 'new' carries the idea of novelty; but when he says, 'I am writing you a new command', newness in an eschatological sense is meant. (vii) *Regressio* is a figure of speech which reiterates things already said and draws distinctions between them (2:18: 'Dear children, this is the last hour; and as you have heard that the antichrist is coming, even now many antichrists have come. This is how we know it is the last hour'. The prophecy is repeated and the distinction made that the present secessionists are the antichrists of prophecy).[35]

Watson goes on to provide examples of amplification effected by *conduplicatio, distributio,* synonymy, epanaphora, *commemoratio, enargeia,* polysyndeton and asyndeton, antithesis, personification, hyperbole, emphasis, and the development of commonplaces. He points out that 1 John uses virtually every known rhetorical technique for amplification. The use of *expolitio* clearly predominates, perhaps because it is a multifaceted technique and one of the central aspects of rhetoric learned in secondary school in the ancient world.[36] The upshot of all this is that we should read 1 John, not trying to discern the flow of the argument as we would in a Pauline letter, but rather recognising that it is, in its structure and rhetorical form, a piece of epideictic rhetoric. It does not seek to prove anything; on the contrary, it seeks to increase the readers' adherence to traditional truths of the Christian community in the face of the threat posed by the secessionists' doctrine and ethics.

Structure. As a piece of epideictic rhetoric, 1 John, not surprisingly, lacks a clear structure. Instead it revisits the same themes over and over, each time amplifying them further. For this reason commentators have great difficulty describing the structure of this letter. Frequently one reads comments about the repetitive nature of the letter and its spiralling structure.

35. Duane F. Watson, 'Amplification Techniques in 1 John: The Interaction of Rhetorical Style and Invention', *JSNT* 51 (1993) 100-118.
36. Watson, 'Amplification Techniques in 1 John', 118-23.

31

Brown has suggested that the structure of 1 John mirrors that of the Fourth Gospel, having, as that Gospel does, a prologue (John 1:1-18/ 1 John 1:1-4), followed by two major parts (John 1:19–12:50, the book of signs; John 13:1–20:29, the book of glory/1 John 1:5–3:10; 1 John 3:11– 5:12), and then an epilogue/conclusion (John 21/1 John 5:13-21). Within the two major parts Brown identifies units based on such things as repeated phrases (the 'if we claim . . .' of 1:5–2:2), repeated forms of address ('dear children' in 2:28–3:10), and what he calls inclusions ('spirits' in 4:1-6). Whether this is the best way to uncover the structure of the letter or not, it does usefully identify the units which make it up.

The analysis of 1 John provided below (p. 49) does not seek to trace any developing argument through the letter because there isn't one. Instead it represents an analysis of the letter in terms of what appear to be its natural divisions.

1 John and Qumran

When the Dead Sea Scrolls were discovered and compared with writings in the NT, scholars noted many parallels between themes developed in 1 John and in the Scrolls. Most of the parallels to 1 John are found in the Manual of Discipline (1QS). These include light and darkness, truth and deceit (1QS 3:19/1 John 1:5, 8; 2:4, 21-22; 3:17-19); the division of people into two groups, sons of light (1QS 3:13, 24, 25/1 John 1:7) and sons of darkness (1QS 1:10/1 John 1:7), who are distinguished by these pairs of opposites. They are motivated by two spirits, the spirit of truth and the spirit of deceit (1QS 3:18, 19/1 John 4:6), the spirits of light and darkness and the angels or princes of light and darkness (1QS 3:20-25/1 John 3:8-10). In addition, there are parallel emphases upon brotherly love (1QS 2:24-25; 5:4, 24-25/1 John 2:7-11; 3:10-14), community (1QS 1:1; 3:12; 5:1; 8:1, 5, 19/1 John 1:3-7), knowledge (1QS 4:22; 9:17-18/1 John 4:2, 6), confession of sin (1QS 1:23-26/1 John 1:8-10), and idols (1QS 2:11, 17; 4:5/ 1 John 5:21).[37]

While there are a number of parallels, as illustrated above, we cannot say that the Dead Sea Scrolls have had any direct influence on the thought of 1 John. What they share in common are concepts often found in the great religions. Further, 1 John differs in the most significant ways from the Dead Sea Scrolls, most clearly, of course, in the place given to Jesus Christ.[38]

37. Thomas A. Hoffman, '1 John and the Qumran Scrolls', *BTB* 8 (1978) 117-22.
38. Hoffman, '1 John and the Qumran Scrolls', 122-24.

Major Theological Themes

We will deal with major theological themes as they arise in the commentary which follows. Here we will simply offer a summary statement. In seeking to describe these major theological themes we must first take note of the points the author himself wished to emphasise. These are all related to his rejection of the secessionists' teaching and behaviour and his desire to reassure his readers. Other significant themes will emerge along the way.

What the Author Affirmed While Rejecting Secessionist Teaching. First, in response to secessionist claims to be intimate with God the author insists that those who truly know God do right, avoid sin, and love their fellow believers. Second, in response to secessionist teaching concerning the person of Christ the author insists on the real humanity of Jesus as the Christ, the Son of God, come in the flesh. Third, in response to the secessionist teaching concerning the work of Christ, the author argues that he came 'not by water only, but by water and blood'; that is, Christ not only has a baptising ministry, but he also made the atoning sacrifice for our sins through his death on the cross.

What the Author Affirmed While Reassuring His Readers. The author's primary aim in writing 1 John was to reassure his readers, whose confidence had been shaken by the activities of the secessionists. Assurance, then, is a pervading theme in the letter, and the grounds of assurance that the author provides tend to be objective and ethical rather than subjective and doctrinaire. The readers' assurance is to be grounded on God's testimony about his Son, their own godly living, loving action and concern for fellow believers, their obedience to the love command, and the Spirit's testimony to Christ (see 'A Note on the Bases of Assurance', pp. 198-200).

Linked to the readers' loving action and their acceptance of God's testimony is a corresponding assurance that God will hear their prayers. If they convince their hearts to be generous to needy fellow believers, then they will experience confidence before God when they pray, and know that they will receive what they ask of him. Likewise, believing in the name of the Son of God results in confidence in approaching God, so that whatever they ask for according to his will they will receive.

In seeking to reassure his readers the author had to remind them that they, too, were recipients of the anointing from God. They, too, had the Holy Spirit, who taught them all things they needed to know concerning Christ, so that they did not need any of the teachings of the secessionists. They had received the Spirit of truth, the one who bore true testimony to Jesus (see 'A Note on the Role of the Spirit', pp. 151-55).

What the Author Taught along the Way. In the process of refuting the secessionist teaching and reassuring his readers, the author makes a number of statements from which we can infer certain things about his understanding of other important themes. The most important of these is the nature of God. The author of 1 John highlights three characteristics of God. First, God is light, and in him there is no darkness of sin (1:5). This means that those who know God will walk in the light (1:7), they will not continue in sin because they are born of God (3:9; 5:18), and they will do what is right (3:10). Second, God is love (4:7). He has lavished his love upon believers by making them his children (3:1). His love was revealed in the sending of his Son as the atoning sacrifice for sins so that people might live through him (4:9-10). Those who have been born of God, who have experienced his love, will love others in practical ways (3:17; 4:7, 12); and while no one has ever seen God, when believers love one another they show that God lives in them and they in God (4:12, 16). Third, God is revealed as the Father of Jesus Christ (1:2, 3; 2:22, 23, 24; 4:14). To love the Son is to love the Father (5:1). God has borne testimony to his Son (5:9-11), and those who believe that testimony dwell in God (4:15) and have eternal life (5:11).

The theme of eternal life is pervasive throughout 1 John. It appears first in the preface concerning the Word of life, where the author says that the eternal life which was with the Father has been revealed to us in his Son, Jesus Christ (1:2). The Fourth Gospel (5:26) says that the Father has life in himself and has given the Son also to have life in himself. This throws light on what the author means when he says that whoever 'has' the Son has eternal life (5:11-13). Those who have the Son, who have eternal life, are those who may be said to have been born of God, and the evidences of this are avoidance of sin, love of fellow believers, and belief that Jesus is the Christ (2:29; 3:9; 4:7; 5:1, 4, 18) (see 'A Note on Eternal Life', pp. 184-87).

Another important theme is the atonement. The author makes mention of, or alludes to, the atonement in four places in the letter. The first of these is 2:2, where the author speaks of Christ as 'the atoning sacrifice *(hilasmos)* for our sins, and not only for ours but also for the sins of the whole world'. The next reference is found in 3:8b: 'The reason the Son of God appeared was to destroy the devil's work', that is, the proliferation of sin. Another reference appears in 4:10: 'This is love: not that we loved God, but that he loved us and sent his Son as an atoning sacrifice *(hilasmos)* for our sins.' A final allusion to the atonement is found in 5:6, where the author insists that Jesus 'did not come by water only, but by water and blood', a reference to the importance not only of Jesus' (the Spirit's) baptising ministry but also of his vicarious death. From all this we may conclude that the author viewed the death of Christ both as the proof of God's love and as an atoning sacrifice for sin, by which the devil's work was destroyed. When one seeks to understand what is meant by 'the atoning sacrifice' *(hilasmos)* in 1 John 2:2 and 4:10, he or she can rule out neither the idea of expiation nor propitiation as possible meanings. It is only the context of *hilasmos* in these texts that can provide the answer. As we argue in the commentary on 2:2 below, the context of that verse does support the idea of propitiation, though this must not be thought of in pagan terms as the overcoming of the wrath of a hostile god because, as 4:10 makes clear, it was God himself who provided his Son as the atoning sacrifice for our sins (see 'A Note on *Hilasmos*', pp. 75-76).

Still another theme which receives considerable emphasis in 1 John is that those who are born of God do not sin. They cannot sin because they are born of God, or because God's 'seed' remains in them. The children of God are distinguished from the children of the devil on this basis: those who do right are of God, while those who commit sin are of the devil (3:4-10). Such teaching, however, stands in apparent contradiction to what the author says in 1:8-9: 'If we claim to be without sin, we deceive ourselves and the truth is not in us. If we confess our sins, he is faithful and just and will forgive us our sins and purify us from all unrighteousness'. The tension between these two parts of the letter is best resolved by recognising that sin in chapter 3 is defined as *anomia,* which in context is to be understood as rebellion, and is related to the devil's opposition to God. It is impossible for those born of God to have any part in *anomia* (see 'A Note on Sinless Perfectionism', pp. 126-32).

One can find references and allusions to the Holy Spirit in several places in 1 John. Most of what the author says about the Holy Spirit refers to his role as true witness to Jesus Christ. In face of the claims of the secessionists to have received special revelations from the Spirit, the author reminds his readers that they have 'an anointing from the Holy One', the Holy Spirit, who teaches them all they need to know so that they do not need the secessionists to teach them. The Holy Spirit taught them the truth about Christ in the gospel message which they received at the beginning of their Christian lives, and they should remain committed to that teaching (2:20-27). In 3:24b–4:6 the readers are told about the Spirit of truth and the spirit of falsehood, and how to distinguish between the two. Where the Spirit of truth is at work, people acknowledge that Jesus Christ has come in the flesh, something denied by those in whom the spirit of falsehood (the spirit of antichrist) is operating. A similar statement is found in 4:13-16, where the Spirit is related to the true confession of Jesus Christ as the Son of God. In 5:6-8 the Spirit is once more presented as the witness to the truth about Christ: there are three who bear witness in this passage, the Spirit, the water, and the blood, and these all agree (see commentary *ad loc.*). Finally, in 3:9 believers are said to be not able to commit sin *(anomia)* because God's seed remains in them. This is a bold metaphor, but when unpacked it refers to the work of the Spirit in believers (see 'A Note on the Role of the Spirit', pp. 151-55).

INTRODUCTORY MATTERS RELATED TO 2 JOHN

Authorship

Unlike 1 John, this letter *does* begin with the usual A to B greeting formula, and the author *does* identify himself, but not as clearly as we, modern readers, might like. He introduces himself simply as 'the elder' (v. 1). External evidence suggests that there was someone known as 'the elder John', distinct from the apostle John, who also lived in Ephesus, and who may have been responsible for the writing of 2 John (and 3 John). As in the case of 1 John, a citation of a statement of Papias by Eusebius, and Eusebius's own interpretation of that statement, constitute the evidence for the existence of a second 'John', the elder, in Ephesus (see above, pp. 13-14).

As we also noted earlier in this Introduction (see p. 14 above), the reference to the two Johns, the apostle and the elder, makes way for the later belief, reported by Jerome, that the elder, not the apostle, was the author of 2 and 3 John.

Despite this late tradition, it has to be emphasised that there are many similarities between 1 John and 2 John which have obvious implications for the authorship of 2 John, and these have led scholars to suggest that the same author is responsible for both letters.[39] First, the elder deals with the same historical situation as that reflected in 1 John. He speaks of those who 'have gone out into the world' and 'do not acknowledge Jesus Christ as coming in the flesh'; people who 'run ahead' and 'do not continue in the teaching of Christ' (vv. 7, 9; cf. 1 John 2:19, 22-23). Sec-

---

39. So, e.g., tentatively, Smalley, *1, 2, 3 John,* xxii. This is also the working hypothesis adopted by Brown, *The Epistles of John,* 19. So, too, Schnackenburg, *The Johannine Epistles,* 276.

ond, he brands these false teachers as antichrists, as does the author of 1 John (v. 7; cf. 1 John 2:18, 22). Third, the elder stresses the great importance of the love command, which was received at the beginning along with the gospel, just as the author of 1 John does (vv. 4-6; cf. 3:11, 23; 4:7, 21; 5:1-4a). Fourth, the elder, like the author of 1 John, finds his joy in seeing his children walking in the truth of the gospel (v. 4; cf. 1 John 1:3-4). However, the fact that the elder who wrote 2 John did not hesitate to identify himself, whereas the author of 1 John, like the author of the Fourth Gospel, refrains from doing so, could point in the opposite direction. The matter is difficult to decide. If we are swayed by the similarities between 1 and 2 John and conclude that the same author wrote both, we must fly in the face of later tradition. On the other hand, if we accept later tradition we are still left with the task of explaining how there could be such similarities between the letters if the authors were different. This commentary adopts the view that all three letters were written by the same person; in other words, it gives more weight to internal evidence than to relatively late tradition.

A couple of other things can be said about the elder. First, his self-references, when he is distinguishing himself from his readers, are entirely in first person singular form (unlike 1 John, where the author uses the first person plural in some places to distinguish himself from his readers while associating himself with other eyewitnesses of the incarnate Christ). Second, the paraenetic nature of the letter (it contains both encouragement and dissuasion) indicates that the elder is on friendly terms with his readers and that they consider him to be a friendly superior.[40] Beyond this it is difficult to go, though Strecker suggests that he was 'the principal authority of the Johannine circle',[41] and Brown that he was 'a disciple of the disciples of Jesus'.[42]

Addressees

The introductory greetings (vv. 1-3) are addressed to 'the chosen lady *(eklektē kyria)* and her children'. The rest of the letter has these people in mind, even though what is said is addressed sometimes to the 'lady' *(kyria)* using the second person singular (vv. 4-5, 13), and sometimes to both the lady and her children using the second person plural (vv. 6-12).

---

40. Duane F. Watson, 'A Rhetorical Analysis of 2 John according to Greco-Roman Convention', *NTS* 35 (1989) 108.
41. Strecker, *The Johannine Letters*, 219.
42. Brown, *The Epistles of John*, 650-51.

Brown lists five interpretations for the meaning of 'elect lady': (i) the lady Electa, referring to a certain Babylonian lady named 'Electa'; (ii) 'the noble Kyria'; (iii) 'dear lady', a colourless term of courtesy addressed to an individual woman; (iv) an elect lady, meaning the church at large; (v) an elect lady and her children, a symbolic reference to a church in a town at some distance from the community centre in which the author is living. Brown, like many others, adopts the fifth option.[43] Klauck points out that Bauer, Arndt, and Gingrich's *A Greek-English Lexicon of the New Testament* is misleading when it cites Hellenistic sources (which include references to *kyria ekklēsia*) in support of an interpretation of *eklektē kyria* as lady congregation. The references cited refer to an Athenian assembly and provide no support for a metaphorical interpretation of the *kyria ekklēsia*. Nevertheless, Klauck agrees with most modern commentators that *eklektē kyria* does refer to the congregation, and he finds support for this interpretation in the many references in the OT and Apocrypha to Israel as wife, bride, mother, daughter, etc.[44] In this commentary we take 'the chosen lady and her children' to mean a church and its members. The 'lady' has a 'chosen sister' in the place from which the elder writes, whose 'children' send her their greetings (v. 13).

The elder rejoices that some of the 'children' of the elect lady are living by the truth (v. 4) On the surface, this might imply that some were not, that some had already succumbed to the deceit of the secessionists (cf. vv. 7-9). But there is no indication elsewhere in the letter that this is the case, so it is best to regard the elder's statement as expressing joy over those he has heard are walking in the truth, without implying that others are not.

Opponents

As we have already mentioned, there are similarities between the false teachers mentioned by the author of 1 John and those the elder warns his readers about in 2 John. Like those mentioned in 1 John, the false teachers of 2 John are described as those 'who do not acknowledge Jesus Christ as coming in the flesh' and are accordingly branded antichrists (v. 7; cf. 1 John 4:2-3). They are further described as people who run ahead and do not continue in the teaching of Christ (v. 9). These people are said to 'have gone out into the world' (v. 7; cf. 1 John 2:19), a technical expression de-

---

43. Brown, *The Epistles of John*, 651-55.
44. Hans-Josef Klauck, '*Kyria ekklēsia* in Bauers Wörterbuch und die Exegese des zweiten Johannesbriefes', *ZNW* 81 (1990) 135-38.

noting the activity of missionaries.[45] They were apparently on the road between a number of churches because the elder says, 'If anyone comes to you and does not bring this teaching ["the teaching of Christ" as it was received at the beginning], do not take him into your house or welcome him' (v. 10). While this is pretty scant information, as one would expect in such a brief letter, it is, nevertheless, enough to indicate that the false teachers of 2 John are the same as those the author of 1 John sought to expose. Therefore the things said in the discussion of the false teachers of 1 John above also apply to those the elder warns his readers about in 2 John.

Purpose and Time of Writing

The elder's primary purpose in writing was to warn his readers about the deceivers, and of the dire consequences of welcoming them and accepting their teaching: they would lose the reward for which they (we) have worked (v. 8), by 'running ahead' and failing to continue in the teaching of Christ they would no longer 'have' either the Father or the Son (v. 9), and by welcoming these deceivers and accepting their teaching they would become partakers in their wicked work (v. 11). Vouga notes that the elder does not provide any new arguments against the false teachers. He is content to quote 'a string of ready made formulae taken directly from the Gospel or from the first Epistle'.[46]

The elder has a second, related purpose in writing: to remind the 'lady' of the command that they had from the beginning, that they love one another (v. 5). The elder is concerned to ensure that the secessionists do not succeed in alienating this 'lady' from fellowship with him.[47]

The letter may also have been intended as a forerunner to a personal visit, during which the elder will speak face to face with the 'lady', thus cementing the fellowship threatened by the secessionists, and so completing both his joy and hers (v. 12). However, it is possible, as Watson suggests, that this stated intention may be no more than an epistolary convention.[48]

There are obvious parallels between the elder's purpose in writing 2 John and the purpose of the author of 1 John in writing that letter. Both are concerned to counteract the teaching of people who have seceded

45. François Vouga, 'The Johannine School: A Gnostic Tradition in Primitive Christianity?' *Bib* 69 (1988) 372.
46. Vouga, 'The Johannine School', 373.
47. Cf. Vouga, 'The Johannine School', 372.
48. Watson, 'A Rhetorical Analysis of 2 John', 129.

from a Christian community and who are propagating teaching which denies that Jesus Christ has come in the flesh. Both are intent upon maintaining fellowship with their readers, and both realise that it is only by so doing that their own joy can be made complete.

If the elder who wrote 2 John also wrote 1 John, then clearly he wrote 2 John around the same time as 1 John, and in it he dealt, albeit more briefly, with the same sort of problem precipitated by the same people. If 1 John was a circular letter sent to a number of churches in the area around Ephesus in the early part of the last decade of the first century, then 2 John could be a letter sent to one of these churches shortly after the sending of the circular letter to warn members of an impending approach by the secessionists, and the need to adopt a practical strategy (refusal of hospitality) to limit their operations. If the elder was not responsible for the writing of 1 John, then we would have to say that he wrote 2 John to deal with the same problem confronted in 1 John (the propaganda of the secessionists and its effect upon the orthodox believers), and that he appears to have been acquainted with the contents of 1 John, as well as the contents of the Fourth Gospel. Like 1 John, 2 John was probably written in the early part of the last decade of the first century.

Genre, Rhetorical Form, and Structure

There is no doubt that 2 John fits into the genre of a typical Greco-Roman letter. It begins with the normal A to B address formula ('the elder to the chosen lady and her children . . .') (v. 1), followed by a greeting ('grace, mercy and peace from God the Father . . .') (v. 3), and then an expression of the writer's pleasure in remembering his readers ('it has given me great joy to find some of your children walking in the truth . . .') (v. 4). In the body of the letter that follows the elder urges his readers to continue with him in practising love for one another (vv. 5-6), and warns them about the false teachers and the evil consequences that would follow if they assisted them by providing hospitality (vv. 7-11). The letter closes with an epistolary commonplace indicating the writer's desire to see his readers face to face rather than write more at this time (v. 12) and the final greeting (v. 13).

Watson classifies 2 John as 'a letter of exhortation and advice, and the subtype of such letters, the paraenetic letter'.[49] He classifies it rhetorically as a deliberative letter because it manifests several of the typical features of deliberative rhetoric: (i) the letter is clearly intended to 'advise

---

49. Watson, 'A Rhetorical Analysis of 2 John', 107.

and dissuade' (v. 5); (ii) the letter is future oriented (dealing with the imminent arrival of the secessionists) (v. 10); (iii) the elder makes use of the *topoi* (themes) usually found in deliberative rhetoric, that is, 'what is advantageous and harmful, expedient and inexpedient'; (iv) the letter is paraenetic, and paraenetic letters are usually deliberative.[50]

Watson analyses 2 John as follows: vv. 1-4: *praescriptio/exordium*, in which the elder seeks to gain his readers' goodwill; v. 5: *narratio*, outlining the main concerns of the elder; vv. 6-11: *probatio*, containing the 'constraints' the author brings to bear to get the readers to implement his concerns; v. 12: *peroratio*, which normally repeats and emphasises the points made in the *narratio* and *probatio* and which is here simply an expression of the elder's desire to have face-to-face contact; v. 13: the epistolary closing, with its reference to 'the children of your chosen sister', which forms an *inclusio* with the opening greeting and serves to strengthen the relationship between the two communities, thus 'creating positive pathos'.[51]

Wendland suggests that, following the opening greetings (vv. 1-3), the body of the letter is arranged in two sections, the first largely positive (vv. 4-6), the second largely negative (vv. 7-11), and then the whole is concluded on a positive note in which the elder speaks of his desire to meet face to face with his readers (vv. 12-13).[52]

The analysis of 2 John used in this commentary may be found on p. 49 below.

Major Themes

Being such a brief letter, 2 John does not develop any major theological themes of its own. It repeats in much briefer form ideas found in 1 John (e.g., the importance of obedience to the love command and the failure of the secessionists to acknowledge Jesus' coming in the flesh). One new idea introduced in 2 John is the matter of hospitality; 2 John shows how providing it to the secessionists would involve the readers in promoting their 'wicked work' (see 'A Note on Hospitality', pp. 215-16).

---

50. Watson, 'A Rhetorical Analysis of 2 John', 109.
51. Watson, 'A Rhetorical Analysis of 2 John', 113-29.
52. E. R. Wendland, 'What Is Truth? Semantic Density and the Language of the Johannine Epistles (with Special Reference to 2 John)', *Neot* 24 (1990) 316.

INTRODUCTORY MATTERS RELATED TO 3 JOHN

Authorship

Like 2 John, this letter begins with the standard A to B address formula in which the author identifies himself as 'the elder' (v. 1). He writes from within a community of 'friends' *(philoi),* who join him in sending greetings (v. 15). In a couple of places he associates others with himself in what he writes: in vv. 9-10 he says that a certain Diotrephes 'will have nothing to do with *us'*, and is 'gossiping maliciously about *us'*, and in v. 12 he says of a certain Demetrius that *'we* also speak well of him, and you know that *our* testimony is true'. In the context of 3 John, these first person plural forms are probably best understood to denote the elder and the 'friends' who send their greetings along with his own (v. 15), who together constitute the church (v. 6) in the place ('here') from which the elder writes (v. 15).

The striking similarities of language, content, and style between 2 John and 3 John indicate that the same person was responsible for writing both letters: in both the elder expresses his joy that the 'children' are 'walking in the truth' (2 John 4; 3 John 4); in both the addressees (the 'chosen lady' and Gaius respectively) are described as those whom the elder loves 'in the truth' (2 John 1; 3 John 1); and both conclude with virtually identical statements (2 John 12: 'I have much to write to you, but I do not want to use paper and ink. Instead, I hope to visit you and talk with you face to face'. 3 John 13-14a: 'I have much to write you, but I do not want to do so with pen and ink. I hope to see you soon, and we will talk face to face').

As we noted in the comments on the authorship of 2 John above, internal evidence suggests that 2 John was written by the same person who wrote 1 John; the same may be said about 3 John.[53] However, we also noted there some external evidence suggests that there was someone known as 'the elder John', distinct from the apostle John, who also lived in Ephesus, and who was responsible for the writing of 2 John and 3 John. The position adopted in this commentary, giving the greater weight to internal evidence, is that the same person wrote all three letters.

---

53. Bernhard Bonsack, 'Der Presbyteros des dritten Briefs und der geliebte Jünger des Evangeliums nach Johannes', ZNW 79 (1988) 62, believes that the beloved disciple who wrote the Fourth Gospel and functioned as an authoritative teacher of the Christian community could have designated himself as 'the elder' when he wrote 3 John at a later time.

Addressee

The letter is written to Gaius, whom the elder repeatedly addresses as 'dear friend' *(agapēte)* (vv. 1, 2, 5, 11), and whom he regards as spiritually sound (v. 2). Gaius is known to be faithful to the truth (v. 3) and faithful in providing hospitality (vv. 5-7). Gaius, like the elder, is associated with a group of Christian friends *(philoi)* to whom the elder sends his greetings (v. 15), and together with Gaius these friends probably constitute the 'church' in the place where Gaius lived, and the church to which the elder had written previously in the letter mentioned in v. 9 (probably now lost).

Gaius must have been a person of means because he was in a position to provide hospitality to itinerant missionaries, indicating that he occupied a house of significant proportions. The elder did not hesitate to call on him to continue this ministry of hospitality, which also suggests that he must have been a person of some means.

A number of people named Gaius are mentioned in the NT. In Acts a Gaius from Macedonia was one of Paul's travelling companions (Acts 19:29), and there is a Gaius from Derbe (Acts 20:4). There was also a Gaius among the early converts of the apostle Paul in Corinth (1 Cor 1:14). He was probably the same person whom Paul mentioned as the one 'whose hospitality I and the whole church here enjoy' when he wrote Romans from Corinth (Rom 16:23). We cannot be sure whether the Gaius to whom the elder wrote 3 John is to be identified with one of these people or with none.

Itinerant Missionaries

It is clear from references that the elder makes in 3 John that itinerant Christians moved between the Christian communities to which he and Gaius respectively belonged. The 'brothers' who had been recipients of Gaius's hospitality were most likely members of the elder's community and reported to it (vv. 5-6), and regarded his community as their base. They had gone out 'for the sake of the Name', most likely as itinerant preachers; and, following the pattern laid down by Jesus (Matt 10:10-11), they depended on the hospitality shown to them by people like Gaius in the places they visited (vv. 7-8). Demetrius, who is commended by the elder and those associated with him (v. 12), was probably an itinerant preacher from the same community.

Diotrephes and the Elder

In 3 John there is no mention of secessionists as there is in 1 and 2 John. The only opponent of the elder is one Diotrephes. The elder had written (probably on behalf of the church of which he was a part) an earlier letter to the church of which Gaius was a part (v. 9a). Some think the letter to which the elder refers is 2 John, but this is unlikely because nothing in 2 John constitutes a letter of recommendation for travelling missionaries — all it does is warn against providing hospitality to the heretical teachers. There is no appeal in the letter which Diotrephes would have rejected. This earlier letter is probably now lost.

In this lost letter the elder asked the church to provide hospitality to itinerant missionaries setting out from his own church. But this request had been refused, and the elder's honour had been damaged by malicious gossip originating from Diotrephes. In connection with the writing of this letter the elder says: 'I wrote to the church; but Diotrephes, who loves to be first, will have nothing to do with us' (v. 9), and adds that Diotrephes has been 'gossiping maliciously about us' (v. 10a). Diotrephes's opposition to the elder manifested itself in his refusal 'to welcome the brothers' (the itinerant preachers), and in his expelling from the church those who wanted to welcome them (v. 10b). The exact nature of the conflict between Diotrephes and the elder has been variously interpreted.

First, some have suggested that the conflict is one of ecclesiastical authority. Diotrephes has been regarded as an authoritarian bishop in the early church who abused his powers of excommunication.[54] Adolf Harnack saw in Diotrephes the first of the monarchical bishops known to us by name.[55] Taeger adopts an opposite view, arguing that it was the elder's desire to impose his own leadership and teaching authority on another church that led to the conflict reflected in 3 John. According to him, Diotrephes stood for the original 'Johannine' form of church order in which each member had an unmediated relationship to Christ through the Spirit-Paraclete, and he resisted the elder's attempt to impose something else. It was the elder, not Diotrephes, who was moving towards monarchical leadership within the church.[56] Storm argues that when Diotrephes ignored or suppressed the elder's letter and refused hospital-

---

54. Theodore Zahn, *Introduction to the New Testament* (repr., Minneapolis, Minnesota: Klock & Klock, 1953) 3:375-78.

55. Adolf Harnack, 'Über den dritten Johannesbrief', TU 15 (1897), 16ff., cited by Jens-W. Taeger, 'Der konservative Rebell: Zum Widerstand des Diotrephes gegen den Presbyter', ZNW 78 (1987) 268.

56. Taeger, 'Der konservative Rebell', 286-87.

ity to the brethren, he was in fact rejecting the authority of the spiritual community of which the elder was the spiritual and moral leader. The real issue between the elder and Diotrephes, then, was over the question of authority within Diotrephes' local congregation. In his view, the authority of the elder was moral and spiritual, while that of Diotrephes was brutally practical. Storm cites Perkins with approval, namely, that in a time when the author's community was breaking up (evidence: the breaking away of the secessionists and their missionary activity), when the *koinōnia* no longer existed, Diotrephes believed that no one (including the elder) had the right to require support for travelling missionaries.[57]

Second, others have argued that the conflict between the elder and Diotrephes is to be interpreted as a struggle for doctrinal orthodoxy. Walter Bauer argues that Diotrephes was the heretic, and the elder the one standing for the orthodox faith.[58] Bonsack adopts a similar position, arguing that the elder was the head, the authoritative witness of the truth, in one of several places where 'Johannine' groups lived. He worked with fellow Christians and possessed a certain weight for Christians of other groups. However, he was rejected by Diotrephes (who claimed the first place in his own local group) because of the deviant form of universal Christianity which he represented. He (the elder) hoped, through a discussion, to win back recognition for the truth in Diotrephes' place.[59] Ernst Käsemann also regards the issue between Diotrephes and the elder as one of theology, but argued that it was Diotrephes, not the elder, who stood for the traditional beliefs, and it was the elder who was introducing new ideas.[60]

Third, Price argues that the conflict between Diotrephes and the elder arose because of a regrettable misunderstanding. He offers the following scenario: Members of the elder's church, unknown to him, had adopted a docetic type of Christology and were propagating it in other churches (including Diotrephes' church) without the elder's knowledge. Diotrephes was shocked when he heard their teaching and assumed that the elder, whose emissaries he took them to be, had become a heretic. Diotrephes expelled the missionaries. Subsequently another team from the elder's church, who did not share the commitment to the docetic teaching, turned up in Diotrephes' church, and because they were deemed to represent the

---

57. Melvin R. Storm, 'Diotrephes: A Study of Rivalry in the Apostolic Church', *ResQ* 35 (1993) 196-98, 201.

58. Walter Bauer, *Orthodoxy and Heresy in Earliest Christianity* (Philadelphia: Fortress, 1971) 93.

59. Bonsack, 'Der Presbyteros des dritten Briefs', 46-50.

60. Ernst Käsemann, 'Ketzer und Zeuge. Zum johanneischen Verfasserproblem', *ZTK* 48 (1951) 310-11. So, too, Strecker, *The Johannine Letters*, 262-63.

heretical elder, they were summarily expelled also. News of this got back to the elder, and he sent off a letter to Diotrephes' church, but this letter (mentioned in 3 John 9) was suppressed by Diotrephes, who assumed that it was heretical. Next the elder sent another letter (3 John) to Gaius (probably carried by Demetrius, whom it commended) thanking Gaius for his hospitality, condemning the actions of Diotrephes, and promising to make a visit himself. Finally, the elder did make his visit and found out the truth of the matter (his own church members had, unknown to him, been propagating heresy in Diotrephes' church). The elder then agreed with Diotrephes to implement a policy of noncooperation with the Docetists. Upon returning home, the elder expelled the Docetists from his own community and began to write letters to the other churches urging the same policy of noncooperation (2 John). Later he concluded that it would be better to do this by one circular letter in which he set out his theological grounds for this (1 John).[61]

Fourth, Brown offers the following reconstruction: Diotrephes, like the elder, was the host of a house church, and these house churches were in the habit of providing hospitality to travelling missionaries. However, when the secession took place and the secessionist missionaries began their activities, the situation became quite difficult. The elder sought first to contain the heretical teachings of the secessionists by urging his readers to test the spirits and call for a correct christological confession. This proved insufficient to deal with the situation, and he then called upon his readers not to provide hospitality to the secessionist missionaries. Diotrephes went a little further, refusing hospitality to all itinerant missionaries (including those who had gone out in good faith from the elder's own house church), and hence animosity arose between the elder and Diotrephes.[62]

In seeking to evaluate these various options, one must first note that there is no reference to doctrinal matters at all in 3 John, and it is therefore unlikely that the issue between Diotrephes and the elder was doctrinal. To support a doctrinal option we would have to assume that Diotrephes was associated with the secessionists mentioned in 1 John and 2 John. This is possible, but there is no evidence to back it up. Price's reconstruction is attractive because of its ingenuity, and it is feasible. However, there is very little evidence to support the scenario he suggests. The only approach which has support in the text of 3 John is that which interprets the conflict in terms of ecclesiastical authority.[63] The elder says: 'I wrote

---

61. Robert M. Price, 'The Sitz-im-Leben of Third John: A New Reconstruction', *EvQ* 61 (1989) 114-19.

62. Brown, *The Epistles of John*, 738.

63. So, too, Brown, *The Epistles of John*, 107; Schnackenburg, *The Johannine Epistles*, 296-99.

to the church, but Diotrephes, who loves to be first, will have nothing to do with us' (lit. 'does not receive us', *ouk epidechetai hēmas*) (v. 9). The elder uses the same verb *(epidechomai)* in the next verse when referring to Diotrephes' refusal to 'welcome the brothers', meaning provide them with hospitality. The use of the verb here in v. 9 is metaphorical: Diotrephes did not welcome the elder in that he did not accede to the request made by the elder in his letter. Diotrephes rejected the elder's authority by refusing his request to provide hospitality to travelling missionaries.

Purpose and Time of Writing

The elder who wrote 2 John is clearly the same person who wrote 3 John. Therefore, it is tempting to suggest that the elder's purpose in writing was the same in both cases: to confront the threat posed by the secessionists' teaching. If this was the case, then we could say that the elder's dispute with Diotrephes was theological. Diotrephes would represent the secessionist point of view, and therefore he refused hospitality to those who came with the elder's recommendation because he disagreed with the elder on matters of theology. The elder would then have written 3 John to expose Diotrephes' actions, and seek to limit his influence in support of the secessionists.

But as we have already noted, there is no evidence in 3 John itself that the conflict between Diotrephes and the elder had a theological basis. For this reason it is best to regard the basic reason for this letter to Gaius as being to ensure that he continued his good work of providing hospitality, and to indicate to him that Diotrephes' refusal to accept his recommendation, and the dishonour heaped upon the elder by this action, would not go unchallenged.

The elder's purpose in writing 3 John can be described as threefold, corresponding to the three sections of the letter. It was intended to: (i) reinforce Gaius's commitment to the noble work of providing hospitality to travelling missionaries, something he was already doing (vv. 5-8); (ii) draw attention to the intolerable behaviour of Diotrephes and to foreshadow the steps the elder intended to take in response to it (vv. 9-10); and (iii) commend Demetrius (v. 12).

We cannot know for sure in what order 2 John and 3 John were written, but the similarities of expression in the two letters suggest that they were written at about the same time — probably in the early part of the last decade of the first century.

Genre, Rhetorical Form, and Structure

Like 2 John, 3 John falls clearly into the category of a typical GrecoRoman letter. It opens with the usual A to B address formula (v. 1) followed by expressions of good wishes for Gaius's health, and the elder's pleasure in receiving good news of Gaius's faith (vv. 2-4). The body of the letter, consisting of three parts, follows (vv. 4-12), and then the conclusion with final greetings (vv. 13-14).

Stowers says that 3 John is essentially a letter of recommendation for travelling missionaries, but one which displays a freedom of composition not found in the papyrus letters. It also contains a short invective in vv. 9-10 and an exhortation in vv. 11-12.[64] Watson argues that 3 John is a mixed letter exhibiting characteristics of the friendly letter, the advisory letter, the letter of commendation, the letter of praise, the letter of encouragement, and the letter of vituperation. From a rhetorical point of view, it is an epideictic letter, one which is designed to increase Gaius's commitment to values already embraced by him, that is, extending hospitality to travelling missionaries.[65] Watson analyses the body of the letter rhetorically as: (i) *praescriptio* as *exordium* (v. 1), (ii) *exordium* (vv. 2-4), (iii) *narratio* (vv. 5-6), (iv) *probatio* (vv. 7-12); (v) *peroratio* (vv. 13-14), and (vi) postscript as *peroratio* (v. 15).[66]

The analysis used in the commentary which follows may be found on p. 49.

Major Themes

No new theological themes are introduced in 3 John. The issue of hospitality, introduced in 2 John, is found again in 3 John. The one new feature of 3 John is the reference to the 'brothers' who 'went out' 'for the sake of the Name', 'receiving no help from the pagans'. This provides evidence that it was not only some of the secessionists who were moving about among the churches; orthodox missionaries were also on the road, and they were adopting the modus operandi commanded by Christ to be observed by those whom he sent out on the Galilean mission (i.e., receiving support from those to whom they ministered).

---

64. Stanley K. Stowers, *Letter Writing in Greco-Roman Antiquity* (Philadelphia: Westminster, 1986) 156.

65. Duane F. Watson, 'A Rhetorical Analysis of 3 John: A Study in Epistolary Rhetoric," *CBQ* 51 (1989) 482-85.

66. Watson, 'A Rhetorical Analysis of 3 John', 486-500.

ANALYSES

Analysis of 1 John

1:1-4	A preface concerning the Word of life
1:5–2:2	Claims to know God tested by attitudes to sin
2:3-11	Claims to know God tested by obedience
2:12-14	Encouragement for believers of different levels of maturity
2:15-17	Warnings against loving the 'world'
2:18-27	Warnings against being deceived by the secessionists
2:28–3:10	Distinguishing the children of God from the children of the devil
3:11-24	The gospel demand to love one another and confidence in prayer
4:1-6	Testing the 'spirits'
4:7–5:4a	Claims to love God tested by love for fellow believers
5:4b-12	Accepting God's testimony and eternal life
5:13-21	Concluding reassurance for the readers and an exhortation to pray

Analysis of 2 John

vv. 1-3	Opening greetings
vv. 4-6	Walking in the truth
vv. 7-9	Denial of the truth
vv. 10-11	Do not receive those who deny the truth
vv. 12-13	Final greetings

Analysis of 3 John

v. 1	Opening greetings
vv. 2-4	Rejoicing that Gaius walks in the truth
vv. 5-8	Gaius commended for his hospitality
vv. 9-10	Diotrephes' opposition to the elder
vv. 11-12	The elder's commendation of Demetrius
vv. 13-15	Final greetings

Commentary on 1 John

1:1-4 A PREFACE CONCERNING THE WORD OF LIFE

This letter, written to urge the readers not to be led astray by those who had seceded from the Christian community and to reassure them that they are in the truth, seeks to achieve its purpose by strengthening the readers' commitment to what they already know, that is, the message of the gospel of Jesus Christ which they heard from the beginning. It is in line with this purpose that the author begins his letter with a reminder of the origins of the gospel, the message concerning 'the Word of life' (of which he is a firsthand witness) which constitutes the basis of the fellowship in which he wants them to continue.

1:1 This 'Word of life' is described first of all as **that which was from the beginning** *(ho ēn ap' archēs)*. Modern-day readers of the NT can hardly avoid seeing here an allusion to teaching found in the prologue of the Fourth Gospel: 'In the beginning was the Word' *(en archē ēn ho logos)*. In the context of the prologue of John's Gospel 'the beginning' means the time before the creation of the world. However, in the context of the opening verses of 1 John, 'the beginning' has a different meaning. The expression 'that which was from the beginning' functions as one of a series of relative clauses descriptive of the 'the Word of life', which the passage, as it unfolds, makes quite clear refers to the Word of life incarnate in Jesus Christ. The net result is that when the author describes the Word of life as 'that which was from the beginning', he is in fact speaking primarily of the Word of life incarnate in Jesus Christ, not the Word existing with God prior to the foundation of the world. Nevertheless, the echoes of the prologue of the Gospel found in this statement may imply an identity between the Word of life incarnate in Jesus Christ and the one whom the

51

Fourth Gospel speaks of as being with God in the beginning before the foundation of the world.

Second, the 'Word of life' is described as that **which we have heard**. It is sometimes suggested that this does not imply a firsthand hearing of Jesus' preaching by the author, but only a hearing of the message of Jesus handed down by others. Taken on its own, 'we have heard' could mean this.[1] However, the immediate context of the expression in 1:1 makes it clear that an actual firsthand hearing of the proclamation of Jesus is implied. What was heard is associated with what was seen with the eyes and touched with the hands, expressions which, as we shall see, imply firsthand sense perception. This is in line with the statement in v. 5, where the author speaks of 'the message we have heard *from him*'.

Third, the 'Word of life' is described as that **which we have seen with our eyes** (*ho heōrakamen tois ophthalmois hēmōn*). This expression, found only here in the NT, is used to reinforce the claim that the proclamation of the Word of life comes from one who is an eyewitness.[2] This is supported by the fact that all but one of the 91 uses of expressions combining forms of the verb 'to see' and the words 'with the eyes' in the LXX imply sense perception, that is, a direct personal acquaintance with the object said to have been seen.

Fourth, the 'Word of life' is described as that **which we have looked at** (*ho etheasametha*). The verb *theaomai* is used 22 times in the NT. The 19 uses outside 1 John all denote unambiguously a physical seeing with the human eye. One of the three uses in 1 John (4:12: 'no one has ever seen God') also relates unambiguously to seeing with the human eye. There is little reason, therefore, to think that the other two uses in 1 John, found here in 1:1 and in 4:14 (in both places the author claims to be among those who saw the Word of life/the Son), should be understood in any way other than actual physical seeing with the human eye.

There does not appear to be any notable difference in meaning between the verb 'to see' (*horaō*) and the verb 'to look at' (*theaomai*) used here in v. 1, but the different tenses used in each case represent different emphases by the author: the perfect (in the case of 'we have seen with our eyes') focuses on the status of the author as one of the eyewitnesses, and

---

1. This is the case in a number of other places in the Johannine letters (cf. 1 John 2:7, 24; 3:1; 2 John 6) where the same verb (*akouō*) is used to denote the readers having heard the word of the gospel and the love commandment, and there is no suggestion that they heard these things firsthand from Christ.

2. The author emphasizes his status as one of those who actually saw with his eyes the Word of life by using a perfect form of the verb 'to see' here.

the aorist (in the case of 'we have looked at') simply narrates the seeing itself.

Fifth, the 'Word of life' is described as something which **our hands have touched** *(hai cheires hēmōn epsēlaphēsan).* The expression 'to touch with the hands' is found only here in the NT, but the verb 'to touch' *(psēlaphaō)* occurs in three other places: in Luke 24:39 and Heb. 12:18, where it denotes a physical touching (with the hands), and in Acts 17:27, where it has the metaphorical sense of feeling after God (something made clear by the context). The verb is found 15 times in the LXX, where it is used predominantly to denote actual touching (with the hands). In the present context the author is clearly using the verb to mean actual touching with the hands. By doing so he claims that his proclamation rests on the experience of not only seeing, but also of having touched with his own hands the Word of life.

It is clear from the foregoing that when the author says, **we proclaim[3] concerning the Word of life,** he has in mind something much more than a spoken message.[4] He proclaims the Word of life which he has heard, seen, and touched. As will become clear in what follows, he proclaims a message that has been embodied in a person — the person of Jesus Christ.

A Note on the Language of Sense Perception

Brown includes a lengthy discussion of the identification of 'we' in 1:1, and in particular a discussion of the question whether 'we' were eyewit-

3. The words 'we proclaim' have been added by the translators of the NIV to provide a smooth translation. There is no corresponding equivalent expression in the Greek text.

4. J. Emmette Weir, 'The Identity of the Logos in the First Epistle of John', *ExpTim* 86 (1974-75) 118-20, notes the two possible interpretations of *logos* in this verse: (i) the gospel of Christ or (ii) Christ himself, as in the case of the prologue of John's Gospel. He argues that the latter is the correct interpretation because: (i) In both Gospel and epistle we find the notion of the *logos* being from the beginning. (ii) In both the preposition *pros* is used to express the relationship of the *logos* to God. (iii) In both the *logos* is the source of life, something that, in the Gospel of John, is supported by 14:6. (iv) The claim made by the writer of the epistle to have existential knowledge of the *logos* is appropriate only if the *logos* is a person. K. Grayston, '"Logos" in 1 Jn 1', *ExpTim* 86 (1974-75) 279, contends that Weir may be right about *logos* in 1 John meaning Christ himself as it does in the prologue of John's Gospel, but the points he makes in support of his view need correction: (i) 1 John does not say that the *logos* was from the beginning, and the beginning in 1 John is not necessarily the realm of the eternal. (ii) In 1 John it is the life, not the *logos*, which is *pros* the Father. (iii) His appeal to John 14:6 to make a point about the *logos* is weak. (iv) It is not obvious that existential knowledge is a concept which can only be used of a person, and not of the gospel message.

nesses of the Word of life.[5] Brown, who argues that 'we' were not eyewitnesses but a 'School of tradition bearers', appeals to a number of ancient texts to illustrate how the language of sense perception could be used where sense perception was not involved. It is important to review this evidence, and so the texts to which he appeals are reproduced below together with a brief comment on their significance.

Tacitus, *Agricola* 45:

It was not his [Agricola's] fate to see the Senate-house besieged, the Senate surrounded by armed men, and in the same reign of terror so many consulars butchered, the flight and exile of so many honourable women. Mettius Carus was still rated at one victory only; Messalinus' rasping voice was confined to the Alban citadel; Baebius Massa was still, as before, on trial. A little while and our hands it was which dragged Helvidus to his dungeon; it was we who were (put to shame) by the look which Mauricus and Rusticus gave, we who were soaked by the innocent blood of Senecio. Nero after all withdrew his eyes, nor contemplated the crimes he authorised.

In this text the speakers do use metaphor when they say 'our hands it was which dragged Helvidus to his dungeon' and we 'were soaked by the innocent blood of Senecio'. Nevertheless, they are still acknowledging that they, unlike Agricola, were eyewitnesses of the terrible events they narrate. This text, then, is the testimony of eyewitnesses and provides no precedent for interpreting 1 John 1:1 otherwise.

2 Peter 1:18:

We ourselves heard this voice that came from heaven when we were with him on the sacred mountain.

In this text the author claims to have actually heard the voice from heaven that spoke to the disciples on the Mount of Transfiguration. The only way the implied claim to be an eyewitness here can be denied is to regard 2 Peter as pseudonymous. If it is not pseudonymous, this text also provides no precedent for interpreting 1 John 1:1 as the voice of the 'Johannine School' and not the voice of an eyewitness.

Polycarp, *Philippians* 9:1:

Now I beseech you all to obey the word of righteousness, and to endure with all the endurance which you also saw before your eyes, not

5. Raymond E. Brown, *The Epistles of John* (AB 30, New York: Doubleday, 1982) 158-61.

only in the blessed Ignatius, and Zosimus, and Rufus, but also in others among yourselves, and in Paul himself, and in the other Apostles.

Here Polycarp urges the Philippians to follow the examples of obedience to the word of righteousness (probably meaning the instructions given to them about facing persecution and martyrdom) that they 'saw before their eyes' in the endurance of people they knew, that is, the endurance of Ignatius, Zosimus, Rufus, and others among themselves. Clearly Polycarp was referring to their actual observance of the sufferings of these people. He goes on to cite the example of Paul and the other apostles, whose sufferings the readers had probably not witnessed, and they would know that Polycarp was speaking metaphorically at this point. This text does, then, speak about genuine eyewitness experience, and where it speaks metaphorically the meaning would be obvious. This text provides no precedent for interpreting 1 John 1:1 metaphorically, for that text gives no indication whatever that it is to be read metaphorically.

Irenaeus, *Against Heresies* 5.1.1:

For in no other way could we have learned the things of God, unless our Master, existing as the Word, had become man. For no other being had the power of revealing to us the things of the Father, except His own proper Word. For what other person "knew the mind of the Lord," or who else "has become His counsellor"? Again, we could have learned in no other way than by seeing our Teacher, and hearing His voice with our own ears, that, having become imitators of His works as well as doers of His words, we may have communion with Him, receiving increase from the perfect One, and from Him who is prior to all creation.

Here Irenaeus does speak of 'seeing our Teacher, and hearing His voice with our own ears', something which must definitely be taken as metaphorical, for Irenaeus (A.D. 120-202) lived and wrote well after the time of Christ. But what is true about Irenaeus's writings cannot be said about 1 John 1:1. Everyone would know that Irenaeus was speaking metaphorically, whereas in the case of 1 John 1:1 the clear inference that must be drawn is that the author is using the language of sense perception in a straightforward manner.

Gregory Nazianzen, *Oration* 39:1-4:

At his birth we duly kept Festival, both I, the leader of the Feast, and you, and all that is in the world and above the world. With the Star we ran, and with the Magi we worshipped, and with the Shepherds we were illuminated, and with the Angels we glorified Him, and with Sim-

55

eon we took Him up in our arms, and with Anna the aged and chaste we made our responsive confession.

In this text, Gregory (ca. A.D. 325-91) is clearly speaking in liturgical fashion. It was in the feast, as it were, that they ran with the star, worshipped with the Magi, and glorified Christ with the angels. This text provides no precedent for reading 1 John 1:1 metaphorically.

Amos 2:6-16:

This is what the LORD says: "For three sins of Israel, even for four, I will not turn back [my wrath]. They sell the righteous for silver, and the needy for a pair of sandals. They trample on the heads of the poor as upon the dust of the ground and deny justice to the oppressed. Father and son use the same girl and so profane my holy name. They lie down beside every altar on garments taken in pledge. In the house of their god they drink wine taken as fines. "I destroyed the Amorite before them, though he was tall as the cedars and strong as the oaks. I destroyed his fruit above and his roots below. "I brought you up out of Egypt, and I led you forty years in the desert to give you the land of the Amorites. I also raised up prophets from among your sons and Nazirites from among your young men. Is this not true, people of Israel?" declares the LORD. "But you made the Nazirites drink wine and commanded the prophets not to prophesy. Now then, I will crush you as a cart crushes when loaded with grain. The swift will not escape, the strong will not muster their strength, and the warrior will not save his life. The archer will not stand his ground, the fleet-footed soldier will not get away, and the horseman will not save his life. Even the bravest warriors will flee naked on that day," declares the LORD.

In the midst of this prophecy the Lord says to Israel: 'I brought you up out of Egypt, and I led you forty years in the desert to give you the land of the Amorites' (2:10). These words, relating to the experience of the Exodus generation, are addressed through Amos, an eighth-century (B.C.) prophet, to the Israel of his day. Clearly the prophet is addressing Israel as a nation and reminding her of the history of God's dealings with her, before exposing her present failings. Amos 2:10 clearly provides no precedent for interpreting 1 John 1:1 in a metaphorical way.

Overall, then, the texts cited by Brown as precedents for not interpreting 1 John 1:1 as a claim to be providing eyewitness testimony fail to achieve this aim. There is no compelling reason to reject the view that the author is claiming to be an eyewitness of the things he proclaims.

A Note on 'From the Beginning' (*ap' archēs*)

The expression 'from the beginning' (*ap' archēs*) occurs ten times in the Johannine letters (1 John 1:1; 2:7, 13, 14, 24 [2x]; 3:8, 11; 2 John 5, 6), and in various connections: (i) It is used here in 1:1 in connection with the 'Word of life' that was heard, seen, and handled at the beginning by the eyewitnesses. (ii) In 2:24 it denotes the message of the gospel as it was first heard by the readers of the Johannine letters. (iii) In 2:13, 14 it refers to Christ, who is known by the readers as the one who was from the beginning, that is, the incarnate one (see commentary *ad loc.*). (iv) It is used in 3:8 in connection with the devil, who is described as sinning from the beginning. (v) It is used most frequently in relation to the command to love one another, which the readers heard as part of the gospel message from the beginning (1 John 2:7ff.; 3:11; 2 John 5, 6).

1:2 In this verse the author states clearly what is implied in the previous verse, that is, that **the life appeared** (it had to have appeared, otherwise he could not have seen it, touched it, etc.). The author reiterates that **we have seen it**, and then adds, we **testify to it** and **we proclaim to you the eternal life, which was with the Father**. As we already noted, this reference to eternal life 'which was with the Father' (*hētis ēn pros ton patera*) is an allusion to the teaching found in the prologue of the Fourth Gospel, where the Logos is described as the one who 'was with God' (*houtos ēn . . . pros ton theon*), which in its context means being in the closest relationship with him (cf. John 1:1, 18). The expression 'eternal life' here, then, does not denote an impersonal quality of life that comes from the Father, but refers to the Word of life, the Son of God, who was with the Father prior to his incarnation, and in whom eternal life is found (cf. 1 John 5:11-12). It was the eternal life which was with God from the beginning which, the author says, **has appeared to us** incarnate in Jesus Christ (see 'A Note on Eternal Life', pp. 184-87). Depicting God as Father as the author does here is consistent with the way Jesus' own relationship to God is repeatedly expressed in the Fourth Gospel, where Jesus refers to God as his Father more than a hundred times.

1:3 By saying, **we proclaim to you what we have seen and heard**, the author simply reiterates what he has already affirmed in vv. 1-2. He then goes on to explain his reason for proclaiming what he has seen and heard: **so that you also may have fellowship with us**. The author's purpose is to ensure that his readers persist in the fellowship they have with him. To have fellowship with him is the alternative to having fellowship with the secessionists. In this context 'fellowship' denotes, not only a personal relationship with the author, but also partnership with him in his work of proclamation (see 'A Note on the Meaning of "Fellowship" (*koinōnia*)', pp. 59-61). To have fellowship with the secessionists would involve partnership with them in their (evil) work, as 2 John 11 indicates. To encourage his readers to persist in their fellowship with him and his (good) work, the author reminds them that **our fellowship is with the Father and with his Son, Jesus Christ**. Christian fellowship is primarily a fellowship with God the Father through Jesus Christ his Son. The priority of the Father in this statement reflects the Johannine understanding of things. In the Fourth Gospel even eternal life is defined in similar terms: 'Now this is eternal life: that they may know you, the only true God, and Jesus Christ, whom you have sent' (John 17:3).

Jesus is here described as the Son (*huios*) of God, a term used for him, and him alone, 22 times in 1 John. When the author refers to believers as God's children, he never uses the word 'son' (*huios*), as, for example, Paul does (Rom 8:14, 19; 9:26; 2 Cor 6:18; Gal 3:7, 26; 4:6, 7; 1 Thess 5:5), but consistently uses the word 'child' (*teknion* or *teknon*). This appears to be his way of marking the fundamental distinction between Jesus as the Son of God and believers as God's children. This is the first time in the letter that the term 'Christ' is found. It is used in two ways in the letter. First, here and in 2:1; 3:23; 4:2; 5:6, 20 it is used as part of the expression 'Jesus Christ', which functions as a full name for Jesus. Second, it is used as part of the confessional formula 'Jesus is the Christ', where it points clearly to the fact that Jesus was the (Jewish) Messiah (2:22; 5:1). What the author is saying in this verse is that to have fellowship with him is to have fellowship with God (which also involves fellowship with his Son) and to share in the work of God. As will become apparent in v. 6, the secessionists also claimed to have fellowship with God, but this is a claim which the author rejects.

1:4 The preface of the letter concludes with the author's reason for writing as he does: **We write⁶ this to make our joy complete** (*kai tauta graphomen hēmeis, hina hē chara hēmōn ē peplērōmenē*).⁷ On first reading it seems strange for the author to say that his purpose in writing is to bring

---

6. A present tense form of the verb 'to write' is used here (as it is consistently in the earlier part of the letter [2:1, 7, 8, 12, 13]), indicating that at this point the author presents himself as in the process of writing what he hopes will complete his joy. (Later in the letter [2:14, 21, 26; 5:13] he consistently uses the aorist tense to speak about what he writes, indicating that at those points he is thinking of his writing as one complete act.)

7. Some manuscripts read 'we write these things to you (*hymin*) to make your (*hymōn*) joy complete' instead of 'we (*hēmeis*) write this to make our (*hēmōn*) joy complete'. However, *hēmeis* and *hēmōn* are the harder readings and have stronger external support, while still making good sense when the overall context of the letter is borne in mind: The author's own joy can only be complete when he knows that his readers hold fast to the truth of the gospel as he proclaims it to them (cf. 2 John 4; 3 John 4).

his own joy into a state of completeness — we might expect him to say that it is to bring the joy of his readers into a state of completeness — nevertheless it is an understandable motivation. The author recognises that his own joy in Christ cannot be complete if fellow believers for whom he feels some responsibility are in danger of departing from the truth by becoming involved in another *koinōnia,* one which he will soon prove to be bogus because it does not really involve *koinōnia* with the Father and the Son (vv. 5-7). In 2 John 4 and 3 John 4 a similar sentiment is expressed: The elder's joy comes from knowing that others walk in the truth.

As we noted at the beginning of the commentary on the prologue (1:1-4), the author's purpose in this passage was to remind his readers of the origins of the gospel, that it was a message concerning 'the Word of life', and that this is what constitutes the basis of the fellowship they share and in which he wants them to continue. It may be possible, as Brown suggests, that the author is also consciously correcting secessionist distortions of the prologue of the Fourth Gospel (with which this prologue has many affinities), especially by stressing that experience of the Word of life is mediated through the proclamation of the message that was entrusted to eyewitnesses, and not in any other way.[8]

A Note on the Meaning of 'Fellowship' *(koinōnia)*

The term 'fellowship' *(koinōnia)* is found only four times in 1 John (and not at all in 2 John, 3 John, or the Fourth Gospel). All four occurrences of the word are found in vv. 3, 6, and 7, where the author is concerned to bring his readers into fellowship with those who (truly) proclaim 'the Word of life', which also involves fellowship with the Father and the Son. The author does this against the background of what he believes is the false claim of the secessionists to have fellowship with God, and their attempt to lead his readers astray and presumably to incorporate them into their fellowship. The context of the introduction of the term *koinōnia* into 1 John, then, suggests that it was not a characteristic term employed by the author, but rather one used by his opponents and one he took up and used in his effort to deny what they claimed, that is, that they have fellowship with God without having fellowship with other believers (those belonging to the author's group).[9] Fellowship with God, he insists, means fellowship 'with us'.

We also need to discuss what exactly is meant by 'fellowship'

8. Brown, *The Epistles of John,* 178, 182.
9. So John Painter, 'The "Opponents" in 1 John', *NTS* 32 (1986) 54.

(koinōnia), as far as it concerns the relationship between the author and his readers. Perkins suggests that behind the author's references to *koinōnia* in this letter lies its use as a technical term in the early Christian mission, in particular the Pauline mission (cf. Gal 2:9; Phil 1:5; 3:10; Phlm 6). In the Pauline letters the term *koinōnia* is one of a cluster of technical terms connected with the Roman *societas*, a legally binding association of equal partners based on their mutual assent to a common purpose. Perkins does note that *koinōnia* is much more than a legally binding association for Paul and his associates.[10] Nevertheless, she argues, it is this concept of a mutual commitment to a common purpose which lies behind the use of the term *koinōnia* in both the Pauline letters and 1 John. Interpreted along these lines, 1 John 1:3 explains that the purpose of the author is to elicit his readers' commitment to his *koinōnia* (rather than that of the secessionists). In 2 John 11 (assuming that letter was written by the same person) he urges his readers not to assist the rival *koinōnia* by providing hospitality, and so sharing *(koinōnei)* in their wicked work.[11]

There do appear to be some parallels between the *koinōnia* which Paul and the Philippians enjoyed and that which the author of 1 John wanted to share with his readers on the one hand, and the Roman *societas* on the other. However, as 1:7 indicates, the author thinks of the establishment of fellowship between believers not as something based on mutual assent to a common purpose, but rather as something created as people walk in the light as God is in the light. That fellowship, once established, may then find expression in a commitment to a common purpose (such as partnership with the author in his proclamation of the Word of life by providing hospitality for orthodox itinerants sent out with his recommendation), but it would be wrong to say that it is based simply upon mutual assent to a common purpose.

Further, a study of the occurrences of *koinōnia* in the NT as a whole indicates that while there are places where the idea of commitment to a common task may be involved (Gal 2:9; Phil 1:5; 3:10; Phlm 6; 1 John 1:3), there are other places where the expression denotes a personal relationship without there being overtones of commitment to a common task (Acts 2:42; 1 Cor 1:9; 2 Cor 6:14; 13:14; Phil 2:1; 1 John 1:6, 7), and yet others where it denotes sharing financially with people in need (Rom 15:26; 2 Cor 8:4; 9:13; Heb 13:16), and one where it denotes fellowship with other believers and the Lord in the Eucharist (1 Cor 10:16).

Koinōnia in 1 John 1:3, 6, 7 appears to denote a personal relationship

---

10. Pheme Perkins, '*Koinōnia* in 1 John 1:3-7: The Social Context of Division in the Johannine Letters', *CBQ* 45 (1983) 633-34.

11. Perkins, '*Koinōnia* in 1 John 1:3-7', 636-37.

with the author or with God, and may, in 1:3 in particular, include the idea of commitment to a common task, that of the proclamation of the Word of life.[12]

A Note on the Use of First Person Forms

In the commentary on vv. 1-4 above, the author of 1 John is referred to in the singular number, even though he uses the first person plural pronoun for self-reference in these verses. However, in the letter as a whole, the author's self-references occur in first person singular as well as first person plural forms. When he refers to himself as the writer of the letter, the author regularly uses the first person singular (2:1, 7, 8, 12, 13, 14, 21, 26; 4:20; 5:13), with only one exception (1:4). When he writes about having heard the message from the lips of Christ, or having seen him and touched him, or about bearing witness to the message of eternal life, he always uses the first person plural form (1:1-3, 5; 3:11; 4:14; 5:20); he also does so when he speaks about Christian experience (so, e.g., 1:6, 7-10; 2:1-3, 5, 28; 3:1-2, 14, 16, 18-19, 21-24; 4:9-13, 16-17, 19; 5:2-3, 14-15, 18-20). One important conclusion which may be drawn from the above is that, while the author writes this letter as an individual, nevertheless, when he testifies to the eternal life proclaimed by and embodied in the incarnate Christ, he always associates himself with other firsthand witnesses (see the discussion of authorship of 1 John in the Introduction, pp. 9-11). Possibly he does this to strengthen his readers' confidence in the message which he proclaims to them in the face of the questions that have been raised in their minds by the secessionists.

1:5–2:2 CLAIMS TO KNOW GOD TESTED BY ATTITUDES TO SIN

1:5 Having claimed, in vv. 1-4, that he was numbered among the eyewitnesses of the Word of life, and having said that it was this Word of life which he proclaims to his readers, the author, in this verse, defines the content of his message. It is this definition of the message in 1:5 which provides basis for the ethical implications the author makes in 1:6–2:2. He

---

12. Excursuses on *koinōnia* are provided by Georg Strecker, *The Johannine Letters* (Hermeneia, Philadelphia: Fortress, 1996) 20, and Rudolf Schnackenburg, *The Johannine Epistles* (Tunbridge Wells, Kent: Burns & Oates, 1992) 63-69.

begins by saying, **This is the message**[13] **we have heard from him and declare to you.** The writer indicates again that it is as one who has heard the Word of life, 'from him' *(ap' autou)*, that is, from Christ, that he now declares to his readers.[14] Then he defines the content of this message as **God is light.** His message is essentially one about the character of God.[15] The author does not intend to define what God is in himself, but to provide a basis for ethical application. If God is light, those who truly know God will walk 'in the light' (1:7). Having said that 'God is light', using a strong double negative *(ou mē)*, the author states the same thing negatively: **in him there is no darkness at all.** The metaphor of light and darkness is used frequently in the NT and in a variety of ways (see 'A Note on Light and Darkness', pp. 65-66), and in every case the context provides the clue to its meaning. Here the author says, 'God is light; in him there is no darkness at all' so that he can immediately draw out its ethical implications. This he does as he states three claims made by the secessionists and his own counterhypotheses in 1:6–2:2.

In 1:6-10 we meet three conditional sentences all introduced in a similar way (v. 6: 'If we claim to have fellowship with him . . .'; v. 8: 'If we claim to be without sin . . .'; v. 10: 'If we claim we have not sinned . . .'), which reflect the author's understanding of the claims of the secessionists. In setting out the nature of these claims (and his counterhypotheses), the author not only addresses the false teaching of his opponents, but also reveals what he means by saying that 'God is light; in him there is no darkness at all.'

1:6 In this verse the author sets forth the first of his three conditional sentences, which portrays what he understands to be the position of his opponents. He begins by saying, **If we claim to have fellowship with him, yet walk in the darkness. . . .** Here the author projects a situation in which a claim is made to have fellowship with God even though the claimants continue to walk in darkness. In the light of comments made on 1:4 above and the note on the meaning of *koinōnia* which follows it, we may say that the secessionists' claim to 'have fellowship' with God probably involved not only the claim to know God but also the claim to participate with God in the task of proclaiming the Word of life. (What

---

13. The author uses the Greek word *angelia;* nowhere does he use the word *euangelion,* which is commonly used elsewhere in the NT for the gospel message.

14. In 4:21 there is another indication that the message of the gospel, and the love command handed down with it, originated 'from him [Christ]' (lit. 'and this is the command we have from him [*ap' autou*], that he who loves God should love his brother also').

15. As is usual in both OT and NT, the character of God is expressed in terms of his actions, not his essence. In this respect the author's view differs from the pagan Greek view, which focuses more on the essence of God's being than on his activities. Cf. C. H. Dodd, *The Johannine Epistles* (London: Hodder and Stoughton, 1946) 107-10.

the author means by walking 'in the darkness' is discussed along with the meaning of walking 'in the light' below.)

The author completes his conditional sentence by saying that if the situation he projects prevails, then it may be said of those who make this claim that they **lie and do not live by the truth** (lit. 'we do not do the truth', *ou poioumen tēn alētheian*). They are guilty of two offences. First, they are guilty of lying about their relationship with God. According to the message heard from Christ, God is light, there is no fellowship between light and darkness, and therefore their claim to have fellowship with God (while walking in darkness) is false. Second, they are guilty of 'not doing the truth'. The expression 'to do the truth' is found only here in 1 John, but it also occurs in John 3:21 ('But whoever lives by the truth [lit. 'does the truth', *poiōn tēn alētheian*] comes into the light, so that it may be seen plainly that what he has done has been done through God'). In that context, 'to do the truth' is the opposite to 'doing evil' (John 3:20), which suggests that here in 1 John 'doing the truth' means living in the light of the truth and seeking to avoid sin. It is not enough to claim to know God (as the secessionists did); people must also live in the light of that truth, putting it into practice and avoiding sin. We learn something of what this means from the positive counterhypothesis which follows.

1:7   The counterhypothesis is also expressed in the form of a conditional sentence, which begins: **But if we walk in the light, as he is in the light. . . .** In 1:5 the author said, 'God is light', but here he says that God 'is in the light', which indicates that he is going to use the metaphor in an ethical fashion. A situation is now projected which is opposite to the one projected in 1:6. Here he is speaking of people who walk in the light, as God is in the light. What it actually means to 'walk in the light' and to 'walk in the darkness' is not explained in this letter. Probably the best explanation of what it means is to be found in the Fourth Gospel:

> And this is the judgment, that the light has come into the world, and people loved darkness rather than light because their deeds were evil. For all who do evil hate the light and do not come to the light, so that their deeds may not be exposed. But those who do what is true come to the light, so that it may be clearly seen that their deeds have been done in God. (John 3:19-21, NRSV)

This suggests that 'walking in the light' involves a willingness to be open towards God and his revelation in Christ, while 'walking in the darkness' involves a refusal to do this.[16] The author of 1 John, however, is less con-

16. Cf. Charles P. Baylis, 'The Meaning of Walking "in the Darkness" (1 John 1:6)', *BSac* 149 (1992) 214-22, who concludes that 'walking "in the light" means receiv-

cerned to define what walking in the light or the darkness means than he is to explain the consequences of doing so. As noted in the commentary on 1:6, the consequences of walking in the darkness while claiming fellowship with God are that 'we lie and do not live by the truth'. The consequences of walking in the light are spelled out in 1:7. These are twofold:

The first consequence is, **we have fellowship with one another**. As people walk in the light with God, they have fellowship with one another. This statement comes as something of a surprise. We might expect the consequence to be that people who walk in the light would have fellowship *with God*. After all, that is what is denied to those who walk in darkness. However, the author says the first consequence is that we have fellowship *with one another*. This is not to say that those who walk in the light do not have fellowship with God, but rather to assert that those who do have fellowship with God as they walk in the light will also have fellowship with one another. Or, to put it another way, there is no real fellowship with God which is not expressed in fellowship with other believers. It would appear from what is to come later in this letter that this unexpected statement about the consequence of walking in the light is made to rule out the claim of the secessionists who say they do have fellowship with God while not sharing fellowship with other believers (in this case, with those of the author's persuasion).

The second consequence is **the blood of Jesus, his Son, purifies us from every sin**. As people walk in the light with God, the blood of his Son Jesus 'purifies' them from their sins. When the author speaks of the 'blood of Jesus' he is referring to his violent death on the cross,[17] and it this death which provides purification[18] from sins for those who walk in the light with God. By his use of the present tense for the verbs 'to walk' and 'to purify', the author represents both the walking and the cleansing as ongoing activities. One lesson that may be learned from this second

---

ing God's revelation of Himself through His Son, and receiving eternal life and forgiveness of sins', while 'walking "in the darkness" is walking in death, rejecting that revelation' (222).

17. There are two other places in the letter (5:6, 8) where the author refers to the blood of Christ, and these are best understood in terms of his death also.

18. The verb 'to purify' *(katharizō)* is found only here and in 1:9 in the Johannine writings. It is found 18 times in the Synoptic Gospels, where it refers to ritual purification of people or objects; three times in Acts, where it relates to making Gentiles acceptable to God; three times in the Pauline corpus, where it denotes cleansing from moral defilement; four times in Hebrews, where it is used to describe the cleansing of sanctuaries (twice) and the cleansing of the conscience (twice); and once in James to denote cleansing oneself from the practice of evil deeds. The common factor in these uses of *katharizō* in the NT is that they all denote, in one way or another, purification which makes people or things acceptable in God's sight.

consequence is that walking in the light does not mean that those who do so never sin, but that they do not seek to hide that fact from God. They 'walk in the light' with him, and the result of their doing so is that the blood of his Son Jesus purifies them from their sins. Purification from sin, when unpacked, is virtually equivalent to forgiveness of sins, as the use of these two concepts in parallel in 1:9 indicates (the two concepts are also found in parallel in Jer 33:8: 'I will cleanse them from all the sin they have committed against me and will forgive all their sins of rebellion against me'). That the concomitant of walking in the light is being purified from every sin suggests that walking in the darkness might best be interpreted here, not simply as walking in ignorance, but as walking in sin.

A Note on Light and Darkness

The words 'light' *(phōs)* and 'darkness' *(skotia/skotos)* are used extensively in metaphorical ways in the NT, far more often in fact than they are used literally. The light and darkness metaphors are used with the following meanings: (i) *life and death* (Matt 4:16; Luke 1:79; John 1:4); (ii) *the light of witness* (Matt 5:14, 16; Luke 8:16; 11:33; John 5:35; Acts 13:47); (iii) *Jesus, the light of revelation to the world* (Luke 2:32; John 1:7-8; 8:12; 9:5; 12:35-36, 46; (iv) *good and evil behaviour* (Matt 6:23; Luke 11:35; 22:53; John 1:5; 3:19-21; Rom 13:12; 2 Cor 6:14; Eph 5:8-14; 1 John 1:5-7; 2:8-11); (v) *openness and secrecy* (Matt 10:27; Luke 12:3; 1 Cor 4:5); (vi) *truth and falsehood* (John 1:9; 8:12; 2 Cor 11:14; Jas 1:17); (vii) *God's kingdom and the devil's kingdom* (Luke 16:8; Acts 26:18, 23; Eph 6:12; Col 1:12-13; 1 Thess 5:4-5; 1 Pet 2:17); (viii) the darkness of eternal punishment (Matt 8:12; 22:13; 25:30; Jude 13); and (ix) *the light of the glory of God* (1 Tim 6:16; Rev 21:23-34; 22:5).

As Strecker notes in his 'Excursus: Light and Darkness',[19] God is compared with light in the OT (e.g., Ps 27:1; 36:9) and is the creator of light (Gen 1:3-5; Isa 45:5-7). In the Dead Sea Scrolls the children of light and the children of darkness are contrasted (e.g., 1QS 1:9-10), and the opposition of light and darkness is found in gnostic writings as well (e.g., *Poimandres* 1.1-6; *Pistis Sophia* 1.32, 2-3, 21). The light and darkness motif in 1 John is dependent on the Fourth Gospel (John 1:4-5; 8:12; 9:5; 12:35-36, 46), which in turn owes most to the OT. In the Fourth Gospel, however, Christ, not God, is the light, probably because of the christological emphasis of this Gospel — over and over again what the OT predicates of God is predicated of Jesus in the Fourth Gospel ('I am the light of the

---

19. Strecker, *The Johannine Letters*, 26-28.

world'; 'I am the good shepherd'; 'before Abraham was born, I am'; 'I am the resurrection and the life').

1:8 Having stated his counterhypothesis to the first claim, the author moves on to state, in another conditional sentence, a second aspect of what he believes to be the false teaching of the secessionists. And this comes as a natural follow-on from what he has said in the first counterhypothesis. This conditional sentence begins: **If we claim to be without sin . . .** (lit. 'If we say that we do not have sin [*hamartian ouk echomen*] . . .'). The making of the claim is presented as a complete act (using the aorist tense), but what is claimed, 'to be without sin', is presented as an ongoing action (by the use of the present tense). Contrary to what is sometimes asserted, the words 'If we claim to be without sin . . .' are not here intended to reflect an assertion on the part of the secessionists that they have a sinless nature; that they are free from the sin principle which operates in other human beings.[20] The expression 'to have sin' (*echō hamartian*) is found only here in 1 John, but it occurs four times in the Fourth Gospel (John 9:41; 15:22, 24; 19:11), and in each case it means to be guilty of sins. Allowing this usage to guide us, we would have to say that what the secessionists were claiming was, not that they were by nature free from the sin principle, but that they were not guilty of committing sins,[21] by which they probably meant they had not sinned since they came to know God and experienced the anointing.

The conditional sentence is then completed: [If we claim to be without sin,] **we deceive ourselves and the truth is not in us**. While making the claim 'to be without sin' is presented as a complete act, the concomitant self-deception is presented as ongoing.[22] The statement, 'the truth is not in us', has a parallel in 2:4, where the author says that the person who claims to know God but does not keep his commands is a liar and 'the truth is not in him'. There 'the truth is not in him' appears to be synonymous with 'he is a liar'. If this is the case, then here in verse 8 the statement, 'the truth is not in us', probably means the same, and may be taken as synonymous with deceiving oneself.

It is worth noting that to claim to have fellowship with God while walking in darkness makes a person a liar (1:6); to claim to be without sin involves lying to oneself (1:8) and makes God out to be a liar as well (1:10).

---

20. So, e.g., Schnackenburg, *The Johannine Epistles*, 80.
21. So, e.g., Brown, *The Epistles of John*, 205.
22. The present subjunctive, *planōmen (heautous)*, is used in the apodosis, indicating that the author is presenting the self-deception as ongoing.

A Note on Truth

The word 'truth' *(alētheia)* occurs nine times in 1 John. In 1:6 it appears as part of the expression 'to do the truth', which is the opposite to 'doing evil'. In 1:8 and 2:4 it is found in the expression 'the truth is not in us/him', where it is related to lying. In 2:21 the 'truth' is something which the author's readers 'know', that is, the truth of the message which was heard at the beginning by the eyewitnesses and handed on to the readers. 1 John 2:21 asserts that 'no lie comes from the truth', and the idea here is that christological errors propagated by the secessionists are not of the truth, that is, they are not in accordance with the message handed down from the beginning. In 3:18 the readers are urged to love 'with actions and in truth', and here 'in truth' means 'truly'. Loving in truth is virtually synonymous with loving in action. It is by loving 'in action and in truth', the author says in 3:19, that 'we know that we belong to the truth'. To 'belong to the truth' appears to have personal overtones: it means belonging to God. The final two uses of the word 'truth' relate to the Spirit. In 4:6 the Holy Spirit is called 'the Spirit of truth' and distinguished from the spirit of error, and in 5:6 the Holy Spirit is one who bears witness along with 'the water and the blood', and, the author adds, 'the Spirit is the truth'. At a minimum this constitutes a guarantee of the truthfulness of the Spirit as witness alongside 'the water and the blood', but it may also imply that, as truth is personified in Jesus in the Fourth Gospel, so it is personified in the Spirit (and in God; cf. 3:19) in 1 John.

From this survey of the use of the word 'truth' in 1 John, it is clear that the Johannine understanding of truth (involving 'doing the truth', not lying, understanding the message of salvation, acting truly in love, belonging to the truth, and truth personified in the Spirit) is different from Greek notions of truth (that which conforms to reality or logical facts). It is also different from the OT idea of truth as faithfulness and loyalty. There exist some parallels in gnostic writings where the enlightened are said to be indwelt by truth, and in the Dead Sea Scrolls where there are references to the sons/men of truth (1QS 4:5-6; 1QpHab 7:10), and where the Holy Spirit is associated with the truth (1QS 4:21).[23] But none of these parallels comes near the Johannine idea of truth personified in Christ/God/the Spirit, who communicates not only his message but himself to human beings. De la Potterie, commenting on truth in the Fourth Gospel, sums it up well:

> The Johannine idea of truth, then, is quite different from the intellectualist conception of the Greeks, for whom the truth was the reality,

---

23. See Schnackenburg, *The Johannine Epistles,* 81.

the essence of being, that is revealed to the spirit. In hellenistic dualism, this reality is transferred to the sphere of the divine, and consequently cannot be attained except by escaping from the world, and fleeing to the realm of light; but the cosmic dualism underlying this conception is liable to cut the world off from God. For John, on the other hand, truth is found in the word of the Father turned to mankind, incarnate in Christ, illuminated through the action of the Spirit. What men are required to do with respect to the truth is not to win it by intellectual endeavour; it is to receive and enter into it in faith, to submit to it and to live by it.[24]

1:9   Having described his opponents' claim (to be without sin) and the concomitant reality (their self-deception), the author now puts forward a counterhypothesis in another conditional sentence. The sentence begins with the words, **If we confess our sins. . . .** The author projects a situation in which people acknowledge their sins in an ongoing way.[25] He portrays authentic Christian living as involving honest and ongoing acknowledgement of one's sins.[26]

Confession of sin is not a theme that is found often in the NT. It is found in only four other places. It occurs in the Synoptic accounts of the ministry of John the Baptist when people came confessing their sins to be baptised by him (Matt 3:6; Mark 1:15). It is also found in James 5:16, where, in the context of praying for the sick, people are urged to confess their sins and pray for each other that they may be healed. People in Ephesus confessed their 'evil deeds' and burned their magical books during the ministry of Paul in that city (Acts 19:18).[27] In each of these cases confession of sin was public, not private (i.e., not just between the individual and God). It may then be the case that here in 1:9 the author also has in mind public confession of sin.[28]

---

24. Ignace de la Potterie, 'The Truth in Saint John', in *The Interpretation of John*, ed. John Ashton (Philadelphia/London: Fortress/SPCK, 1986) 64. Cf. Brown, *The Epistles of John*, 199-200.

25. Indicated by the use of the present tense of the verb 'to confess'.

26. This is obviously in tension with what the author says in 3:6-9; 5:18 about those being born of God not sinning and in fact being unable to sin because God's 'seed' remains in them. This is a very real problem. It is discussed in 'A Note on Sinless Perfection', pp. 126-32.

27. There are several OT references to confession of sin, some private (Ps 51:3-4), some public (2 Sam 12:13). Most notable is the confessing of the nation's sin on the Day of Atonement (Leviticus 16).

28. Strecker, *The Johannine Letters*, 32, regards this as an open question; Brown, *The Epistles of John*, 208, appears to favour public confession, citing also *Did.* 4:14: 'In the congregation thou shalt confess thy transgressions, and thou shalt not betake thyself to prayer with an evil conscience. This is the way of life.'

The conditional sentence is then completed: [If we confess our sins,] **he is faithful and just and will forgive us our sins and purify us from all unrighteousness**. Here the author sets forth two aspects of God's response to people who confess their sins: God forgives their sins and purifies them from all unrighteousness. God's forgiveness means that he no longer holds people's sins against them; he cancels their 'debt' (cf. Matt 6:9-15; 18:21-35). God's purifying them 'from all unrighteousness' (cf. 1:7, 'purifies us from every sin') means that he removes the defilement which their sins had produced. When the metaphor of defilement is unpacked, it also denotes the removal of the impediment to fellowship with God through forgiveness of sins (cf. Ps 51:1-2). Both verbs, being aorist subjunctive in form, portray forgiveness and purification as complete, rather than ongoing actions.

In forgiving and purifying, the author says, God is both 'faithful' and 'just'. The context does not make exactly clear what the author means by saying that God is 'faithful' *(pistos)* when he forgives and purifies. In the OT individuals speaking in later books (Num 14:18; Neh 9:17; Pss 86:15; 103:8; 145:8; Joel 2:13; Jonah 4:2; Nah 1:3) keep harking back to Exodus 34:6-7 ('The LORD, the LORD, the compassionate and gracious God, slow to anger, abounding in love and faithfulness, maintaining love to thousands, and forgiving wickedness, rebellion and sin') because they know God will be faithful in fulfilling his promise to forgive. In the NT there are only three places where God is said to be faithful in doing something or other. These are 1 Corinthians 1:9; 10:13 and 2 Corinthians 1:18. In each case God's faithfulness is expressed in providing for his people in various ways (presenting believers blameless on the Day of our Lord Jesus; providing a means of escape from temptation; and remaining true to his word by fulfilling his promises). It would seem reasonable, then, to infer from these references that God's faithfulness is his trustworthiness in fulfilling the commitments he has made to his people. A similar meaning would be entirely appropriate here also: God is faithful to believers in that he is carrying through on his commitment to forgive and purify those who confess their sins, something which necessitated the giving of his Son to be the atoning sacrifice for their sins (4:9-10, 14).[29]

The author says that God is not only faithful but also 'just' *(dikaios)*

29. Judith M. Lieu, 'What Was from the Beginning: Scripture and Tradition in the Johannine Epistles', *NTS* 39 (1993) 461-67, suggests that this text, which stresses that forgiveness proceeds from God's faithfulness, may well reflect the influence of Exod 34:6 tradition. Lieu traces the effects of this tradition through Num 14:18-19; Neh 9:17; Pss 86:15; 103:8; 145:8; Dan 9:9; Joel 2:13; Jonah 4:2; Nah 1:3; Sir 2:1; 1QH 6:8-9, and suggests it reaches right through to 1 John 1:9.

when he forgives and purifies those who confess their sins. The adjective 'just'/'righteous' *(dikaios)* is found in four other places in this letter (2:1, 29; 3:7, 12). In 2:1 Jesus Christ, who speaks to the Father in our defence, is described as 'the Righteous One' *(dikaios)*. In 2:29 the readers are re-minded that if, as they know, God is righteous *(dikaios)*, they may also know that 'everyone who does right has been born of him'. What we find in 3:7 is very similar: 'He who does what is right is righteous *(dikaios)*, just as he [God] is righteous *(dikaios)*'. And finally in 3:12 Cain is said to have murdered his brother, 'because his own actions were evil and his brother's were righteous *(dikaios)*'. From the author's use of *dikaios* else-where in this letter, it is clear that to be righteous means to act in a righ-teous way. So when he says that God is righteous when he forgives sin and purifies sinners, he means that in doing so God is acting righteously. What seems to lie behind this is the problem of how God can be said to be righteous when he forgives the guilty. It is a problem which the apostle Paul had to deal with when explaining his gospel in Romans 3:21-26, and his resolution of the problem was that God can be both just and the justifier of sinners because he set forth Christ as the atoning sacrifice *(hilastērion)* for their sins. The author of 1 John does not state the matter as clearly as Paul does, but it is plain that he, too, understands God to be righteous in forgiving those who confess their sins because he sent his Son to be the atoning sacrifice *(hilasmos)* for those sins (cf. 2:2: 'He is the atoning sacrifice *[hilasmos]* for our sins'; 4:10: 'This is love: not that we loved God, but that he loved us and sent his Son as an atoning sacrifice *[hilasmos]* for our sins').

1:10　The author now moves on to restate in other words, and in a third conditional sentence, the second aspect of what he believes is the false teaching of the secessionists. The conditional sentence begins: **If we claim we have not sinned. . . .** The secessionists claim to be people who have not sinned. This probably does not mean they claimed absolutely to have never sinned. More likely it means that they claimed not to have sinned since they came to know God and experienced the anointing. The only difference between this expression of their claim and the earlier statement of it in 1:8 is that here the author presents what is claimed, not as an ongoing achievement of not sinning as before, but as a condition of not having sinned (indicated by his use of the Greek perfect tense). The essential meaning of what is projected is the same in each case, but it is presented differently.

The conditional sentence is then completed: [If we claim we have not sinned,] **we make him out to be a liar, and his word has no place in our lives**. In v. 8 the author said that the claim to be without sin involved the claimant in self-deception; here in v. 10 he adds that the claim to have

70

not sinned involves making God a liar. He does not say why this is so, but it may be safely assumed that this is the case because God declares the human race to have sinned (something that may be inferred from the author's statement in 4:10 that God 'sent his Son as an atoning sacrifice *for our sins*'). If God, then, may be said to regard all people as having sinned, to deny this makes him a liar. It would also indicate that 'his word has no place in our lives'.[30] In this way the author further undercuts the claims of the secessionists to know God or have fellowship with him.

The author does not immediately provide his rejection of their claim with a positive counterhypothesis as he did in the case of the previous two claims. Instead, in 2:1-2 he addresses his readers directly, and in a pastoral fashion urges them not to commit sin. He assures them at the same time that, should they fail in this respect, God has provided an atoning sacrifice for their sins. While his pastoral concern appears to be to the fore here, 2:1-2 also functions as the positive counterhypothesis to the false claim of the secessionists mentioned in 1:10.

2:1a Turning his attention away from the secessionists' claims, the author now addresses his readers directly: **My dear children, I write this** [lit. 'these things'] **to you so that you will not sin**. Several matters call for comment. First, the readers are addressed as 'my dear children' *(teknia mou)*,[31] and this reflects something of the relationship the author believes he has with his readers. It reflects the affection in which he holds them and the more senior position which he occupies in relation to them. Second, the author, who up to this point in the letter has consistently used the first person plural in self-designations, now adopts the first person singular as he addresses his readers directly. Third, 'these things' which the author says he is writing about refer to the situations projected either for condemnation or commendation in 1:6-10, considerations which the author believes are sufficient to stiffen his readers' resistance to sinning. Fourth, it is clear that when the author says, 'I write this to you so that you will not sin', he is not adopting here the position he criticised in 1:8, 10 (i.e., his opponents' claim that they have not sinned), because in 2:1b

---

30. There are parallels to this expression in John 8:37, where Jesus says to his Jewish adversaries: 'Yet you are ready to kill me, because you have no room for my word', and in John 5:37-38, where he says to them: 'And the Father who sent me has himself testified concerning me. You have never heard his voice nor seen his form, nor does his word dwell in you, for you do not believe the one he sent.' By way of contrast Jesus says of his disciples: 'For I gave them the words you gave me and they accepted them.'

31. Brown, *The Epistles of John*, 214, notes that the author uses the plural of *teknion* (2:1, 12, 28; 3:7, 18; 4:4; 5:21) or *paidion* (2:14, 18) for direct address to his readers, but uses the plural of *teknon* (3:1, 2, 10; 5:2) when speaking about the children of God. This is probably just a stylistic variation.

he speaks about the provision God has made for the occasions when believers do sin.

2:1b   The author recognises the possibility of believers committing sin when he begins his next sentence with the words, **But if anybody does sin. . . .** The author projects a situation in which believers yield to temptation and commit sin, though he gives no indication concerning what the nature of this sin might be.

The concomitant to this projected situation is both surprising and encouraging for believers, for the author notes that if anyone sins **we have one who speaks to the Father in our defense — Jesus Christ, the Righteous One.** The English expression 'one who speaks . . . in our defense' translates a single Greek word: *paraklētos*. This word is found only here in 1 John, and four times in the Gospel of John. It is found nowhere else in the NT, and not at all in the LXX. In the Gospel of John the word consistently denotes the Holy Spirit, who was to be sent to be with the disciples on earth when Jesus returned to the Father. However, in 1 John *paraklētos* is used of Jesus Christ himself, and is used in connection with his function in heaven.[32]

In seeking to understand the meaning of *paraklētos* in this verse, it is helpful to begin with the meaning of the word in the ancient Hellenistic texts. Deissmann provides references to these texts,[33] in which the *paraklētos* is consistently portrayed as an advocate, one who speaks on behalf of the accused (not in the professional sense we use it today, but as a friend or patron who speaks up in favour of the accused). In the Fourth Gospel one of the functions of the Holy Spirit as *paraklētos* is to testify in favour of Jesus over against a hostile world. The *paraklētos* acts as an advocate for Jesus (John 16:7-11). In a similar fashion, in 1 John Jesus functions as our *paraklētos*, speaking up on our behalf in the presence of his Father when we sin. He is our advocate with the Father.[34]

---

32. The way the author expresses himself here, saying, literally, 'we have an advocate with the Father' *(pros ton patera)*, recalls both John 1:1, where the Word is said to be in the presence of the Father *(pros ton theon)*, and 1 John 1:2, where eternal life is said to have been in the presence of the Father *(pros ton patera)* and now revealed to us.

33. See Adolph Deissmann, *Light from the Ancient East: The New Testament Illustrated by Recently Discovered Texts of the Graeco-Roman World* (London: Hodder and Stoughton, 1927) 336-37.

34. Kenneth Grayston, 'The Meaning of *Paraklētos*', *JSNT* 13 (1981) 70-75, 79-80, has surveyed the usage of the word *paraklētos* in early Greek writings (dating from the fourth century B.C. to the third century A.D.) in order to answer two outstanding questions about its use and meaning: (i) 'whether *paraklētos* is a legal word sometimes used more generally or a word of more general meaning sometimes applied in legal proceedings'; (ii) 'what function a legal *paraklētos* might have'. He concludes that '*paraklētos* was a word of general meaning which could appear in legal contexts, and

Jesus Christ, the advocate, is described as 'the Righteous One' *(dikaios)*. The term 'righteous' *(dikaios)* is found in four other places in the letter (1:9; 2:29; 3:7, 12), and in each case the term is related to righteous behaviour. Thus it would seem that it is used in the present context to indicate that it is the One who has acted righteously, who now stands in the presence of the Father to speak on behalf of those who have not acted righteously. However, Jesus Christ is much more than an advocate who intercedes for those who have sinned, as becomes apparent in the next verse.

2:2   He is the atoning sacrifice *(hilasmos)* **for our sins.** The author emphasises that Jesus Christ is not only our advocate who speaks in our favour in the presence of God despite our sins, but that he is also the atoning sacrifice for those sins. In the first case he appears as an advocate in court, in the second as a sacrificing priest in the temple. And, as the author will explain later in the letter (4:10), it was because of the Father's love for us that he sent his Son to make this atoning sacrifice.

What does the author mean by the term *hilasmos,* translated as 'atoning sacrifice' here? The word is found in only two places in the NT, both of them in this letter (2:2 and 4:10). It occurs six times in the LXX (Lev 25:9; Num 5:8; Ps 129:4 [= 130:4 ET]; Ezek 44:27; Amos 8:14), and in every case except Amos 8:14 it relates to the removal of guilt because of sin, which in most places (Ps 129:4 and Amos 8:14 are the only exceptions) is effected through sacrifice (see 'A Note on *Hilasmos*', pp. 75-76). What is not clear in these references is whether the atoning sacrifice deals only with the removal of sin or whether it also removes God's anger towards sinners. The use of the cognate verb 'to make atonement' *(exilaskesthai)* in the LXX (see comments in 'A Note on *Hilasmos*', p. 76) indicates that atonement in the OT may be described as either the cleansing and forgiving of the sinner, or appeasing God's wrath.

Clues as to what the author meant by saying that Jesus Christ is 'the atoning sacrifice for our sins' in 2:2 will have to be sought within the immediate context. And the idea of the atoning sacrifice here is in juxtaposition with the idea of advocacy. Jesus is the one who speaks to the Father in our defence when we sin. This suggests that he is, as it were, pleading for mercy for sinners, and this in turn suggests that his role as the atoning

---

when it did the *paraklētos* was a supporter or sponsor'. Commenting on 2:1 ('But if anybody does sin, we have one who speaks to the Father in our defense — Jesus Christ, the Righteous One'), Grayston says: 'This corresponds to the situation described by Philo where a person who had displeased the emperor needs a sponsor to propitiate him. In John's teaching, when a Christian has sinned the Father observes that the sinner is sponsored by Christ and is persuaded not to reject him and withdraw his truth.' Cf. Strecker, *The Johannine Letters,* 37.

sacrifice is to secure that mercy; that is, he is, in this context, the propitiation for our sins.[35] This, of course, must be balanced by the fact that in 4:10 the author declares that God himself sent his Son to be that atoning sacrifice. There is no hint of the pagan notion of propitiation overcoming the reluctance of an arbitrary deity. For God himself takes the initiative in providing the propitiatory sacrifice which is needed if our sins are to be forgiven.

The author is not content to say that Jesus Christ is the atoning sacrifice 'for our sins' (meaning the sins committed by believers; cf. 2:1), but adds, **and not only for ours but also for the sins of the whole world** *(kosmou)*. The word *kosmos* occurs 23 times in 1 John, and its meaning varies according to the context. In one place it means the natural world (3:17), in several places it bears a locative sense — the place into which various ones go or in which they live (4:1, 4, 9, 14, 17; cf. 2 John 7), in other places it denotes 'worldly' values or attitudes that are opposed to God (2:15-17 [6x]; 5:4 [2x], 5), and in yet other places it denotes the unbelieving world — people who are opposed to God and believers, and who are under the power of the evil one (3:1, 13; 4:5 [3x]; 5:19).[36] When the author says that Jesus Christ is the atoning sacrifice for 'the sins of the whole world', that includes not only our sins (i.e., the sins of believers) but the sins of the unbelieving world as well.

It is not easy to explain what the author means by saying that Jesus Christ is the atoning sacrifice 'for the sins of the whole world'. It is not unique within the Johannine writings, for in John 1:29 the Baptist hails Jesus as 'the Lamb of God, who takes away the sin of the world', and in 1 John 4:14 we read that 'the Father has sent his Son to be the Saviour of

35. Strecker, *The Johannine Letters,* 39, n. 17, argues that the idea of propitiation cannot be excluded in this context because 'it accords with the preceding argumentation', in particular the reference to the blood of Jesus (1:7) and purification (1:9). The idea of a life given for propitiation of the sins of others is also found in 4 Macc 6:26-29, where the dying martyr asks that his punishment might suffice for his people, that his blood might effect their purification, that his life might be accepted in exchange for theirs. There is, of course, a great difference between the death of the martyrs (who though godly were yet sinners themselves) and the death of Christ (who is described as the righteous one).

36. *Kosmos* is used 78 times and with a similar range of meanings in the Fourth Gospel: for the natural world (1:10; 11:9; 17:5, 24; 21:25); with a locative sense (1:9, 10; 3:17; 6:14; 8:23 [2x]; 9:5, 39; 10:36; 11:27; 12:25, 46; 13:1 [2x]; 16:21, 28 [2x], 33; 17:11 [2x], 13, 15, 18 [2x]; 18:36 [2x], 37; for 'worldly' values or attitudes opposed to God (12:31 [2x]; 14:30; 16:11, 33; 17:14 [2x], 16 [2x]); and for the world of people who are opposed to God and believers and are under the power of the evil one (1:10, 29; 3:16, 17 [2x]; 4:42; 6:33, 51; 7:4, 7; 8:12, 26; 9:5; 12:47 [2x]; 14:17, 19, 22, 27, 31; 15:18, 19; 16:8, 20; 17:6, 9, 14, 23, 25). In addition to these uses, there are two places in Fourth Gospel where *kosmos* is used in a way not found in 1 John, i.e., where it denotes the world of people in a quite neutral way (12:19; 18:20).

the world'. That Jesus offered the atoning sacrifice 'for the sins of the whole world' cannot mean that all people's sins are automatically forgiven so that all are the inheritors of eternal life, even if they do not believe in the name of the Son of God. The author himself rules out such an idea elsewhere in his letter. For example, in 5:11-13 he says that those who have the Son have eternal life, but those who do not have the Son do not have life. Having the Son involves believing in the Son, so that those who do not believe in him cannot be said to have him, and therefore they cannot be said to have eternal life. While we can say what Jesus Christ being the atoning sacrifice 'for the sins of the whole world' does not mean, it is more difficult to say what it does mean, for the author gives us no clues. We might suggest that Jesus Christ is the atoning sacrifice for the sins of the whole world because his death was sufficient to deal with the sins of the whole world, but that his sacrifice does not become effective until people believe in him.

A Note on *Hilasmos*

As noted above, the word *hilasmos* is found in only two places in the NT, both in 1 John: in 2:2 and again in 4:10. There has been extended debate among scholars concerning the meaning of *hilasmos*. Does it denote the removal of guilt and the purifying of the sinner (expiation),[37] or the appeasing of God's anger towards sinners (propitiation),[38] or God's action in offering propitiation to humanity.[39] Most important in deciding the matter are the contexts in which the word is used in 1 John. Before examining these it is worth noting the use of the *hilasmos* in the LXX.

Hilasmos is found six times in the LXX, indicated by the italicised words in the descriptions of its use in the relevant texts which follow: Lev 25:9, referring to the Day of *Atonement*; Num 5:8, used in connection with the ram with which people make *atonement* for their sins; Ps 129:4 (ET 130:4), where the psalmist rejoices that God does not keep a record of sins and that there is *forgiveness* with him; Amos 8:14, a strange use of the word referring to those who swear by the *shame* of Samaria; Ezek 44:27,

---

37. C. H. Dodd, 'HILASKESTHAI, Its Cognates, Derivatives, and Synonyms, in the Septuagint', *JTS* 32 (1931) 360; T. C. G. Thornton, 'Propitiation or Expiation?' *ExpTim* 80 (1968-69) 54-55; Brown, *The Epistles of John*, 217-22.

38. Leon Morris, *The Apostolic Preaching of the Cross* (3rd ed., London: Tyndale, 1965) 206; David Hill, *Greek Words and Hebrew Meanings: Studies in the Semantics of Soteriological Terms* (Cambridge: Cambridge University Press, 1967) 37-38.

39. Henri Clavier, 'Notes sur un mot-clef du Johannisme et de la soteriologie biblique: *hilasmos*', *NovT* 10 (1968) 303.

referring to the *sin offering* a priest must make for his own sins; 2 Macc 3:33, referring to the high priest presenting the *offering of atonement*. In addition to these six occurrences of *hilasmos* there is one more in a variant reading in Dan 9:9, which speaks of the mercies and *forgivenesses* of the Lord. These usages do not decide the issue. Even though most of them relate to atonement and forgiveness, it is not clear in these texts whether atonement relates to the removal of sin or to appeasing God. Because the use of the word *hilasmos* itself in the LXX does not decide the matter, it is worthwhile checking the way cognate words are used.

The cognate noun *hilastērion* is found 28 times in the LXX, all of which refer to the mercy seat in the tabernacle except for one in Amos (9:1), which the NIV translates as 'the capitals', and three in Ezekiel (43:14, 17, 20), which the NIV translates as 'ledge'. *Hilastērion* occurs twice in the NT: once in Rom 3:25 to denote Christ as the atoning sacrifice set forth by God, and the other in Heb 9:5 to denote the mercy seat in the tabernacle.

The cognate verb *hilaskomai* is found 12 times in the LXX, where it nearly always means to forgive (people their sins). It is found twice in the NT, once in Luke 18:13, where it means to forgive, and once in Heb 2:17, where it means to make atonement for sins.

The cognate verb *exilaskesthai* is not found at all in the NT, but is found 105 times in the LXX in 97 verses. These include several texts in which *exilaskesthai* denotes atonement that involves cleansing the sinner (e.g., Lev 12:7, 8; 14:18, 20, 29, 31, 53; 15:30; Num 8:21); many others where atonement effects forgiveness (e.g., Lev 4:20, 26, 31, 35; 5:10, 13, 16, 18; 6:7; 19:22; Num 15:28; Ps 65:3; 78:38; 79:9; Isa 22:14; Jer 18:23; Ezek 16:23); and several more where atonement means removal of wrath (Gen 32:20; Exod 30:12; 32:30; Num 8:19; 17:11 [ET 16:46]; 35:31; Prov 16:4; Isa 47:11). What this suggests is that the notion of atonement in the OT is best understood comprehensively to include both the cleansing and forgiveness of the sinner, and the turning away of God's anger. This in turn suggests that neither the idea of expiation nor that of propitiation can be ruled out as possible meanings for *hilasmos* in 1 John 2:2 and 4:10. It is therefore the context of *hilasmos* in these texts that provides the best guide. As we argued in the commentary on 2:2 above, the context of that verse does support the idea of propitiation, though the notion of propitiation must not be thought of in pagan terms as the overcoming of the wrath of a hostile god, because, as 4:10 makes clear, it was God himself who provided his Son as the atoning sacrifice for our sins.

2:3-11 CLAIMS TO KNOW GOD TESTED BY OBEDIENCE

In 1:6–2:2 the author dealt with the claims made by the secessionists to have fellowship with God while still walking in darkness; while claiming not to have sinned. In 2:3-11 he continues to deal with the claims of the secessionists, but here he focuses upon the claim they make to know God while not keeping his commands. This section begins with a positive statement of the assurance true believers have of knowing God when they obey his commands. This is followed by three statements, each one introduced with the same expression ('The one who says . . .', *ho legōn* . . .), though unfortunately the NIV translation obscures this similarity (2:4: 'The man who says . . .'; 2:6: 'Whoever claims . . .'; 2:9: 'Anyone who claims . . .'). Each of these statements reflects, directly or indirectly, what the author believed the secessionists falsely claimed and is followed either by a direct rebuttal or by a counterstatement which embodies the characteristics that should be found in those who make such claims.

2:3 This section begins with a positive statement: **We know that we have come to know him if we obey his commands**. The NIV omits the words 'by this *(en toutō)* [we can be sure]', which point the readers forward to what is to follow, that is, it is by obeying his commands that we may be sure we know him. Ongoing assurance that we are people who know God is dependent upon ongoing obedience to his commands. A number of questions need to be answered if we are to understand this verse properly.

First, what does the author mean by 'knowing' him? To 'know' God is a virtually universal religious longing. Brown points out that in the Greek classical period knowledge of God was sought through the exercise of human reason, but in the Hellenistic period people sought this knowledge through the mystery religions, while in Israel the knowledge of God was derived from revelation.[40]

In 1 John, the verb 'to know' *(ginōskō)* is used in a number of different contexts where 'knowing' has various shades of meaning: (i) knowing something to be the case (2:3, 5, 29; 3:19, 24; 4:6, 13; 5:2); (ii) knowing (or not knowing) Jesus Christ and/or God the Father (2:4, 13, 14; 3:1, 16; 4:7, 8); (iii) not knowing believers (3:1); (iv) knowing facts (3:20); (v) knowing, that is, recognising the Spirit (of truth) or spirit of error operating in a person (4:2, 6); (vi) knowing the love of God (4:16); and (vii) knowing the truth (personified in Jesus) (5:20; cf. 2 John 1). The author uses *ginōskō* with the first of these meanings when he says, 'we know'

---

40. Brown, *The Epistles of John*, 277-78.

(i.e., we know it to be the case), and with the second meaning when he continues, 'that we know him'. Knowing him is not knowing facts about him, nor simply being able to recognise him operating in circumstances or in other people; it is knowing him personally for oneself.[41] For the author of 1 John knowing God involves fellowship with him (1:4), walking in his light (1:7), and being 'in him' (2:5-6). However, as will become very evident as the letter unfolds, the author is more concerned to unpack the moral concomitants of knowing him than he is to define the nature of that knowledge itself. And in this context, the moral concomitant he highlights is obedience to his commands.

The second question that needs to be answered is, To whom does the author refer when he speaks about knowing 'him'? Is he referring to God the Father, or to Jesus Christ, his Son? To answer this question we need to look to the wider context. In 1:5-7 the author makes analogous statements. He writes: 'God is light. . . . If we claim to have fellowship with him yet walk in darkness, we lie and do not put the truth into practice. But if we walk in the light . . . the blood of Jesus, his Son, purifies us from every sin.' The author's main concern here is with bogus claims to have fellowship with *God*. Jesus Christ, the Son, is introduced in a secondary way, as the one whose blood cleanses the sins of those who walk in the light as God is in the light. If we allow this pattern to guide us in the interpretation of 2:3, we will understand 'him' in this verse to denote God the Father. Such an approach is supported by the fact that later in this same chapter the author deals with the false claims of those who say they know God while holding inadequate opinions about his Son (cf., e.g., 2:22-23).

The third question to be answered is, What does the author mean by 'his commands'? He uses the word 'command' *(entolē)* 14 times in 1 John. Sometimes it is found in singular form, other times in plural form. When he uses the singular form, it always refers explicitly to Christ's command that his followers should love one another (2:7 [3x], 8; 3:23 [2x]; 4:21). The plural form occurs where there is no explicit reference to Jesus' command (2:3, 4; 3:22, 24; 5:2, 3 [2x]), though in all but two of these references the context indicates clearly that Jesus' love command is in mind. The exceptions are 2:3, 4, where the evidence that people know God is that they keep his commandments and walk as Jesus walked. At first sight this could be taken to refer to God's law, especially the Ten Commandments,

41. It is helpful at this point to compare John 14:9: 'Don't you know me *(ouk egnōkas me)*, Philip, even after I have been among you such a long time?' Here, knowing Jesus involved more than even being closely acquainted with him (something Philip had experienced); it involved perceiving his true identity; a true but not complete understanding of his nature.

which Jesus observed during his incarnate life.[42] But there is no hint else-where in the letter that the author is concerned about obedience to the Mosaic law. And in 3:21-23 he speaks about God answering believers' prayers because they obey his commands, and then continues: 'and this is his command: to believe in the name of his Son, Jesus Christ, and to love one another as he has commanded us' (3:23). God's commands are that we believe in Christ and do what he commands, and this letter high-lights Jesus' command to love one another. It may be best, therefore, to in-terpret the reference to 'his commands' in this verse in that light also.

The thrust of 2:3, therefore, is that it is those who, like the readers, believe in Jesus Christ, God's Son, and obey his command to love one an-other who truly know God. The secessionists who claim to know God but do not keep his command by implication do not know God.

2:4 Having stated positively the assurance of knowing God that is possible for those who obey his commands, the author now refutes those who claim to know God while not obeying his commands. This he does in the first of the three statements introduced with the words, 'the one who says'/'the man who says' *(ho legōn):* **The man who says, "I know him,"** **but does not do what he commands. . . .** The author uses the perfect tense of the verb 'to know' *(egnōka)* to depict his opponents' claim to be people who know God. The concomitant behaviour of the claimants is depicted as ongoing disobedience to God's commands by the use of the present tense in the expression, 'does not do' *(mē tērōn).* As suggested above, the com-mands of God the author has in mind are to believe in his Son and do what he commands. Anyone claiming to be a person who knows God, while dis-obeying what he commands, the author says, **is a liar, and the truth**[43] **is** **not in him**. The statement, 'the truth is not in him', is synonymous with 'he is a liar'. Underlying this whole verse is the recognition that people can have no authentic relationship with God if they do not obey his com-mands. This does not mean, of course, that those who know God will never fail to obey God's commands, but rather that those who know God will not be characterised by disobedience to his commands.

2:5a Having refuted the secessionists' claim to know God while they disobey God's commands, the author continues: **But if anyone** **obeys his word, God's love is truly made complete in him** (lit. 'Whoever keeps his word, truly in this one the love of God is perfected'). The NIV

---

42. Both Brown, *The Epistles of John,* 280-81, and Strecker, *The Johannine Letters,* 40, n. 22, think there may be some reference to the Decalogue in 2:6.

43. Some manuscripts omit the article, having 'truth' rather than 'the truth', and still others have 'the truth of God'. The last is clearly an expansion and has little external support. The reading without the article is not supported by as weighty manuscripts as the reading with the article.

mistakenly renders this as a conditional sentence. In fact it is a statement, as the literal rendering indicates. A number of other matters call for comment. First, the tenses of the verbs are again important. The verb 'obeys'/ 'keeps' is in the present tense, depicting obedience as ongoing, and the verb 'made complete'/'is perfected' is in the perfect tense, thus depicting those who obey God's word as people in whom God's love is perfected.

Second, the expression 'the love of God' (NIV: 'God's love') here is susceptible to a number of interpretations, each of which is represented elsewhere in the letter: (i) God's love for believers (4:9); (ii) believers' love for God (5:3); and (iii) the love which comes from God and is expressed through believers to others (3:17; 4:7). The indications are that the second option, believers' love for God, should be adopted here, because a very similar statement is made about obedience and the love of God in 5:3 (lit.: 'For this is the love of God, that we keep his commands'; NIV: 'This is love for God: to obey his commands'), in which 'the love of God' is clearly intended to be understood as believers' love for God.[44]

Third, if it is correct to say that 2:5 speaks about those in whom love for God is perfected, we need to know what kind of perfection of love the author has in mind. The verb the author uses, *teleioō*, often bears (as the NIV translation of this verse reflects) the meaning 'to complete' something. Thus, for example, in John's Gospel Jesus speaks repeatedly, using *teleioō*, of completing the work(s) assigned to him by his Father (4:34; 5:36; 17:4). There are three other places in 1 John (apart from 2:5a) where the verb *teleioō* and the idea of the love of God occur side by side, and in each case the idea of perfection as the completion of something makes good sense: In 4:12 (God's love for us completes its work in us when we love one another); 4:17 (God's love for us completes its work with us when we have confidence on the day of judgement); 4:18 (perfect love casts out fear, so that it may be said that those who fear have not been perfected in [God's] love [for them], that is, God's love has not yet completed its work in them). This suggests that what the author wishes to say in the present context is that our love for God completes its work when we obey his command to love one another.

2:5b The words of 2:5b, **This is how we know we are in him** (*en toutō ginōskomen . . .*), could be linked with what precedes, and so form, with the opening words of 2:3 ('by this we can be sure we know him', *kai en toutō ginōskomen . . .*), an *inclusio* for 2:3-5.[45] Alternatively they could be

---

44. Brown, *The Epistles of John*, 257, does not express a preference, but says the expression must include God's love for believers.

45. So, e.g., Schnackenburg, *The Johannine Epistles*, 98. So, too, Brown, *The Epistles of John*, 258, but he holds that 2:5b also functions as a transition to 2:6.

linked with what follows, and thus pave the way for what is to come in 2:6 (so NIV). In favour of the latter alternative is the fact that the words 'this is how we know we are in him' foreshadow the concept of remaining in him, which is developed in 2:6. Also supporting this approach is the fact that the first of the author's statements beginning with the words 'the one who says'/'the man who says' *(ho legōn)* (2:4) is preceded by a positive statement about assurance beginning with the words 'by this we know . . .' *(kai en toutō ginōskomen . . .)* (2:3). If we do connect 2:5b with what follows rather than with what precedes, then the second of the author's statements beginning with the words 'the one who says' *(ho legōn)* (2:6) is likewise preceded by a positive statement about assurance beginning with the words 'by this we know . . .' *(en toutō ginōskomen . . .)* (2:5b). For these two reasons it is probably better to read 2:5b with what follows rather than with what precedes it. If this is the case, we must look for the meaning of the statement, 'This is how we know we are in him', by examining what follows in 2:6.

2:6 This verse then spells out the basis on which people may 'know they are in him'. It begins, **Whoever claims to live** *(menein)* **in him. . . .** This is the second time a statement in this section is introduced with the words 'the one who says'/'whoever claims' *(ho legōn)*. The primary function of these words is to introduce a positive statement of the characteristics of those who do indeed 'live in him'. They could possibly have the secondary function of stating those characteristics which are *not* found in the lives of the author's opponents. The author uses present tense forms of the verbs to depict both the making of the claim *(ho legōn,* 'Whoever claims') and what is being claimed *(autō menein,* 'to live in him') as ongoing actions.

What it means here 'to live in him' is not easy to define. The general concept is found ten times in the letter (2:5, 6, 27, 28; 3:6, 24; 4:13, 15, 16; 5:20). Sometimes it is part of a broader concept: the mutual indwelling of believers in God and God in believers (3:24; 4:13, 15, 16). In two places where this mutual indwelling is mentioned, the author says believers can be assured of it because of the Spirit whom God has given to them (3:24; 4:13). All this suggests that when the author speaks about living in God, as he does here in 2:6, or of being in God, as he does in 2:5b, it is something more than keeping God's commands that he has in mind. It is the new and very real spiritual existence that believers enjoy, and which is effected through the agency of the Spirit, who bears witness to the truth.

The author completes his positive statement of the characteristics of those who live in God by saying, [Whoever claims to live in him] **must walk as Jesus did** (lit. 'must himself walk as he walked'). As the literal translation indicates, this passage is not as unambiguous as the NIV rendering suggests. However, if the interpretation of 'his commands' adopted above is correct, then we may say that the NIV has caught the sense correctly. In general terms the thrust of the whole section 2:3-6 would then be: Those who keep God's commands may have assurance that they are people who know God; those who claim to know God while not obeying his commands are liars; those who say they live in God must walk as Jesus walked, that is, keeping God's commands to them as Jesus obeyed God's commands to him.

Before making the third of the statements in this section introduced with the words 'he who says'/'anyone who claims', *ho legōn* (2:9), the author addresses his readers directly in 2:7-8 and writes about the new command. These verses are transitional, moving the readers from the general requirement of obedience to God's commands (2:3-6) to the specific obligation to love fellow believers (2:9-11).

2:7 The transitional section begins: **Dear friends, I am not writing you a new command but an old one.** By addressing his readers as 'dear friends' *(agapētoi)* — the first of six times he does so in this letter (2:7; 3:2, 21; 4:1, 7, 11) — the author reveals again the affectionate regard in which he holds his readers. He assures his friends that he is not urging them to keep some new command of which they have never heard before.[46] Rather, it is an old one which they know well; it is one, he says, **which you have had since the beginning.** The 'beginning' is the time when the readers first heard the gospel; something that is made plain when the author defines the command: **This old command is the message you have heard.** The old command is none other than the message that they heard at the beginning, that is, the gospel message by which they were made children of God. It was the command to believe in God's Son, Jesus Christ, and, as we learn later in the letter, that included the obligation to do what Jesus commanded (cf. 3:23). Within the author's community it appears that the love command was handed on alongside the gospel message itself.

2:8 On the surface of things, what we find in this verse stands in direct contradiction to what we find in 2:7. How can the author say, 'I am not writing you a new command' (2:7), and then immediately afterwards say, **Yet I am writing you a new command?** The clue to resolving this apparent contradiction is to be found in John 13:34, where Jesus says, 'A new commandment I give you: Love one another.'[47] The command to

---

46. Brown, *The Epistles of John*, 264, suggests the author may be denying a secessionist charge that he was introducing a command that was not part of the received tradition.

47. The only other place in the NT where the expression 'a new command' *(entolē kainē)* is found is in 2 John 5, where again the author denies that what he is writing is a 'new command').

love one another was described by Jesus himself as a 'new command'. However, the ministry of the historical Jesus was for the author long past. So the 'new command' of Jesus was the 'old command' for the author and his readers, and it was something his readers had heard long ago, when they first received the gospel. The striking juxtaposition of what appear to be contradictory statements, then, is the author's way of saying that he is not imposing some novel obligation upon his readers, but only recalling them to what they have known from the very beginning of their Christian walk.

Of this new command the author goes on to say, **its truth is seen in him and you**. The NIV provides a paraphrase rather than a translation at this point. Literally translated, the text would read: 'which [thing] is true in him and in you'. The 'thing' here must refer to the old/new command. So here, then, the author not only says that the old/new command is 'true in him' (denoting here Jesus Christ) but also that it is true 'in you' (denoting the readers). This statement involves an unusual use of the word 'true' (*alēthes*). In the papyri the word consistently means 'true' as opposed to 'false' in relation to statements of fact, or 'truthful' as opposed to 'untruthful' in relation to persons,[48] and this is its normal range of meaning in the NT as well (Matt 22:16; Mark 12:14; John 3:33; 4:18; 5:31, 32; 7:18; 8:13, 14, 17; 10:41; 19:35; 21:24; Rom 3:4; 2 Cor 6:8; Phil 4:8; Tit 1:13; 2 Pet 2:22; 1 John 2:27; 3 John 12). However, there are a few places in the NT where *alēthes* is used with the meaning 'real 'or 'genuine' (John 6:55; Acts 12:9; 1 Pet 5:12). This latter meaning comes closest to what is demanded by the context in 2:8, but still does not really fit properly. The sense of *alēthes* demanded in this context is something like 'truly expressed'. And the sense of the whole clause is that the author writes a new command 'which finds true expression in Jesus Christ and in his readers' (and so the NIV paraphrase is true to the sense of the clause after all).[49] This verse reflects something of the author's perceptions concerning his readers. They are not only his 'dear friends' (2:7); they are also people in whom he believes the original message is bearing genuine fruit. In this respect they differ markedly from the secessionists, in whom, the author is convinced, such fruit is lacking. It is noteworthy that the author does not hesitate to say that the old/new command is finding true expression in his readers, as it did in Christ.[50] It is a re-

48. Cf. MM *ad loc.*

49. Andrew Persson, 'Some Exegetical Problems in 1 John', *NotesTrans* 4 (1990) 18-19, argues that the antecedent for the expression 'its truth' in 1 John 2:8 is 'the whole of the preceding clause'. 'He is saying: "I claim that this command is new and you can see that my claim is true both in him and in you."'

50. Schnackenburg, *The Johannine Epistles,* 105, observes that '1 John does not share our modern squeamishness about hurting our "humility" by such self-confidence.'

flection of the sense early Christians had of living in the new age, as the author goes on to point out.

The old/new command finds true expression in Jesus Christ and his readers, the author says, **because the darkness is passing and the true light is already shining**. In 1 John the expression 'darkness' is found seven times (*skotia* 6x, and its synonym *skotos* 1x), and the various contexts in which it is found indicate that it stands for either sinful behaviour (1:5; 2:11) or the realm in which sinful behaviour predominates (1:6; 2:8, 9, 11). The darkness which the author here says is passing away is the realm in which sinful behaviour predominates, or what he later describes as 'the world and its sinful desires' (2:17). The darkness is passing away because the true light has begun to shine. The true light here is best understood to refer to Jesus Christ himself. In the Fourth Gospel, Jesus Christ is the true light coming into the world which the darkness cannot overcome (John 1:4-9; cf. 8:12; 9:5; 12:35-36, 46), and there can be little doubt that 'the true light that is already shining' in 1 John 2:8 is a reference to Jesus Christ also, even though the explicit identification is not made.[51]

When the author says the darkness is 'passing', he uses the verb *paragō*. This is found a total of ten times in the NT, seven times (in the active voice) in the Gospels, where it always refers to someone passing by a person or a place (Matt 9:9, 27; 20:30; Mark 1:16; 2:14; 15:21; John 9:1), and three times elsewhere (once in the active voice and twice in the passive voice), where it refers to something passing away, that is, coming to an end. The first of these (intransitive, active voice) is in 1 Cor. 7:31, where it is 'the 'form of the world' that is said to be coming to an end, which in context means that the time has grown short and the end of the present evil age is drawing near. The second (transitive, passive voice) is here in 1 John 2:8, where it is 'the darkness' that is coming to an end, and the third (transitive, passive voice) is in 1 John 2:17, where it is 'the world and its desires' that will come to an end.[52] These also refer to the passing of the present evil age because the powers of the new age were being felt since the true light began shining with the coming of Jesus Christ. Using present tense verbs in 2:8, the author depicts both the passing away of the darkness and the shining of the true light as ongoing events. These concurrent ongoing events form the context in which the new/old command is finding its true expression in the readers.

2:9 Following the transitional verses, 2:7-8, in which the author

51. Schnackenburg, *The Johannine Epistles,* 106, prefers to explain the true light, not directly in terms of the coming of Christ, but as the light that now 'radiates from Christians through the way they live'.

52. There does not appear to be any significant difference in meaning between the intransitive present active and the transitive present passive forms of *paragō*.

addressed his readers directly and wrote about the old/new command, he now takes up the theme of love for fellow believers, something which he believes the secessionists are not practising. The author has just said in 2:8 that 'the darkness is passing and the true light is already shining', and in this verse he deals with the secessionists' claim to be in the light (while they hate fellow believers). It is with the secessionists in mind that he says, **Anyone who claims to be in the light. . . .** This is the third of the statements in this section (2:3-11) which begin with the words 'the one who says'/'anyone who claims' *(ho legōn)*, and by which the author introduces the claims of the secessionists. These are claims to 'know him' (2:4), to 'live in him' (2:6), and now to 'be in the light' (2:9). All of these claims the author takes to be claims to intimacy with God, even the last, because, as 1:7 indicates, God is 'in the light'.[53] In the mouths of the secessionists, however, the claim to be 'in the light' may have had gnostic connotations ('either by virtue of possessing a nature which partook of the essence of light, or through mystical experience').[54]

Earlier, the author implied that the secessionists walked in the darkness of sin, despite their claims to have fellowship with God (1:6). Here he is more specific about the sin: [Anyone who claims to be in the light] **but hates his brother is still in the darkness**. The incompatible accompaniment to their claim is described, not just in general terms such as walking in darkness, but explicitly as their ongoing hatred (indicated by the use of the present tense of the verb 'to hate') of fellow believers. It is their hatred of fellow believers which shows they are 'still in the darkness'.

There is one particular matter that needs addressing at this point. Does the author imply here that his opponents actually hated all the 'brothers', that is, all believers? It would be highly unlikely that they did so, for surely they did not hate one another. It is more likely that the brothers they hated were the author himself and those who belonged to his group. If this is the case, we are confronted in this verse with evidence of a very sad split within early Christianity, one which manifested itself, at least on one side, in an active hatred of other believers.

2:10 Having stated in 2:9 the claim of the secessionists (to be in the light), their concomitant behaviour (hating fellow believers), and his own view of their real situation (they are still in the darkness), the author now states, in 2:10, his counterhypothesis: **Whoever loves his brother lives in the light**. The light of Jesus Christ is already shining, and the proper behaviour of people who live in that light is love for fellow believers. One

---

53. So Brown, *The Epistles of John,* 289.
54. So, e.g., John Painter, *John: Witness and Theologian* (London: SPCK, 1975) 121.

important outcome of living in the light is then stated: **and there is nothing in him to make him stumble** (lit. 'and there is nothing to cause stumbling in him/it'). As the literal translation indicates, the text could read, 'and there is nothing to cause stumbling in it [i.e., in the light]'. However, this would be to state the obvious. It is in the darkness that people are likely to encounter things to make them stumble, not in the light. It is better, therefore, to interpret the verse to mean that there is nothing in the people who walk in the light that will cause them to stumble.

It is the Greek word *skandalon* which is translated as the thing which causes stumbling in this verse. In the NT *skandalon* is found 15 times, always with the meaning of causing some sort of harm to a person. It can denote (i) that which causes people to fall into sin (Matt 13:41; 16:23; 18:7; Luke 17:1; Rom 14:13; 16:17; 1 John 2:10; Rev 2:14); (ii) that which causes people to be scandalised so that they fail to accept the truth as it is in Jesus Christ (Rom 9:33; 1 Cor 1:23; Gal 5:11; 1 Pet 2:8); or (iii) even a means of judgement (Rom 11:9). The first meaning fits the context here best. The author is saying that in the lives of those who walk in the light there is nothing to cause them to fall into sin. What 'sin' the author has in mind is not specified, but in the context of 1 John it is probably the sin of the secessionists: their denial that Jesus is the Christ, the Son of God come in the flesh who gave himself to be the atoning sacrifice for our sins, and their aberrant behaviour, culminating in their leaving the Christian community to plunge back into the realm of darkness, the 'world'.[55]

2:11 Having stated in 2:10 his positive counterhypothesis, the author now turns his attention to the behaviour of the secessionists again with the words: **But whoever hates his brother is in the darkness and walks around in the darkness.** This repeats and expands what was said in 2:9. Those who hate their fellow believers are described not only as being in darkness but as walking about in it. What this involves is made clearer as the author continues: **he does not know where he is going, because the darkness has blinded him.**[56] As noted above (see commentary on 2:8), in 1 John the expression 'darkness' stands for either sinful behaviour (1:5; 2:11) or the realm in which sinful behaviour predominates (1:6; 2:8, 9, 11). Here in 2:11 the word 'darkness' is used with both of these meanings. People who hate fellow believers walk in the realm in which sinful behaviour predominates, and their own sinful behaviour, in this case their hatred, blinds their eyes so that they do not know where they

---

55. Cf. Brown, *The Epistles of John*, 291.

56. This recalls John 12:40, where the evangelist cites Isa 6:10 to show that the rejection of Jesus by his kinspeople was in fulfilment of prophecy ('He has blinded their eyes and deadened their hearts'). Cf. Lieu, 'What Was from the Beginning', 472-74.

are going.[57] Those who do not walk in the light of Jesus Christ that is already shining must walk in the darkness. They do not have the truth to guide them, so they do not know where they are going (cf. John 12:35).[58]

2:12-17 AFFIRMATION AND EXHORTATION FOR BELIEVERS

In this section, the author once more addresses himself directly to his readers, introducing his remarks with the words, 'I write to you'.[59] First, he addresses them in turn as those whose sins are forgiven, who know him who is from the beginning, and who have overcome the evil one in order to affirm and encourage them (2:12-14). Second, he urges them not to love the 'world' or what is in it because it is passing away. Instead, it is implied, they are to do the will of God because those who do so 'live forever' (2:15-17).

In the first part of this section the author twice addresses his readers as 'children', 'fathers', and 'young men', and each time in that order. The question is raised whether, by so doing, the author is addressing three different groups among his readers and portraying three different levels of maturity attained by them. Are some mere infants in their knowledge of God, while others have already grown to spiritual adolescence and

57. The verb 'to blind' (typhloō) is found only three times in the NT, here, in John 12:40, and in 2 Cor 4:4. The agent of blinding and the nature of the blindness varies: In 1 John 2:11 'darkness' blinds the eyes so that people do not know where they are going; in John 12:40 (where Isa 6:10 is cited) it is God who blinds the eyes so that the Jews do not believe in Jesus, and in 2 Cor 4:4 the god of this world blinds the minds of unbelievers so that they fail to see the light of the gospel of the glory of Christ. Of the three, only 1 John 2:11 relates blindness to moral failure, while the other two relate it christologically: as failure to recognise who Jesus really is.

58. J. M. Lieu, 'Blindness in the Johannine Tradition', NTS 34 (1988) 90-92, points out correctly that the blindness motif (drawing upon Isa 6:9-10) is applied differently in the Fourth Gospel (John 9:39-41; 12:40) than it is in 1 John 2:11. In the former it is applied christologically and is related to Jewish rejection of Jesus, whereas in the latter it is applied to moral behaviour and the Christian community, in particular the failure of the secessionists to love fellow believers.

59. In 1:1–2:13 the expression 'I write (graphō) to you' is always found in the present tense (1:4; 2:1, 7, 8, 12, 13 [2x]), but after that, in 2:14–5:21, it is consistently found in the aorist tense (2:14 [3x], 21, 26; 5:13). By changing from the present to the aorist tense the author changes from speaking of his writing as an ongoing action ('this letter I am writing to you . . .') to speaking of it as a complete action ('this whole letter I write to you . . .'). Why he does so is beyond our ability to explain, except perhaps to say that it is a stylistic device to enhance the rhetorical effect of his statements.

have proved their strength against the evil one, while yet others are quite senior, able to be described as those 'who know him who is from the beginning'? Attractive as this interpretation might first seem, it is not supported by a closer examination of the text. This will become evident in the detailed comments below. At this point it is sufficient to point out that throughout the letter the author repeatedly addresses *all* his readers as children (2:1, 12, 14, 18, 28; 3:7, 18; 4:4; 5:21), and therefore it seems unlikely that here in 2:12-13 that same designation would denote only mere infants in the knowledge of God. It is more likely that when the author addresses the 'children' he is addressing all his readers (in line with the use of the word 'children' in the rest of the letter) and that these readers fall into two, not three, different groups: those who may be described as 'young men' and those who may be described as 'fathers'.[60]

2:12   I write to you, dear children. The author addresses his readers, as he does many times in this letter (see references above), as 'dear children' *(teknia)*.[61] This designation reflects something of the author's attitude towards his readers, the affection in which he holds them, and his own more senior standing in relation to them. He then adds, [I write to you, dear children,] **because** [that] **your sins have been forgiven**.[62] The author has spoken already about forgiveness for those who confess their sins (1:9), something which clearly applies to all true believers. This supports the view that 'children' here applies not to one group among the readers, those who are less mature than others, but rather to all believers, for all know the blessing of forgiveness. The author writes to his children as those who have been forgiven **on account of his name**. God is the one who forgives sins, and he does so on account of his name (i.e., the name

60. That the readers are addressed as 'fathers' and 'young men', both masculine terms, reflects a first-century way of speaking, but does not exclude female readers.

61. When the author addresses his readers as children he uses mostly the word *teknion* (2:1, 12, 28; 3:7, 18; 4:4; 5:21), but occasionally the word *paidion* (2:14, 18). In 1 John there appears to be no significant difference between the two words.

62. The NIV here (and in 2:13a and 2:13b) renders the Greek word *hoti* as 'because', suggesting that the reason the author wrote to the 'children' (and the 'fathers' and 'young men') was because their 'sins have been forgiven' (because they 'have known him who is from the beginning' and because they have 'overcome the evil one'). An alternative rendering of *hoti* is 'that', which is preferable here. Rendered this way the author writes to affirm that their 'sins have been forgiven', etc. Brown, *The Epistles of John*, 318, supports this second alternative, while I. Howard Marshall, *The Epistles of John* (NICNT, Grand Rapids: Eerdmans, 1978) 136-37, prefers the former but notes that 'Greek readers did not make the sharp distinction between the two uses of the conjunction which springs to the mind of the grammarian!', a point also made by Strecker, *The Johannine Letters*, 57. B. Noack, 'On I John II.12-14', *NTS* 6 (1959-60) 236-41, also argues that *hoti* in all these clauses should be translated as 'that', resulting in the following translation of this first clause: 'I write to you, dear children, that your sins have been forgiven'.

of Jesus, his Son). To do something on account of the name of a person is the same as doing it on account of that person.[63] Forgiveness 'on account of the name' is shorthand for what is spelled out more fully elsewhere, i.e., God forgives our sins because of Jesus Christ, the one whom he sent as the atoning sacrifice for our sins (2:2; 4:10).

2:13a   I write to you, fathers. The author now addresses himself to the 'fathers'. There is only one other place in the NT where believers are referred to as fathers. This is in 1 Tim 5:1, where Timothy, as a young pastor, is given advice concerning the way he should relate to older men in the church at Ephesus: 'Do not rebuke an older man harshly, but exhort him as if he were your father.' Here the designation 'father' is clearly applied to those of more advanced years than the young Timothy, but there is no indication that they are more mature in the faith than Timothy; if anything, the reverse is true (Timothy has a pastoral responsibility towards them).[64] If we take our cue from 1 Tim 5:1, then we can interpret 2:13a as an address to those who are relatively advanced in years (though not necessarily more mature in the faith).[65] The author writes to the fathers, he says, **because [that] you have known him who is from the beginning**. We need to ask, Who exactly is the one they have known; who is the one who is from the beginning? The concept of the beginning is found in several other passages in 1 John and with several different connotations. It refers to: (i) the Word of life, who was in the beginning (1:1, 2); (ii) the devil, who has been sinning from the beginning (3:8); (iii) the beginning of the readers' own discipleship (2:7, 24; 3:11; cf. 2 John 5, 6). Elsewhere, then, in 1 John (and in the Fourth Gospel)[66] the only person re-

63. The expression the 'name' of Jesus is also used in 3:23 ('And this is his command: to believe in the name of his Son, Jesus Christ') and 5:13 ('I write these things to you who believe in the name of the Son of God'), both of which make it clear that the name stands for the person. It is also possible that forgiveness 'on account of his name' may reflect early baptismal formulae; see Brown, *The Epistles of John*, 321.

64. If the second-century tradition that 1 John was produced in Ephesus is correct, there would be added cause to understand 'fathers' in 1 John 2:13 in the same way as it is clearly to be understood in 1 Tim 5:1, 1 Timothy being a letter addressed to Timothy in Ephesus.

65. Brown, *The Epistles of John*, 300, 318, suggests that fathers and young men denote those who have been Christians for longer and shorter times respectively. He believes the description of the fathers as those who 'have known him who is from the beginning' implies that they had been Christians for a long time. However, the text speaks about Christ who is from the beginning, not the fathers having known him from the beginning.

66. The concept is used with four different connotations in the Gospel of John, including the first two listed for 1 John in the main text above: (i) the Word, who was in the beginning (1:1, 2); (ii) the devil, who was a murderer from the beginning (8:44); (iii) the beginning of Jesus' public ministry (6:64; 8:25; 15:27; 16:24); (iv) a nonchronological sense — the beginning (first) of Jesus' signs (2:11).

ferred to as *being* from the beginning is the Word (identified as Jesus Christ). It never refers to the God the Father. For this reason, knowing 'him who is from the beginning' in 2:13 (and 2:14) is best understood as a reference to knowing Jesus Christ. However, when the author of 1 John speaks about Christ being from the beginning, he is referring not to the beginning of time,[67] but to the time when the Word of life was incarnate in Jesus Christ (see commentary on 1:1). In 2:13a, then, the author addresses himself to people of more advanced years who (also) know Jesus Christ.

2:13b   Having addressed the older men, the author now addresses the younger men: **I write to you, young men**. The word for 'young men' (*neaniskos*) is found only here and in the next verse (2:14c) in 1 John. It is not found at all in the other Johannine letters or the Fourth Gospel. It does occur nine times in the Synoptic Gospels and Acts, where it consistently refers to people of fewer years.[68] This suggests that the expression 'younger men' in this verse should be taken in the same way. It does not mean people of greater maturity in their discipleship than the 'children' and of lesser maturity than the 'fathers'. Once again reference to 1 Timothy is helpful, for in that letter Timothy, as a young pastor, is given advice concerning the way he should relate to older men and younger men, older women and younger women, in the church at Ephesus. He is told: 'Treat younger men as brothers' (1 Tim 5:1). In context, the designation 'younger men'[69] clearly denotes those of a similar age to the young Timothy. It is not their similar maturity in the faith that is implied here. If anything, the opposite is the case (Timothy has a pastoral responsibility towards them, as he has towards the 'fathers').[70] If we take our cue from the other uses of *neaniskos* in the NT and the reference to 'younger men' (*neōteroi*) in 1 Tim 5:1, we can interpret 'young men' here in 2:13b as people of lesser years.

The author writes to the 'young men', he says, **because [that] you have overcome the evil one**. The word 'evil' (*ponēros*) is used substantively ('the evil one'), and only substantively, five times in 1 John (2:13,

---

67. Contra Marshall, *The Epistles of John*, 139.

68. See Matt 19:20, 22; Mark 14:51; 16:5; Luke 7:14; Acts 2:17; 5:10; 23:18, 22. In all cases it refers to young people, except Mark 16:5, where it refers to the 'young man' (angel) whom the women found sitting on the stone rolled back from Jesus' tomb.

69. 'Younger men' here translates the Greek masculine plural adjective, *neōterous*.

70. Again, if the second-century traditions that 1 John was produced in Ephesus are correct, there would be added cause to understand 'young men' in 1 John 2:13b in the same way as it is clearly to be understood in 1 Tim 5:1 (1 Timothy was sent to Ephesus), i.e., the author is addressing himself to those who are relatively younger in years than others (though not necessarily less mature in the faith).

14; 3:12; 5:18, 19). The references to 'the evil one' elsewhere in 1 John all refer to the devil (3:12 [cf. 3:8, 10]; 5:18, 19), and this is how the expression should be interpreted here also. We need to know why the young men are described as those who have overcome the evil one. Beyond the present context the author uses the word 'to overcome' *(nikaō)* a further four times (4:4; 5:4 [2x], 5). In 4:4 the readers are said to overcome those who are in the world (the antichrists) because greater is the One who is in them (God)[71] than the one who is in the world (the devil). In 5:4, 5 those born of God overcome the world by their faith. In addition to this, in 5:18 the readers are said to be protected by the One born of God (Jesus Christ) so that the evil one does not touch them. Putting all this together, we can say that the author understands believers' victory over the evil one to be achieved because God himself abides in them (he is greater than the evil one) and his Son, Jesus Christ, protects them, and as a result they are able to overcome the evil one through their faith in God.[72] In the context of 1 John, where the forces of evil are arrayed against the faithful within the author's community through the agency of the secessionists, to overcome the evil one is best understood as rejecting all that the secessionists stand for in belief and behaviour. This the readers do by remaining faithful to the message heard from the beginning.

Having addressed himself to his readers as children, fathers, and young men in 2:12-13, the author proceeds to do this for the second time in 2:14. As noted above, in 2:14 the author switches from the present tense *(graphō)* to the aorist tense *(egrapsa)* when he speaks about writing to them, and he continues to do so in the rest of the letter (2:26; 5:13).[73] The use of the aorist tense indicates that the author is depicting the writing of this letter as a complete action rather than an ongoing process. The author probably adopts first the present tense and then the aorist tense in these contexts as a stylistic device to heighten the rhetorical effect of what he is writing.[74]

---

71. The subject of the indwelling of believers in 1 John is always God (3:24; 4:12, 13, 15, 16), the only exception being 3:19, where the subject is 'God's seed'.

72. J. Edgar Bruns, 'A Note on John 16 33 and I John 2 13-14', *JBL* 86 (1967) 451-53, notes that NT occurrences of the verb *nikaō* and the cognate noun *nikē* are concentrated in the Johannine literature. He suggests that the portrayal of Jesus (and by extension the young men) as the one who gained the victory over the evil one is reminiscent of the cult of Herakles, who was regarded as the conqueror of death and evil. This, he notes, suggests that the author not only sets forth Jesus as the fulfilment of the Jewish system of worship, but also as the one in whom certain pagan aspirations find their fulfilment.

73. There is a variant reading that has the present tense *graphō* instead of the aorist *egrapsa* at 2:14a, but it is poorly attested and clearly represents a later alteration.

74. Strecker, *The Johannine Letters*, 54-56, goes to great lengths to argue that the aorist is used because the author is referring to 'one or more earlier writings, possibly

2:14a   I write to you, dear children, because [that] you have known the Father. In the comment on 2:12 we argued that the designation 'children' has nothing to do with immaturity in the faith, compared with the greater maturity of the 'young men' and the 'fathers'. 'Children' is used throughout the letter as a term of address for all the readers. By addressing them as those who know the Father, the author is, in effect, affirming that they are people who walk in the light, who keep God's commands, and who practise love of fellow believers, for elsewhere in the letter he says that these are the marks of those who truly know God (1:5-7; 2:3, 4; 4:7).

2:14b   I write to you fathers, because [that] you have known him who is from the beginning. Apart from the aorist tense form of the verb 'to write' used here (about which comment has already been made above), 2:14b repeats exactly what we have already read in 2:13a, that is, that the 'fathers' know Jesus Christ, 'who is from the beginning' (see comments on 2:13a).

2:14c   I write to you young men because [that] . . . you have overcome the evil one. Besides the fact that the aorist and not the present tense of the verb 'to write' is used here, 2:14c repeats for the most part what is found in 2:13b, and to this extent it needs no further comment (see comments on 2:13b above). However, 2:14c does expand upon what is found in 2:13b by adding two reasons why the author writes to the young men: **because you are strong, and the word of God lives** [*menei*, lit. 'remains'] **in you.** There are, then, two reasons why the author says the young men have overcome the evil one, but in fact the two are one. They have overcome the evil one because they are strong, and they are strong because the word of God lives in them. How are we to interpret 'the Word of God' here? There are a couple of hints elsewhere in the letter: (i) In 1:1, 'the Word of life' is introduced as the message that is proclaimed to the readers. It is clear from the context (1:1-4) that this message was embodied in Jesus Christ. (ii) In 2:5, those who obey 'his [God's] word' are those in whom God's love is

---

2 and 3 John'. Despite Strecker's protestations, the fact that there is nothing in these two letters anything like what the author writes here militates against this view. Stanley E. Porter, *Idioms of the Greek New Testament* (Sheffield: Sheffield Academic Press, 1995²) 36-37, is closer to the mark when he says: 'Writers tend to compose their letters from their own temporal perspective, using the appropriate verbal aspects (tense-forms) to indicate their personal perspective on the events described. Especially common is to find the aorist used to refer to the entire writing process.' Commenting on this passage, Porter writes: '1 John 2.12-14 (*graphō* [I write] three times, *egrapsa* three times) can be explained at least in part by this analysis. Various theories regarding reference to other letters or to earlier parts of the letter, and so on, are unnecessary if the present tense-forms are seen as making emphatic statements which are recapitulated by the aorist tenses, all referring to the entire epistle.'

truly made complete. In this context the word of God is equivalent to the command of God, and the command of God, we learn from 3:23, is that people 'believe in the name of his Son, Jesus Christ, and love one another'. In 2:14c, then, to have the word of God remain in them means that they allow the message proclaimed by, and embodied in, Jesus Christ to remain in them. Or, as it is put a little later in this chapter, 'See that what you have heard from the beginning remains in you' (2:24). By continuing to allow the word of God to remain/live in them, the young men are strong, and thus have overcome the evil one.

Having come to the end of our discussion of the section 2:11-14 in which the author addresses his readers directly as children, fathers, and young men, we are in a position to make some general comments about the nature and function of this address. First, our detailed examination of the passage supports the view that when the author addresses himself to the 'children' he is addressing all his readers, not only some of them. Second, when he addresses the 'fathers' and the 'young men', he is addressing respectively older people and younger people who together make up his 'children'. What information can be gleaned does suggest that the designations 'fathers' and 'young men' do not imply greater or lesser degrees of spiritual maturity, but rather greater and lesser age levels.[75] Third, what the author says about his 'children' in this passage (their sins are forgiven, they know the Father, they know him who is from the beginning, and they are strong and have overcome the evil one) is very complimentary. It stresses the blessings they have received as children of God, and so functions as a basis upon which the author may proceed to exhort them not to love the world.[76] This he does in the next section, 2:15-17.

75. C. Spicq, 'La place ou le rôle des jeunes dans certaines communautés néotestamentaires', *RB* 76 (1969) 525-26, seems to adopt a similar view, saying that the author attributes appropriate characteristics to the old and the young. The old have the experience and knowledge of the truth appropriate to their mature years, and the young have the vigour, valour, and militancy usually attributed to them.

76. Duane F. Watson, '1 John 2.12-14 as *Distributio, Conduplicatio,* and *Expolitio*: A Rhetorical Understanding', *JSNT* 35 (1989) 97-110, arrives at similar overall conclusions, but by a different route. He sums up his conclusions as follows: 'From a rhetorical standpoint, the questions surrounding 1 Jn 2.12-14 receive more precise answers. The number of groups addressed is two, children being an inclusive category, and fathers and young men being constituent categories. This is indicated by the rhetor's use of *distributio* of the type in which the inclusive category is mentioned. The repetitive nature of the passage is attributable to the use of *conduplicatio* and *expolitio* for amplification and the development of topics. The shift in the tense of *graphein* from present to aorist lends vivacity to the style. It is an element of the amplificatory scheme, the past tense used to portray something present being a noted feature of *conduplicatio*. The passage as a whole is a *digressio* used after argumentation and refutation, serving to praise the audience, elicit their goodwill, enhance style, and amplify topics.'

In the second part (2:15-17) of this section (2:12-17), the author continues the direct form of address to his readers, but rather than complimenting them, he now exhorts them. The exhortation is essentially a negative one ('Do not love the world'), which is teased out in some detail. However, the way the section closes — pointing out the advantages of doing the will of God — reveals the positive alternative to loving the world, and there is here an implied exhortation that the readers do the will of God and live forever.[77]

2:15 The exhortation begins, **Do not love the world or anything in the world**. The present form of the imperative is used in the prohibition, 'do not love' *(mē agapate)*, indicating that the author is presenting the love of the world which he counsels his readers against here as an ongoing action. The love involved in this exhortation carries a different meaning from the love (of fellow believers) mentioned in 2:10. There love is focussed on the well-being of another, whereas here it is focussed on the pleasure and gratification one hopes to receive.[78] The various meanings that the word 'world' carries in 1 John have been listed above (see comment on 2:2). There can be no doubt that in the present context it means 'worldly attitudes or values that are opposed to God' (cf. Jas 4:4).[79] The difference between 'the world' and 'anything [lit. "the things"] in the world' is the difference between the world thought of as a whole and the constituent elements which make it up. What constitutes 'the world' in this context is clarified in 2:16.

Before explaining what constitutes 'the world', the author explains, using a conditional sentence, the consequences of loving 'the world'. He begins, **If anyone loves the world. . . .** The form of the conditional sentence used *(ean + subjunctive in the protasis)* indicates that

---

77. Klaus Berger, 'Die Bedeutung der wiederentdeckten Weisheitsschrift aus der kairoer Geniza für das neue Testament', *NTS* 36 (1990) 415-30, notes that sayings in the Wisdom Text of the Cairo Genizah, dating from ca. A.D. 100 ('The one who finds pleasure in this world will not find the future world . . .' [1.16a]; 'Keep your souls far from desire for it. For that is the opposite of the coming world' [3.3]; 'Exchange your desires for the things of the coming world. For those who love God do not love this world, and they do not love with their eyes' [4.12b-13]), are strikingly similar to what is found in 1 John 2:15-17. The only thing new in 1 John that distinguishes it from the Wisdom Text of the Cairo Genizah is the mention of the Father.

78. Cf. Marshall, *The Epistles of John*, 143.

79. Brown, *The Epistles of John*, 312, 323-25, adopts a position different from most other commentators when he says that the readers are being warned not to be like the secessionists who love the world. The secessionists, he observes, 'concentrate on the incarnation when God showed his love for the world by sending His only Son, but they pay no attention to the salvific import of what happened afterwards during Jesus' ministry when He turned from the world to his own'.

the author is projecting (rather than asserting) a particular situation in which people love the world. The use of the present subjunctive *(agapa)* indicates that the action being projected is ongoing. What it means to love the world becomes evident as this section unfolds, but, in a word, it means to be taken up with all that is in the world (as defined in 2:16) instead of seeking to do the will of God. What the outcome of this projected love of the world would be is stated in the apodosis: **the love of the Father is not in him**. As noted above (see comment on 2:5a), the expression 'the love of God', or, as here, 'the love of the Father', is susceptible to a number of interpretations (our love for God; God's love for us; love which originates with God). But in the present context it is clear that 'the love of the Father' means the believers' love for the Father, because it stands in opposition to believers' love for the world. What the whole conditional sentence conveys, then, is that if people love the 'world', they do not love the Father.

2:16 While not stated explicitly, the main point of this verse is to explain why love for the world is incompatible with love for God. The author does this by showing that those things which make up the world (as he will define them) are antithetical to God. To make his point the author gives a definition of **everything in the world**. This definition involves three elements. The first of these is **the cravings of sinful man** (lit. 'the desire of the flesh' [*hē epithymia tēs sarkos*]). The word "desire" *(epithymia)* is found 38 times in the NT. In only three places does it have positive connotations (Luke 22:15; Phil 1:23; 1 Thess 2:17); in all the rest it has morally negative connotations, as it does in the present context, where the NIV translates it as 'cravings'. This is a general category, and the second and third elements of those things which comprise the world are subcategories.[80] The second of them is **the lust of his eyes** (lit. 'the desire of the eyes'), that is, those sinful cravings which are activated by what people see, and lead to covetousness. Covetousness is one part of what makes up the 'cravings of sinful man' in this context.[81] The third element is **his pride in possessions** (lit. 'pride of life', *alazoneia tou biou*). The word *bios* has a range of meanings, including 'life', 'livelihood', 'living', 'prop-

---

80. Noël Lazure, 'La convoitise de la chair en I Jean, II,16', *RB* 76 (1969) 203-5, agrees that the lust of the eyes and the pride of life are subcategories of the lust of the flesh. However, Lazure argues that all three expressions denote, in one way or another, sexual sin. This is unlikely, especially in relation to the 'pride in possessions', which from all indications relates to material things. Brown, *The Epistles of John*, 326, interprets it as 'human nature incapable of attaining to God unless it is re-created by His Spirit'.

81. Schnackenburg, *The Johannine Epistles*, 122, interprets 'the lust of his eyes' as covetousness, especially 'lustful glances'. Brown, *The Epistles of John*, 326, interprets it as 'seeing only the visible and missing the invisible that is from above'.

erty', and 'possessions'. It is used in 3:17 clearly with the sense of property or possessions, and this is the predominant use of the word in the NT.[82] To construe it here, then, as 'possessions', as the NIV does, not only makes good sense but is also in line with the only other use of the word in 1 John (see 3:17) and the predominant use in the NT.[83] Being puffed up in pride because of one's material possessions is the second of those things which make up the 'cravings of sinful man' in this passage.

It has sometimes been suggested that the three elements of the world mentioned here represent a conscious allusion on the part of the author to the temptation of Eve in the garden: the craving of the flesh for the taste of the fruit itself, the desire of the eyes stimulating her to covet what was forbidden, and the pride of life which would result from eating the fruit when she became 'like God'. This is ingenious, but, if our analysis of the text above is correct, this is not at all what the author had in mind when he wrote these things.

Having described the constituent elements that make up the world, the author reminds his readers that everything in the world **comes not from the Father but from the world**. Everything that makes up the world, those attitudes and values which are defined in 2:16, are 'not from God'. Clearly then, as the author says in 2:15b, 'if anyone loves the world, the love of the Father is not in him'. This is more than enough reason for any believer not to love the world. However, there is another reason why believers should not love the world, and this is spelled out in the next verse.

2:17 The other reason why believers should not love the world is that **the world and its desires pass away**. Using a present tense form of the verb 'to pass away' *(paragetai),* the author depicts the world's passing as an ongoing process. Already in 2:8 he has spoken in a similar vein about the darkness passing away because the true light of Jesus Christ is already shining, and that provides the clue to the meaning here. Because of all that has been set in motion by God through the coming of Jesus Christ, the world is passing away and its days are numbered (cf. 1 Cor 7:31). All that is antithetical to God and his grace is passing away; it is doomed. There is no future in worldliness. While the author says that the world and its desires pass away, he adds, **but the man who does the will of God lives** [lit. 'remains'] **forever**. There will come a time when the

---

82. In the Synoptics it is used 6 times, 5 times meaning material possessions, 1 time meaning one's life. In 1 and 2 Timothy it is found 2 times, in both places meaning one's life.

83. Brown, *The Epistles of John,* 312, 326, describes 'pride in possessions' [*alazoneia tou biou*] as 'the overconfidence of those begotten of the flesh who feel no need to be begotten from above', but this interpretation appears not to take full notice of the meaning of *bios* in 3:17.

world which is passing away will have passed away, but those who do the will of God will not have passed away with it, for they will remain forever.

In the Fourth Gospel Jesus speaks of his doing the will of God five times (4:34; 5:30; 6:38, 39, 40), and in each case it relates in one way or another to his carrying out the mission on which the Father sent him. What the author means by doing 'the will of God' in this context, however, is somewhat different. It is the opposite to all that is involved in loving the world. It means avoiding the 'lust of the eyes' and 'pride in possessions'. Looking beyond the immediate context, doing the will of God in 1 John involves believing in his Son and loving fellow believers (3:23).

Probably the best explanation of what it means to 'remain forever' is to be found in the teaching of Jesus in the Fourth Gospel. Again and again Jesus stresses that those who believe in him (sometimes expressed in terms of eating the bread he gives, or keeping his word, or hearing his voice) shall never perish but shall live and remain forever (6:51, 58; 8:51; 10:28; 11:26).

2:18-27 WARNINGS AGAINST BEING DECEIVED BY THE SECESSIONISTS

In this important section the author turns from encouragement and exhortation to warning. He urges his readers to allow the message they heard from the beginning to remain in them because already there are many antichrists in the world, and the antichrists will try to deceive them. Surprisingly, these antichrists are identified as people who were once members of the author's own Christian community but have seceded from it. The readers' protection against being deceived by these people is threefold. First, they are to remember the truth that they heard from the beginning. Second, they are to recognise the deceivers for what they are: by their denial that Jesus is the Christ, God's Son, they show that they are antichrists. Third, they are to remember that they have an anointing from the Holy One, an anointing which teaches them all things so that they do not need others (namely the secessionists) to teach them anything. As the anointing teaches them, so they are to remain in Christ. The passage has two sections: (i) 2:18-19, in which the author speaks of the coming of antichrists and identifies them as the secessionists; (ii) 2:20-27, where he warns his readers about the secessionists' attempt to deceive them and seeks to arm them against it.

2:18   The author begins by reminding his readers of the time in which they live: **Dear children, this is the last hour**. He addresses them again as 'dear children',[84] reflecting both his affectionate relationship to them and his position as one more advanced in the faith than they. The time in which they live is described as 'the last hour' *(eschatē hōra)*, an expression which is found only here in the NT. However, in several places in the NT expressions such as 'in the last days' *(en tais eschatais hēmerais)* or 'in the last times' *(ep' eschatou tou chronou/tōn chronōn)* are found. In some cases these refer to the whole period begun by the first coming of Jesus and running through to his final parousia (cf. Acts 2:17; Heb 1:2; 1 Pet 1:20). In other cases they refer to the last part of that period, just prior to the final *parousia* (cf. 2 Tim 3:1; Jas 5:3; 2 Pet 3:3; Jude 18). The last part of the period, it is said, will be marked by various difficulties and tribulations (2 Tim 3:1; 2 Pet 3:3; Jude 18). This corresponds with the general thrust of the teaching of Paul in 2 Thess 2:3-4 and of Jesus in Matthew 24 and Mark 13. What the author says in 2:18-27 about the last hour (and the coming of the antichrist) appears to fall into the same category as these other texts, and this indicates the affinity between his teaching and that of other early Christian teachers.

The author believes that he and his readers live in the last hour because what he sees happening around him corresponds with predictions concerning the last hour: **and as you have heard that**[85] **the antichrist is coming, even now many antichrists have come. This is how we know it is the last hour**. By saying, 'as you have heard', he indicates that teaching about the coming of the antichrist(s) was well known to his readers. The actual expression 'antichrist' is found within the NT only in the Johannine letters (1 John 2:18 [2x], 22; 4:3; 2 John 7),[86] and the author of 1 John is probably responsible for coining it.

Moulton and Milligan cite examples to show that the Greek prefix, *anti-*, added to some person's name or title, can mean either (i) the claim to be that person, or (ii) opposition to, equivalence to, or substitution for that person.[87] Jesus taught that *false* Christs would appear in the last days (Matt 24:24; Mark 13:22). In practice there is little difference between a false Christ and an antichrist, for both are opposed to the true Christ. It is

---

84. Here using *paidia*, as also in 2:14, but on all other occasions he uses *teknia* when addressing his readers.

85. 'That' translates *hoti*, and this is the reading of the best manuscripts. Other manuscripts substitute 'the' *(ho)* for 'that' *(hoti)*, and some manuscripts combine both readings to read 'that the' *(hoti ho)*.

86. Polycarp refers to antichrist in a context (Pol. *Phil.* 7:1) which clearly looks back to 1 John 2:18, 22; 4:3 and 2 John 7.

87. MM, 49. Cf. BAG, *'antichristos'*, 76.

very likely, then, that when the author says his readers have heard that antichrist is coming he is referring to the message they heard from the beginning (when they were first instructed in the faith), which included teaching about the coming of the antichrist(s).

A Note on Antichrist

The general concept of a powerful end-time figure opposed to God is found in Jewish apocalyptic writings, and it is probably in these writings that the background to the author's antichrist concept is to be found.[88] Within the NT four main passages reflect this concept, even though only 1 and 2 John use the actual term 'antichrist'. The passages are 2 Thess 2:1-12; Matthew 24/Mark 13; 1 and 2 John, and Revelation 12–13. The information can be most easily presented in tabular form:

2 Thessalonians 2	Matthew 24/Mark 13	1 and 2 John	Revelation 12–13
Man of lawlessness is coming (2:3)	False Christs/ prophets shall come (Matt 24:4-5, 11, 24; Mark 13:22)	Antichrist is coming (1 John 2:18)	John sees the beast rising from the sea (13:1)
He opposes and exalts himself against every so-called god (2:4)			The beast from the sea blasphemes God (13:5-6)
He takes his seat in the temple, and proclaims himself God (2:4)	Desolating sacrilege standing in the holy place (Matt 24:15-16; Mark 13:14)		Humans forced to worship an image of the beast from the sea (13:4)
When I was with you I told you about this (2:5)	I have told you beforehand (Matt 24:25; Mark 13:23)	As you have heard, antichrist is coming (1 John 2:18)	John informs his readers of what is to come (passim)

88. Georg Strecker, 'Der religionsgeschichtlichen Hintergrund von 1 Joh 2,18.22; 4,3 und 2 Joh 7', in *Text and Testimony: Essays on New Testament and Apocryphal Literature in Honour of A. F. J. Klijn*, ed. T. Baarda, A. Hilhorst, G. P. Luttikhuizen, and A. S. van der Woude (Kampen: J. H. Kok, 1988) 249-52, argues that the background to the concept of antichrist is found in the Jewish apocalyptic expectation of an end-time world ruler who would oppose God and be overthrown when God's kingdom would be revealed (cf. Dan 8:11, 13, 25; 9:27; 12:11; 1 Macc 1:54; 2 Macc 9:12; 4QPsDanA[a]; *As. Mos.* 8.1-2; 10.1-2). Cf. Schnackenburg, *The Johannine Epistles*, 135-39.

2 Thessalonians 2	Matthew 24/Mark 13	1 and 2 John	Revelation 12–13
You know what is restraining him (2:6)			
To be revealed in his time (2:6)			
Mystery of lawlessness already at work (2:7)		Now there are already many antichrists (1 John 2:18)	
Lawless one to be slain by Christ at his *parousia* (2:8)			
Coming of lawless one with great signs and wonders (2:9)	False Christs/prophets will show great signs and wonders (Matt 24:24; Mark 13:22)		The beast from the earth performs miraculous signs to deceive the inhabitants of the earth (13:11-14)
To deceive those who perish (2:10)	They lead many astray. They lead astray, if possible, even the elect (Matt 24:4, 11, 24; Mark 13:22)	I write about those who would deceive you (1 John 2:26) Many deceivers have gone out into the world (2 John 7)	The beast from the sea makes war against the saints (13:7)
	They will say, Lo Christ is here . . . (Matt 24:26; Mark 13:21)		
		The antichrists are those who deny Jesus is the Christ (1 John 2:22; 2 John 7)	
		The antichrists are identified as the secessionists (1 John 2:18-19; 2 John 7)	

A number of things significant to our understanding of 1 John 2:18-27 can be seen in the table above. First, it is clear that the coming of a powerful 'antichrist' figure was part of early Christian teaching. Three traditions imply that this information was given 'at the beginning'. Second, in early Christian teaching a distinction was made between the great antichrist figure who will appear near the very end and the lesser antichrist figures whose influence is already being felt. Third, it was widely recognised that the function of both the antichrist figure and those who preceded him was to deceive people. Fourth, in all sources except 1 and 2 John, the antichrist figures attack the church from without. Sometimes the portrayal of these figures has clear political overtones (Matthew/Mark, Revelation). Fifth, only in 1 John are antichrist figures identified as erstwhile members of a Christian community. The evidence for this fifth point is found in 2:19.

One of the questions that arises in respect to the antichrists is whether we are to regard them as purely human phenomena, or whether we are to see behind them some spiritual force. While the passages from Matthew/Mark, 2 Thessalonians, and 1 John might be interpreted in terms of human adversaries alone, Revelation 12–14 certainly cannot. There the 'beast' stands over against human beings. It is probably best to say that while the antichrists are experienced now as human entities, behind them there is another force making war against God and his people.[89] Commenting on this verse, Brown says:

> The author of 1 John has begun a chain of identifications of the Antichrist that would have enormous repercussions in Christian history. While he saw his adversaries as the Antichrist, a century later Tertullian would see his adversaries as the Antichrist, and many centuries later the Reformers would see their enemy (the Pope) as the Antichrist. Often such identifications of the Antichrist with contemporary adversaries were made with the supposition that the biblical writer had seen the future and had predicted the appearance of the adversaries now being encountered. But if the epistolary author demythologized the Antichrist by seeing an apocalyptic expectation of evil fulfilled in a schism that had wracked the Johannine Community, perhaps the time has come to demythologize further his insight by recognizing what he really teaches — not the advisability of

89. Following a study of those NT passages (1 John 2:18; 2 Thess 2:3-10; Revelation 13) in which antichrist type figures are mentioned, Roy Yates, 'The Antichrist', *EvQ* 46 (1974) 50, concludes: 'The lesson here might be that Antichrist, the false prophet, and . . . the forces of evil that assail man on earth can be traced to human pressure groups and to the accumulated and devastating effect of the aggregate of human sin; but beyond these human agents, which are all that we can see, there is another who is making his war upon God. Of course we are faced with difficulties — of being charged with dualism, and of how far we are to demythologize. Nevertheless it seems less than satisfactory merely to equate all these forces of evil with man alone.'

> continuing to identify one's Christian opponents as the Antichrist, but the evil of schism and of doctrinal division in the Christian community.[90]

It is certainly true that 1 John highlights the evil of schism and doctrinal division, something which is always painful when it occurs in the Christian community. It is also true that Christians can be quite unloving, unable to recognise the limited scope of their own understanding of the truth, and therefore much too quick to brand others as 'antichrists'. There is a great need for humility in matters about which Christians differ. However, at times erroneous teaching which is plainly at variance with the truth of the gospel has to be named, and its origins exposed.

2:19   Referring to the antichrists mentioned in the previous verse, the writer says, **They went out from us, but they did not really belong to us.** Those whom the author describes as antichrists were in fact once members of his own Christian community, but they had seceded from it: 'they went out from us'. Their secession, as far as the author is concerned, only showed that they had never really been true members of his Christian community, and this is reiterated in his next statements. First he notes, **For if they had belonged to us, they would have remained with us**, and then he adds, **but their going showed that none of them belonged to us.** If these people had been true members of his community, which they were not, they would have remained as members, and not seceded as they had done. The last clause in the sentence, 'but their going showed that none of them belonged to us', is actually a subordinate purpose clause (introduced by *hina* plus the subjunctive). Translated literally, it would read: 'but [their going was] in order that they be revealed that they all are not of us'. As he looks back on their act of secession, the author understands its purpose to have been that the true colours of the secessionists might be revealed.

As this passage unfolds we discover hints concerning the activities of these people after their secession from the author's community. They denied that Jesus is the Christ (2:22), and they tried to lead the readers of this letter astray (2:26). The author's primary aims are to warn his readers about the secessionists' attempt to deceive them and to arm his readers against them.

2:20   To arm them against the deception of the secessionists, the author begins by reminding his readers of one outstanding resource they have: **But you have an anointing from the Holy One**. The word 'anoint-

90. Brown, *The Epistles of John*, 366.

ing' is found only here and in 2:27 (2x) in the entire NT.[91] The cognate verb 'to anoint' *(chriō)* is found in several other places, where it refers mostly to Jesus being anointed by God with the Holy Spirit (Luke 4:18; Acts 4:27; 10:38), once to Jesus being anointed by God with 'the oil of gladness' (Heb 1:9), and once to Paul being anointed by God, who put his Spirit upon him (2 Cor 1:21-22). Apart from the one metaphorical use of the verb 'to anoint' in Heb 1:9, its consistent use in the NT is in relation to an anointing whose agent is God and whose medium is the Holy Spirit. In the light of this, the cognate noun 'anointing' *(chrisma)* used in this verse to describe the anointing that the readers have from the Holy One is best interpreted as a reference to the Holy Spirit with whom they had been endowed by God (when they first believed), and who confirms to them the truth of the message that they heard at that time (see 'A Note on *Chrisma,* Spirit or Word?' pp. 109-10).

The anointing, the author says, is something they have from 'the Holy One'. This expression is found nowhere else in 1 John, but occurs once in the Fourth Gospel when the disciples say to Christ: 'We believe and know that you are the Holy One of God' (John 6:69). It is appropriate, therefore, to interpret 'the Holy One' here as a reference to Christ. In the Fourth Gospel Christ promises to send the Paraclete to be with his disciples after his own departure, and the Paraclete, Jesus says, will teach them the truth (John 15:26; 16:7, 12-15), just as the author of 1 John reminds his readers that they have an anointing from the Holy One that will teach them also.

The concomitant of having this anointing is, the author says, **all of you know the truth** *(oidate pantes,* lit. 'you all know' — the word 'truth' is not found in the original but has been added by the translators of the NIV). However, at this point in the text there is an important variant reading: *oidate panta* (lit. 'you know all things'). Clearly, there is a significant difference between saying to the readers, 'you all know', and 'you know all things'. While it is difficult to decide between the two readings on the basis of supporting manuscript evidence, Black argues, correctly in my opinion, that, on basis of the overall structure of the passage (2:18-28), the second alternative is the correct one.[92] The statement, 'you know *all things*' (because you have an anointing from the Holy One), in 2:20 is

---

91. Strecker, *The Johannine Letters,* 65-66, provides documentation for the use of the word *chrisma* in the LXX, Jewish apocryphal and pseudepigraphical literature, Josephus, other Greek writings, and the early church fathers (who practised 'chrism', the anointing of people with oil in the baptismal liturgy).

92. David Alan Black, 'An Overlooked Stylistic Argument in Favor of *panta* in 1 John 2:20', *Filologia Neotestamentaria* 5 (1992) 205-8. So also John Breck, 'The Function of *PAS* in 1 John 2:20', *St. Vladimir's Theological Quarterly* 35 (1991) 187-206.

balanced by the statement 'the anointing teaches you about *all things'* in 2:27.

Because they are people who know all things, they do not need the author (2:21), and certainly not the secessionists (2:26-27a), to teach them. The reference to knowing 'all things' here needs to be understood in the context, in which the subject under discussion is the denial that Jesus is the Christ, God's Son come in the flesh. Nothing they need to know about these matters has to be learned from the secessionists. Everything they need to know is taught them by the anointing they have received.

2:21   In the light of the acknowledgement that his readers have an anointing from the Holy One, which means they know all things, the author adds, **I do not write to you because you do not know the truth**, that is, he does not think they are ignorant of the truth and so need him to instruct them by his letter. Rather, he says, [I write to you] **because you do know it**. The statement that the readers already know the truth is in line with the ancient promise of Jer 31:34 that in the last times when God makes a new covenant with his people they shall all be taught of the Lord ('"No longer will a man teach his neighbour, or a man his brother, saying, 'Know the LORD,' because they will all know me, from the least of them to the greatest," declares the LORD'), a promise which is reiterated in the Fourth Gospel when Christ himself declares, 'It is written in the Prophets: "They will all be taught by God"' (John 6:45).

The truth to which the author refers in this context is the truth *about* Jesus Christ, that he is the Christ (Messiah), something the secessionists were denying and thus revealing themselves to be antichrists (2:22-23). While the author says he writes not because his readers do not know the truth but rather because they do know it, nevertheless he does write to warn them about the lies that are being spread around about the person of Christ. This seems to be the thrust of the author's additional explanatory statement: that [he writes] **because no lie comes from the truth**. The secessionists are spreading lies about the person of Christ, and this prompts him to write.

2:22   The liars are now explicitly identified by the nature of their lie: **Who is the liar? It is the man who denies that Jesus is the Christ.** Anyone who denies that Jesus is the Christ is a liar. Already in this letter we have encountered allusions to the claims made by the secessionists concerning their own experience (they have fellowship with God [1:5]; they have not committed sins [1:8, 10]; they live in God [2:6]; they are in the light [2:9]), but in this verse, for the first time, we encounter a reference to their teaching: they deny that Jesus is the Christ. On the surface, this looks like the sort of denial a non-Christian Jew would make, not a Christian. Thus we face something of a dilemma. On the one hand, the author indicates fairly clearly that those who make this denial are erstwhile members of his own community and therefore presumably Christians, and on the other hand the denial they make, as it is presented here, is one that no Christian could make. There are three possible ways to explain this: (i) the secessionists were once Christians but are not Christians any longer, (ii) the secessionists were never really Christians at all, and (iii) the secessionists are Christians and the denial here is not what it first seems.[93] The solution with the least problems is that the secessionists were Christians who once belonged to the author's community, and subsequently left it because they had come to accept a different Christology from that espoused by the author and others in his community. In their own minds they had not ceased to be Christians, but the author believed they had, for no one could hold their Christology and still remain a Christian. The elements of this aberrant Christology are reflected in various allusions the author makes to the beliefs of the secessionists later in the letter. When we put all the elements together, it becomes clear that their Christology involved a denial that Jesus Christ is the Messiah, God's Son, come in the flesh and whose death was real and vicarious (4:2-3, 15; 5:1, 6-8). However, at different places in the letter, the author refers to the whole by mentioning one part. Accordingly, in the present context, the reference to the secessionists' denial that Jesus is the Christ is best read as a shorthand version of the denial that Jesus Christ is the Messiah, God's Son, who has come in the flesh and whose death was both real and vicarious (see commentary on 1:7; 5:6-7).[94]

93. Brown, *The Epistles of John,* 352, 368, offers a fourth: The titles 'Christ' and 'Son of God' were 'virtually interchangeable in Johannine terminology', and these terms were accepted by the secessionists. However, they 'understood them in a way that weakened the human content of the formulas, not the divine'. The issue for the secessionists was not 'on the predicate "the Christ," but on the subject "Jesus" . . . the debate "was whether the man Jesus could be the same person as the divine Christ"'. To be precise, the secessionists may have confessed that the Divine Word (who became flesh but was not really changed by the incarnation) was the Christ. For them to stress that Jesus was the Christ would mean that his humanity and the way he lived were essential for understanding his role as the Christ, the Son of God' (352). Brown adds, 'in this confession "Jesus" means for the author the incarnate Word in his life and death, while the secessionists would acknowledge primarily the preexistent Word as the Christ, the Son of God, with the incarnation adding nothing essential' (368).

94. M. J. Edwards, 'Martyrdom and the *First Epistle* of John', *NovT* 31 (1989) 166, 169, argues: 'That these were men who had failed the trial of martyrdom there can be little doubt. They went out from us, and therefore proved that they were never of us (2:19): the true believer will never succumb to the world' (166), and adds: 'In other parts of the NT there is no doubt that to overcome is to brave the terrors of martyrdom [cf. Rev 2:7, 10, 15, 26; 3:5, 12, 21; 12:11]: it is therefore to the fortitude of his hearers that the writer appeals when he tells them (a) that the world is sure to hate them; (b) that the world is not

The author, having identified the liars by the nature of their lie, then explicitly identifies the liars as antichrists when he says, **Such a man is the antichrist — he denies the Father and the Son.** Anyone who denies that Jesus is the Christ is in fact an antichrist, and his/her denial, as far as the author is concerned, is not only a denial of the true identity of Jesus Christ as the Son of God and Messiah, but is also a denial of God the Father himself. The author does not spell out here why this is so, but from statements he makes later in the letter we can infer that the denial of the Son also involves a denial of the Father because: (i) it was the Father who sent his Son (4:10), and (ii) it is the Father who bears testimony to the Son (5:9-10). All who deny the Son, and so deny the Father, can no longer be regarded by the author as true believers (cf. 2:19: 'they went out from us, but they did not really belong to us . . . their going showed that none of them belonged to us').

2:23 This verse drives home the dire consequences of embracing the secessionist Christology: **No one who denies the Son has the Father.** As already noted above, the secessionists claimed to have fellowship with God (1:5) and even to live in God (2:6), but such claims are empty when made by people who deny that Jesus Christ is God's Son come in the flesh. When people deny the Son, they show that they do not have the Father. The author balances this negative statement with its positive counterpart: **whoever acknowledges the Son has the Father also.** It is those like his readers, who know the truth and acknowledge the Son, who really 'have' the Father.[95] The author's stress upon the connection between denying/acknowledging the Son and a person's relationship with the Father reflects similar statements in the Fourth Gospel (John 5:23; 14:6-7; 15:23).

2:24 The readers had acknowledged Jesus as the Son of God because that truth was part of the message they heard when they first believed. This is what the anointing they had from the Holy One taught them. In the light of the lies that are being spread abroad, the author gives them this exhortation: **See that what you heard from the beginning re-**

---

eternal, therefore weaker and less valuable than they are; (c) that the world will in fact be overcome. The promise of overcoming the world occurs with particular frequency in the fifth chapter (5:4 *bis* and 5:5) and leads to a testimony which is often misunderstood (169).' It is possible that the secessionists had separated themselves from the author's community so as to avoid martyrdom, but while some texts are susceptible to such an interpretation, the clear references the author makes to the secessionists' activities relate to the nature of their doctrinal teachings and their behavioural failings.

95. The author uses present participles in both these clauses ('no one who denies'; 'whoever acknowledges'), indicating that he is presenting the actions in both cases as ongoing rather than complete.

mains in you. One of the strategies that the author urges his readers to employ against the influence of the false teachers is to hold on to the very message of the gospel which they heard at the beginning. Recalling people who are being faced with false teaching to the message of the gospel as they first heard it, and by which they were converted, is a strategy that is also employed elsewhere in the NT (cf. 1 Cor 15:1-11) and needs to be practised today.

The positive benefits of following the exhortation to allow what they heard from the beginning remain in them are then spelled out in a conditional sentence: **If it does, you also will remain in the Son and in the Father** (the NIV has abbreviated the text in translation; literally it reads: 'If what you heard from the beginning remains in you, then you will remain in the Father and in the Son'). This is a nicely balanced conditional sentence in which the author projects a situation in which the message remains in his readers, and they receive the benefit: they remain in the Son and the Father. The emphasis evident in the original language can be represented by the italics in the following simplified paraphrase: 'If *the message you heard* remains in you, *you* will remain in the Son and the Father.' The great positive benefits of allowing the message they heard to remain in them, then, reinforce the exhortation to do just that.

2:25 In this verse the author further explains the blessings promised to those who let that message remain in them: **And this is what he promised us**[96] — **even eternal life** (lit. 'And this is the promise that he promised us, eternal life'). Elsewhere in 1 John eternal life is identified with, or said to be found in, Jesus Christ, God's Son (5:11). He, in fact, is eternal life (5:20), the eternal life that was with the Father from the beginning (1:2). Those who believe in the Son have eternal life (5:13). Those who acknowledge Jesus Christ have the Son (and the Father) (2:23), and those who have the Son have eternal life (5:12). To have the Son, to believe in his name, is to have eternal life in the here and now. But, in line with primitive Christian belief, the author can also speak of eternal life as something 'promised' to believers, something they will experience in the future (2:25). In one place in the Fourth Gospel Jesus says both that believers have already passed from death to life, and that they will hear his voice on the last day and rise out of their graves and live (John 5:24-29).

2:26 In this verse, for the first time in the letter, the author makes quite clear that the readers are being targeted by the secessionists with a view to attracting them to the secessionist teaching, and away from the

---

96. A few manuscripts have 'you' (*hymin*) instead of 'us' (*hēmin*) here, but *hēmin* has better support.

message which they heard from the beginning: **I am writing these things to you about those who are trying to lead you astray.**

2:27a   Here the author returns to the topic with which he began this section (2:20-27) — the anointing which his readers had received: **As for you, the anointing you received from him remains in you.**[97] As noted above, the anointing they had received is the Holy Spirit, and here, in the light of the attempts of the secessionists to lead them astray, the author reminds his readers that the Holy Spirit remains in them. By his Spirit God himself indwells the readers (cf. 3:24b), and this indwelling by God is their most fundamental defence against deception. As the author writes later in the letter, and in an analogous context, 'the one who is in you is greater than the one who is in the world' (4:4).

Because the anointing remains in them, the author says, **you do not need anyone to teach you.** The primary allusion here is to the secessionists who wanted to lead the readers astray. It may be (though this cannot be demonstrated) that the secessionists claimed some special revelation from God to which they appealed in their attempt to influence the readers to adopt their teaching. If this was the case, the reminder that the readers already had an anointing from God, and therefore needed no one else to teach them, would be most apposite. As the author said at the beginning of this section, 'you have an anointing from the Holy One, and you know all things' (2:20). Recognising this, the author insists that when he himself writes to them it is not because he wants to teach them the truth, but because they know the truth (2:21).

2:27b   While the readers do not need anyone to teach them the truth, not the author, and certainly not the secessionists, they do need to be exhorted to stand fast in the truth of the gospel which the Holy Spirit has taught them. **But as his anointing teaches you about all things. . . .** As noted above, the reference to 'all things' here needs to be understood in the context, where the subject under discussion is the denial that Jesus is the Christ, God's Son come in the flesh. Nothing the readers need to know about these matters has to be learned from the secessionists. Everything they need to know is taught them by the anointing they have received. The NIV translation of what follows is rather awkward: [But as his anointing teaches you about all things] **and as that anointing is real, not counterfeit.** This translation moves the focus of attention from the truth of what the anointing teaches to the anointing itself. The text[98] is

---

97. Referring to the reception of the anointing here, the author uses an aorist tense form of the verb, indicating that he is presenting it as a complete act, whereas his reference to this anointing remaining in them involves the use of a present tense form of the verb, which portrays the indwelling itself as an ongoing action.

98. *To autou chrisma didaskei hymas peri pantōn kai alēthes estin kai ouk estin pseudos.*

better translated 'his anointing teaches you about all things and is true and is not a lie' (NRSV). This translation keeps the reader's attention on the truth of what the anointing teaches. Later in the letter the author urges his readers to test the spirits to see whether they are of God (4:1). Here he asserts that what the anointing, the Holy Spirit, teaches them is true, and is not a lie. Accordingly, the author concludes this section by saying, **just as it has taught you, remain** *(menete)* **in him.** Remaining 'in him' on first reading appears to refer to remaining in the anointing (grammatically this is possible). However, the exhortation to remain in him is repeated in the next verse, and there remaining in Jesus Christ is clearly meant, suggesting that the same is the case in this verse. Thus, the thrust of this verse is that as the Holy Spirit has taught them the truth about Jesus Christ, so the readers are to remain in him (Christ).

A Note on *Chrisma*, Spirit or Word?

In the commentary on 2:20 above, we argued that *chrisma* refers to the gift of the Holy Spirit given to people when they believe, which is the interpretation adopted by most recent commentators.[99] De la Potterie argues for another way of interpreting the anointing *(chrisma)* here; one which interprets it as '*God's word*, not as it is preached externally in the community, but as it is received by faith into men's hearts and remains active, *thanks to the work of the Spirit*.'[100] Several points are advanced by de la Potterie in his argument for identifying *chrisma* with God's word: (i) The *chrisma* is something the readers received *(elabon)* when they believed (2:27). The author is using the language of the kerygma, suggesting that the *chrisma* is related to the first announcing of the word and its reception by those who believed. (ii) The *chrisma* is something which teaches believers (2:27). So the *chrisma* denotes the word preached as it has become for believers an interior reality, an object of faith. (iii) The *chrisma* is something believers have received from the Holy One (2:20, 27), suggesting that some transmission has already taken place between Christ and believers, a notion entirely appropriate in relation to the teaching communicated by Christ and transmitted in the church. (iv) The author speaks of having (present tense) a *chrisma* from the Holy One. In John's Gospel, as well as in 1 John, commands are spoken of as things which people have

99. So, e.g., Brown, *The Epistles of John*, 347; Schnackenburg, *The Johannine Epistles*, 141-42; Strecker, *The Johannine Letters*, 65-66.
100. Ignace de la Potterie, 'Anointing of the Christian by Faith', in Ignace de la Potterie and Stanislaus Lyonnet, *The Christian Lives by the Spirit* (New York: Alba House, 1971) 114-15.

(John 14:21; 19:7; 1 John 2:7; 4:21; 2 John 5), and the *chrisma* should be understood along the same lines — in relation to the commandment, the word of God received from Jesus (despite the mystical language of the letter in which people are said to have the Father and the Son). (v) The absolute use of the verb *menein* is found four times in the Letters of John, and always in relation to the word of God or the teaching of Christ (2:14, 27; 3:9; 2 John 5). (vi) The Gospel and Letters of John use a number of references to the interior reality by which we know the truth, and in each case that reality is God's word, albeit expressed in different ways (John 8:31-32; 1 John 2:20-21; 2 John 1-2).[101]

The first four arguments de la Potterie advances in favour of interpreting *chrisma* as God's word can be employed equally well to interpret it as the Holy Spirit. The Spirit (i) is something the readers received when they believed; (ii) teaches believers; (iii) is something they received from the Holy One; (iv) is something they have (present tense).

De la Potterie's fifth argument, that the absolute use of *menein* in the Letters of John refers to the word of God, lacks cogency because (a) although in 1 John 2:14 it is clearly the word of God that abides in the 'young men', that does not determine what it is that 'abides' in people in other contexts; (b) to cite 1 John 2:27, where the 'anointing' is said to abide in and teach the readers, in support of his case is to beg the question; (c) in 1 John 3:9 it is God's 'seed' that abides in believers, and there are good reasons not to interpret this as God's word (see commentary *ad loc.*); (d) the verb *menein* does not occur in 2 John 5.

De la Potterie's sixth argument, that the references to the interior reality by which we know the truth in the Gospel and the Letters of John (John 8:31-32; 1 John 2:20-21; 2 John 1-2) refer to the Word of God also lacks cogency because (a) that it is the *truth* that makes people free in John's Gospel (John 8:31-32) does not help us to identify the *chrisma* in 1 John; (b) that people have a *chrisma* and know the truth (1 John 2:20-21) does not mean that the *chrisma* is the truth; (c) the reference to the truth which lives in us (2 John 1-2) does not necessarily say anything about the way *chrisma* is to be interpreted, and in any case the indwelling truth here may well refer to Christ (see commentary on 2 John 2).

All in all, then, there does not seem to be sufficient reason to abandon the view that *chrisma* in 2:20 refers to the Holy Spirit given to believers when they first believed and who continues to teach them what they need to know.

---

101. De la Potterie, 'Anointing of the Christian by Faith', 99-109.

A Note on the Teaching Authority of the Church

Michl notes that this passage raises the question of who or what it is that guarantees correct belief among members of the church. Is it the teaching authority of the bishops (so Irenaeus), or is it the inner illumination of individual believers by the Holy Spirit? Protestants and Catholics have been divided over this issue for centuries.[102] One resolution of the problem, the conclusion reached by Augustine of Hippo, is that there are both inner and outer forms of instruction. Outer instruction, given to all by the teachers of the church, is not enough. There must also be inner instruction, given by the anointing of Christ, the Holy Spirit, otherwise the external instruction will be understood only externally, and that is not enough.[103]

Michl believes that such an approach is too subjective because it allows people to adopt whatever teaching impresses them. He argues rather that an awareness of the truth is given to the whole church, including those who hold the teaching office and the congregation of the faithful. These stand in an organic union and complement one another. The general faith consciousness of the members and the proclamation of the teachers, through the power and help of the Holy Spirit, lead to an infallible possession of the truth to which it bears witness without error.[104]

Brown notes opposing viewpoints adopted concerning this matter. He cites Bonsirven as a representative of those who believe 4:1-6 supports the necessity of the magisterium of the Pope and councils to set up the criteria for determining the truth, and it is only the application of these criteria that is left to individual believers. As a representative of the opposite opinion Brown cites Plummer, who insists that because all spirits are to be tested the Pope is not excluded. Brown himself correctly observes that the author of 1 John is not concerned with the church as a whole, but with his own community; a community in which the role of authoritative teachers is deemphasised in favour of the Paraclete (John 14:26), the anointing in which all believers participate (1 John 2:27). The idea of a human teaching authority 'would have been an intrusive novelty on the Johannine scene'.[105]

Perhaps the question here is wrongly framed. As far as 1 John is concerned, the connection is not between the Holy Spirit and the teachers

---

102. Johann Michl, 'Der Geist als Garant des rechten Glaubens', in *Vom Wort des Lebens, Festschrift für Max Meinertz*, ed. Nikolaus Adler (Münster: Aschendorffsche Verlagsbuchhandlung, 1951) 146-47.

103. Michl, 'Der Geist als Garant des rechten Glaubens', 148.

104. Michl, 'Der Geist als Garant des rechten Glaubens', 149.

105. Brown, *The Epistles of John*, 509-10.

of the church but between the Holy Spirit and the gospel message as it was heard from the beginning (2:24). The role of the Spirit is primarily as a testimony to the tradition, not as a source of new revelation. Admittedly the tradition is handed down by the witnesses, and to that extent the Holy Spirit confirms the testimony of (true) teachers (see 'A Note on the Role of the Spirit', pp. 151-55).

2:28–3:10 DISTINGUISHING THE CHILDREN OF GOD FROM THE CHILDREN OF THE DEVIL

It is hard to know whether 2:28 is best taken as the conclusion of the previous section or as the beginning of this one. In favour of the former is the fact that 2:28 continues the theme of remaining in him found in 2:27. In favour of the latter, two points can be made: (i) The words 'And now, dear children' appear to mark the beginning of a section in which an additional point is to be made (just as the words 'Dear children' mark the beginning of the previous section (2:18-27), and (ii) the idea of remaining in him so as not to be ashamed before him at his coming, introduced in 2:28, leads naturally into the idea of doing what is right which is the major theme of 2:29–3:10.[106]

2:28   And now, dear children, continue [lit. 'remain'] **in him.** Addressing his readers as his 'dear children' (using *teknia,* not *paidia,* this time), the author expresses again his affection for them, as well as reflecting his sense of being of greater maturity in the faith. The exhortation employs the present imperative of the verb 'to remain' *(menete),* indicating that what the author has in mind here is an ongoing action. The exhortation is to continue 'in him', that is, in Jesus Christ, as the purpose clause which follows makes clear.

The purpose of this exhortation is: **so that when he appears we may be confident and unashamed before him at his coming.** It is the future appearing of Jesus Christ that the author has in mind when he urges his readers to remain in him. The author speaks several times in this letter of the appearing of Jesus Christ. More often than not it refers to his incarnation (1:2 [2x]; 3:5, 8), but in this verse (and in 3:2) it refers to Christ's future appearing. This is also described as his 'coming' *(parousia).* The word

---

106. M.-E. Boismard, 'Une liturgie baptismale dans la prima Petri', *RB* 63 (1956) 200-204, notes certain formal parallels between 1 John 3:1-11 and 1 Pet 1:3-5, 13-23, and suggests that the authors of 1 John and 1 Peter were inspired by the same baptismal liturgy at these places in their letters.

parousia is used extensively elsewhere in the NT, but only here in the Johannine writings. It can refer simply to a person being present somewhere (1 Cor 16:17; 2 Cor 7:6, 7; 10:10; Phil 1:26; 2:12); to Jesus' incarnate presence (2 Pet 1:16); to the future coming of the lawless one (2 Thess 2:9), and to the coming of the Day of God (2 Pet 3:12). But far and away its most frequent use in the NT is in reference to the future coming of Christ as the Son of Man (Matt 24:3, 27, 37, 39) or the Lord (1 Cor 15:23; 1 Thess 2:19; 3:13; 4:15; 5:23; 2 Thess 2:1, 8; Jas 5:7, 8; 2 Pet 3:4; 1 John 2:28). In this verse it is the last of these meanings which the word bears, as the context indicates.

What it means to be confident (lit. 'have confidence', *parrēsia*) in this context is immediately explained as being unashamed (lit. 'not put to shame', *mē aischynthōmen*). The word 'confidence' *(parrēsia)* is found four times in 1 John and refers both to confidence at Christ's coming/in the judgement (2:28; 4:17) and confidence in prayer (3:21; 5:14) (see 'A Note on the Bases of Assurance', pp. 198-200, for a discussion of the uses of *parrēsia* in 1 John).[107] To be confident here, then, is equivalent to not being put to shame. What all this means is best understood in the light of 4:17, where the author speaks about having confidence on the day of judgement. The author's point in 2:28 is that if people remain in Christ (following the teaching they heard from the beginning and which the anointing, the Holy Spirit, continues to teach them), then, when Jesus Christ appears and judges his people, they may be confident and unashamed before him.[108]

2:29 This verse begins a long treatment of the fundamental connection between knowing God and doing righteousness (2:29–3:10), which provides a basis for distinguishing those who are the children of God from those who are the children of devil. This treatment is interrupted in 3:1-3 by an exposition of the greatness of God's love, the immense privilege of being his children, and the hope of being made like Christ at his appearing, but is taken up again in 3:4-10.

The treatment of the connection between knowing God and doing righteousness is introduced with a conditional sentence: **If you know that he is righteous, you know that everyone who does what is right has been born of him**. The 'he' who 'is righteous' is God, and if the readers know that God is righteous they may be sure that everyone who does right is born of him. Those who do what is right, the author says, are people who have been born of him. This is the first of ten uses of the verb 'to

---

107. Cf. Strecker, 'Excursus: *Parrēsia*', in *The Johannine Letters*, 80-81.

108. W. C. van Unnik, 'The Christian's Freedom of Speech in the New Testament', *BJRL* 44 (1961-62) 486, also notes that *parrēsia* here, as in 4:17, means having no shame before God.

give birth to' *(gennaō)* found in 1 John (2:29; 3:9 [2x]; 4:7; 5:1 [3x], 4, 18 [2x]). In every case other than 2:29 God is explicitly mentioned as the one by whom those concerned are brought to birth. Therefore the ambiguous expression 'born of him' in 2:29 must also be interpreted to mean born of God. This confirms that the words 'If you know that he is righteous' refer to God, as indicated above, and not to Jesus Christ, who is the subject of the previous sentence (2:28).

The best clue to what it meant to be 'born of God' as far as members of the author's community were concerned is to be found in two places in the Fourth Gospel: (i) John 1:12-13: 'Yet to all who received him, to those who believed in his name, he gave the right to become children of God — children born not of natural descent, nor of human decision or a husband's will, but born of God'; and (ii) John 3, where Jesus tells Nicodemus that it is necessary to be ' born again' (lit. 'from above'), which is equivalent to being 'born of water and the Spirit', and which in turn is equivalent to being born of the Spirit. Putting all this together, we may say that, for the author, to be 'born of God' was something quite distinct from natural human procreation, something that could not be effected by human action or desire, but only by God himself. It was effected by God through his Spirit in conjunction with faith in Jesus Christ on the part of those concerned.

The author's purpose for including this treatment of the connection between being born of God and doing right was to provide the readers with a way of assessing the claims of the secessionists who were seeking to lead them astray. This becomes evident in the later treatment of this subject (cf. 3:7) following the parenthetical exposition of the theme of the love of God and the hope of the children of God in 3:1-3.

While the section 3:1-3 may be described as parenthetical, it nevertheless picks up two themes found in 2:28-29: the hope of the children of God for Christ's appearing (3:2b), and their need for righteousness/purity of life in the light of that hope (3:3). It is doing righteousness which distinguishes the children of God from the children of the devil, as 3:4-10 makes clear.

3:1 The author begins his parenthesis by urging his readers to recognise the greatness of the love of God: **How great is the love the Father has lavished on us!** (lit. 'Look at the sort of love the Father has given us!'). The exact expression of the love of God the author has in mind here is: **that we should be called the children of God**.[109] In his love, God has

---

109. Taking *hina* + subjunctive to be epexegetical — so Brown, *The Epistles of John*, 388, contra Strecker, *The Johannine Letters*, 87, who reads it as a future reference ('we shall be called . . .').

called us his children. The author includes himself with his readers among those ('we') who are called the children *(tekna)* of God.[110] To be called children of God is an immense privilege because it means that God himself has chosen us to be in his family. The best commentary on what it means to be children of God is found in John 1:12-13 ('Yet to all who received him, to those who believed in his name, he gave the right to become children of God — children born not of natural descent, nor of human decision or a husband's will, but born of God'). Looked at from a human point of view, those who 'receive' Christ, in the sense of believing in him, are children of God. Looked at from the divine point of view, his children are those who are 'born of God', or as Jesus puts it in John 3:8, those who are 'born of the Spirit'. The author not only says that he and his readers are 'called' children of God as an outcome of God's love lavished upon them, but emphasises the reality of this status when he adds, **And that is what we are!**[111]

Those who believe the Word of life may really be the children of God, but that does not mean they will gain any respect from the world. And lest this should cause the readers any distress, the author explains: **The reason the world does not know us is that it did not know him.** The word 'world' *(kosmos)* occurs 23 times in 1 John, and its meaning varies according to the context (see discussion at 2:2). Here, as in a number of other places, it denotes the unbelieving world — people who are opposed to God and to those who believe in his Son. Such 'worldly' people are under the power of the evil one (3:13; 4:5 [3x]; 5:19). It is this unbelieving world which does not know 'us', and it did not know 'him' either. In context, the 'him' whom the world failed to recognise could be interpreted either as God the Father who lavished his love on us and whose children we are (3:1), or as the Son of God whom we shall be like when we see him at his appearing (3:2). The latter interpretation is to be preferred because in the rest of 1 John it is always Jesus Christ come in the flesh whose true identity is in question (2:22-23; 4:2-3; 5:1, 5, 10), never that of the Father. The unequivocal statement of John 1:10 ('He was in the

---

110. In 1 John *teknon* is always and only used to denote children of God (3:1, 2, 10; 5:2). *Teknion* or *paidion* are used as terms of address for the readers. In 2 John *teknon* is used for children of the 'Elect Lady' (1, 4, 13), and in 3 John it is used to refer to believers as children of the elder (4). The word *huioi* ('sons') is never used for believers in the Johannine writings; *huios* is always reserved for Christ.

111. There is a textual variant at this point that omits the words, 'and that is what we are' *(kai esmen)*, but the textual support for it is very thin, whereas the support for its inclusion is overwhelming. Strecker, *The Johannine Letters*, 87, who reads a future orientation in the first part of the verse ('we shall be called . . .'), argues that the words 'and that is what we are' balance what 'we shall be', with a stress on 'what we are' now.

world, and though the world was made through him, the world did not recognise him [the Word = Jesus Christ]') is a parallel to our text interpreted along the lines suggested.

3:2 Addressing his readers once more as **Dear friends** (*agapētoi*), the author goes on to emphasise, by repetition, what he affirmed in the previous verse: **now we are the children of God**. The new element in the repetition is the emphasis on the fact that we are 'now' (*nyn*) children of God. What we are now stands in contrast to what we will be later, so the author adds, **and what we will be has not yet been made known**.[112] While what we will be cannot be fully comprehended now, one thing is known: **But we know that when he appears, we shall be like him**. When Christ appears, the author says, 'we shall be like him'. The nature of our likeness to Christ will be a likeness in respect to ethical purity, as the next verse makes clear. The author then explains the reason for this great change: **for we shall see him as he is**. Elsewhere in 1 John the verb 'to see' is used in reference to the eyewitnesses' encounter with Jesus Christ (1:1-3) and in the denial that those who commit sin have ever 'seen' Jesus Christ, who came to take away sin (3:6). In the first case the seeing involves the physical eyes. In the second case it involves failure to see with the 'eyes' of faith. However, the future seeing spoken of in 3:2 is of a different order: 'we shall see him *as he is*', that is, not seeing him as he was in the days of his earthly ministry, nor seeing him with the eyes of faith, but seeing him as he now is in heavenly glory; and the sight of him, the author says, will be enough to make us pure like him (cf. 1 Cor 13:12; 2 Cor 3:18).

3:3 The author concludes his parenthesis by stating that **everyone who has this hope in him purifies himself, just as he is pure**. The hope[113] of being like Christ in the future expresses itself in an effort to purify oneself to be like him in the present. The verb 'to purify' (*hagnizō*) is found only seven times in the NT. It can have either ceremonial or moral connotations. So in John and Acts it is used consistently in relation to cer-

---

112. F. C. Synge, '1 John 3,2', *JTS* 3 (1952) 79, has suggested a different punctuation of the Greek text of 3:2 that yields the translation: 'Now are we sons of God, and he has not yet been made manifest. What we shall be we know, because if he is made manifest we shall be like him, because we shall see him as he is.' The advantages of this rendering of the text are: (i) it avoids the need to translate the first use of *phaneroō* in the verse impersonally ('what we will be has not yet been made known') and the second personally ('when he appears'), and (ii) it removes the contradiction between not knowing what we will be and knowing that when he appears we shall be like him. The REB has this rendering of the text as a marginal reading.

113. This is the only place in the Johannine writings where the word 'hope' (*elpis*) is found, suggesting that here the author is drawing on other Christian traditions in which the Christian hope was a predominate motif.

emonial purification (John 11:55; Acts 21:24, 26; 24:18). However, in James 4:8 ('purify your hearts, you who are double minded') and in 1 Peter 1:22 ('having purified yourselves by obeying the truth') *hagnizō* definitely denotes moral purification, and this is what it means in the present context where people purify themselves in order to be pure as Christ is pure. That it is the moral purity of Christ which the author has in mind is confirmed by what is said in 1 John 3:5: Christ has appeared to take away our sins, and in him there is no sin.

3:4 Here the author returns to his treatment of the main theme of 2:29–3:10, the fundamental connection between knowing God and doing righteousness, which was interrupted in 3:1-3 by an exhortation to consider the greatness of God's love, the immense privilege of being his children, and the hope of being made like Christ at his appearing.

In contrast to those who do what is right (2:29) and purify themselves (3:3), the author now turns his attention to those who continue in sin: **Everyone who sins** [lit. 'commits sin'] **breaks the law** [lit. 'commits lawlessness', *tēn anomian poiei*]; **in fact, sin is lawlessness** *(anomia)*. The word translated 'lawlessness' *(anomia)* is found only in this verse in 1, 2, and 3 John. It does not here carry the idea of breaking the law, for the whole question of the law is absent from this letter; the word 'law' *(nomos)* is not found at all in 1 John.

De la Potterie, in a most useful article,[114] points out that in the LXX *anomia* translates about 20 different Hebrew words and becomes virtually synonymous with *hamartia* ('sin'). In some places in the LXX *anomia* has Satanic associations, and in two places it is used to translate *Belial* (2 Sam 22:5; Ps 17:4 [ET Ps 18:5]). These things pave the way for the teaching in later Jewish texts that the sins of the people of Israel are brought about by the powers of wickedness — by Satan and his spirits (cf., e.g., *T. Dan* 5:4-6; 6:1-6; *T. Naph.* 4:1; 1QS 3:18-21; 4:9, 19-20, 23). People who commit sins are then called the children/men of iniquity (1QS 3:20; 5:2, 10; 10:20). Among the Gospels only Matthew uses the word *anomia*, and he does so consistently in association with false prophets or others who oppose God's kingdom, and always with some association in the context with the last days or the final judgement (Matt 7:23; 13:41; 23:28; 24:21). In the Pauline corpus the singular form of *anomia* is in all cases but one used to denote a sinful power working in the world, and one to which Christians must not submit themselves (Rom 6:19; 2 Cor 6:14; 2 Thess 2:3, 7). In the NT *anomia* as transgression of the law is completely absent.[115]

---

114. Ignace de la Potterie, '"Sin Is Iniquity" (I Jn 3, 4)', in Ignace de la Potterie and Stanislaus Lyonnet, *The Christian Lives by the Spirit* (New York: Alba House, 1971) 36-55.
115. De la Potterie, '"Sin Is Iniquity" (I Jn 3, 4)', 40-46.

Turning his attention back to 1 John, de la Potterie notes that 3:4 is found in a context in which the behaviour and motivation of the children of God are put side by side. He sets it out in the following way:

And everyone who *has this hope in him* makes himself holy, just as he also is holy (v. 3)
No one who *abides in him* commits sin . . . (v. 6)
He who does what is just *is just* (v. 7)
Whoever *is born of God* does not commit sin . . . (v. 9)

Corresponding to this description of the behaviour and motivation of the children of God is the contrasting description of the behaviour and motivation of the children of the devil. De la Potterie sets this out as follows:

Everyone who commits sin *commits iniquity also* (v. 4)
And *no one* who sins *has seen him, or has known him* (v. 6)
He who commits sin *is of the devil* (v. 8)
Whoever is not just *is not of God* (v. 10)

The parallelism involved requires us to treat as synonymous those things which denote the inner reality of the children of the devil. So, de la Potterie says, '"Not having seen or known God" (v. 6b) is the same as "not being of God" (v. 10); "committing iniquity" must also be synonymous with "being of the devil" (v. 8) and the opposite of "being just" (v. 7)'. Thus de la Potterie concludes: 'We can see, therefore, that the literary structure itself of the passage orientates the interpretation of the word *iniquity* [*anomia*] in v. 4 in a specific way. The term belongs to a series of expressions that describe the spiritual reality of the sinner, his situation, his interior state, and not so much the evil act he commits.'[116]

The next step in his argument is to ask what the author means when he says, 'he who commits the sin *(ho poiōn tēn hamartian)* commits iniquity *(tēn anomian poiei)*'. De la Potterie's answer to this question is that 'it can hardly be anything but the typical sin of the "Antichrists," who reject Christ, the Son of God (2, 22-23)'. In the light of all this, de la Potterie contends, 'the meaning of v. 3, 4 [sic] becomes quite clear. The author wants to warn believers against the sin of the "children of the devil" (v. 10), to which even the faithful remain forever exposed. Whoever commits *the* sin (i.e., the typical sin of heretics), he says, commits not only a morally reprehensible act; he commits *iniquity,* thereby revealing that he is basically a son of the devil (v. 8), someone who is in direct opposition to

---

116. De la Potterie, '"Sin Is Iniquity" (I Jn 3, 4)', 46-49.

Christ and God and who is under the control of Satan. Thus we return to the meaning of *iniquity* which was common in Jewish works of the time and in early Christianity.' This resolution of the problem of the meaning of *anomia* in 3:4, de la Potterie observes, 'fits perfectly into the context of the section 3,1-10. It has an exact parallel in v. 8, a fact that has not been sufficiently noticed: "Everyone who commits sin commits *iniquity* also" (v. 4); "He who commits sin *is of the devil*" (v. 8)'.[117]

3:5 The author now shifts his attention from those who commit sin to the one came to take away sins: **But you know that he appeared so that he might take away our**[118] **sins**. That the author says 'sins', plural, indicates that he is thinking of Christ's appearance to deal with the consequences of the sinful acts of his people (not as often in the Pauline letters, the power of sin itself). In 1 John it is always Jesus Christ, God's Son, who, by his appearance and death, dealt with human sins. He was sent by God to be the atoning sacrifice *(hilasmos)* for our sins (2:2; 4:10), and it is his 'blood' that cleanses us from all sin (1:7). To 'take away sins' here is to be understood as making forgiveness available by offering himself as the atoning sacrifice for those sins. Thus the author can say in 1:9 that God, in the light of Jesus' death ('his blood'), is both faithful and just when he forgives our sins. Our sins 'have been forgiven on account of his name' (2:12). The author can say to his readers that 'you know' these things because they stand at the very heart of the gospel message (cf. 4:9-10) which they heard from the beginning.

Concerning Jesus Christ who appeared to take away sins, the author adds: **And in him is no sin**. This echoes what is said about Jesus in 2:1 ('we have one who speaks to the Father in our defence — Jesus Christ, *the Righteous One*') and in 3:3 ('Everyone who has this hope in him purifies himself, just as *he is pure*'). That Jesus was himself without sin is the consistent testimony of the NT (cf. Matt 3:14; John 8:44; Acts 2:27; 3:14; 4:30; 7:52; 2 Cor 5:21; Heb 4:15; 1 Pet 1:19; 2:22). This affirmation of Christ's sinlessness might imply that the one who was to become the atoning sacrifice for sins (2:2; 4:10) must, like the sacrificial animals of the

117. De la Potterie, '"Sin Is Iniquity" (I Jn 3, 4)', 49-51. Stanislaus Lyonnet, 'The Notion of Sin in the Johannine Writings', in Stanislaus Lyonnet and Léopold Sabourin, *Sin, Redemption, and Sacrifice: A Biblical and Patristic Study* (Rome: Biblical Institute Press, 1970) 42-43, adopts the same approach. Frédéric Manns, '"Le péché, c'est Bélial" 1 Jn: 3,4 a la lumière du Judaïsme', *RevScRel* 62 (1988) 1-9, argues that Jewish tradition leads to the conclusion that *anomia* includes hostility to God that both opposes his rule and abandons his law.

118. The word 'our' *(hēmōn)* is omitted in some manuscripts. Other manuscripts have 'the sins of the world' instead of 'our sins'. Probably the original read, 'so that he might take away sins', and the addition of either 'our [sins]' or '[the] sins [of the world]' was made later.

OT, be without blemish. However, the affirmation of his sinlessness is introduced in this verse for a practical reason: to provide the basis for an important criterion to be used in assessing the claims of people who say they know God. The assessment of such claims is the subject of the next verse (and, in fact, of the whole section 2:29–3:10).

3:6   The fact that there is no sin in Jesus Christ forms the basis of the assertion found in this verse: **No one who lives** [lit. 'remains'] **in him keeps on sinning.** The author uses present tense forms of the verbs 'to remain' and 'to sin', indicating that both the 'remaining' and the 'sinning' in this statement are being viewed as ongoing acts. Where the author speaks of believers 'remaining' in someone, as he does here and in eight other places in this letter, mostly he means remaining 'in God' (3:24; 4:12, 13, 15, 16). In one place he explicitly speaks of remaining 'in the Son and in the Father' (2:24), and in two places it may be inferred from the context that remaining 'in the Son' is intended (2:6, 28). The context of 3:6 seems to indicate that remaining 'in the Son' is intended here also. The possible sinless perfectionist implications of this statement are discussed below (see 'A Note on Sinless Perfectionism', pp. 126-32).

While this interpretation appears to be demanded by the context, it does create problems when we try to understand this verse against the background of the author's criticisms of the secessionists. From other parts of this letter it may be inferred that the secessionists made what the author believed to be false claims to have fellowship with God (1:6), to know God (2:4), to live in/remain in God (2:6 — see commentary on this verse, which provides reasons for understanding it in this way), to be born of God (3:9), and to love God (4:19). However, there are no indications that they claimed to live in/remain in Christ. In fact, the indications are the opposite. From other statements of the author it may be inferred that, while they may once have shared the author's high view of Jesus Christ, they now had little time for him. They denied that Jesus was the Messiah, the Son of God (2:22-23), that he had come in the flesh (4:2-3), and that his death was either real or vicarious (5:6).

The problem is further compounded by the next statement in the verse: **No one who continues to sin has either seen him or known him.** There are no indications that the secessionists would want to claim that they had seen and known Jesus Christ, for, as indicated above, they were denying that Jesus was the Messiah, the Son of God come in the flesh. What they were claiming, as reflected throughout this letter, is that they knew God, and perhaps this is what the author denies implicitly by this statement. If this is the case, then it may be best to interpret vv. 5-6 by saying that in the author's mind the sinlessness of Jesus Christ (emphasised in v. 5) reflects the sinlessness of God, so that any claims by the secessionists to live in/remain in God are vitiated by their ongoing sinful behaviour. Alternatively, it may be that for the author remaining in God is synonymous with remaining in Christ, and therefore he does not always specify one or the other, even when he is refuting the claims of the secessionists for whom the distinction would have been important.

3:7 Addressing them again as **dear children**, the author exhorts his readers: **do not let anyone lead you astray**. As the author saw things, the secessionists were not only living sinful lives themselves, but they were teaching others to do the same. Hence the warning found in this verse. Already in 2:26 the author had warned his readers about those who would deceive them. In that case the warning was related to the denial of the secessionists that Jesus is the Christ, the Son of God. In the present verse the author warns the readers again lest 'anyone' should lead them astray. In this context, the warning relates to moral behaviour: ['Do not let anyone lead you astray.'] **He who does what is right is righteous**. It would appear that those who were trying to lead the readers astray were breaking the nexus between doing what is right and being righteous, or, as the author has already put it, between having fellowship with God and walking in the light (1:5-7), between knowing God and obedience to his word (2:4-6), and between being in the light and loving fellow believers (2:9-11). These earlier allusions to the secessionists' teachings help us to understand what the author means by 'doing what is right'; it means walking in the light as God himself is in the light (see commentary on 1:7), it involves being obedient to his word (see commentary on 2:4-6) and showing love to fellow believers (see commentary on 2:9-11).

The author insists that it is those who are doing what is right, not those who make the sort of claims that the secessionists were making, who are righteous **as he is righteous**. In the context, being righteous 'as he is righteous' means being righteous as Jesus Christ is righteous. In the immediately preceding verses, Jesus Christ is the one who appeared to take away our sins and in whom there is no sin, so that no one who lives in him keeps on sinning (3:5-6), and in the verses which follow immediately after, he is the one who appeared to destroy the works of the devil (whose works had been sinful from the beginning), the result of which is that those born of God do not continue in sin (3:8-9).

Once again we are faced with a problem, because it is unlikely that the secessionists would have been interested any longer in claiming to be righteous as Jesus Christ is righteous, though they probably did make the distorted claim that they were righteous as God is righteous. If this is the case, then it may be best to interpret this verse by saying that, in the author's mind, the righteousness of Jesus Christ reflects the righteousness of God, so that any claims by the secessionists to be righteous as God is righteous would be vitiated by their failure to do what is right as Jesus did. Alternatively, it may be that for the author being righteous as God is righteous is synonymous with being righteous as Jesus Christ is righteous, and he does not need to specify one or the other, even when he is refuting the claims of the secessionists for whom the distinction would have been important.

From all this it may be deduced that the propaganda of the secessionists was not only heretical (denying Christ's true identity) but also immoral (destructive of righteous living).

3:8 To reinforce his exhortation to the readers not to allow themselves to be led astray by those who advocated breaking the nexus between doing what is right and being righteous, or, putting it in other words, saying that one can know God while continuing in sinful behaviour, the author asserts: **He who does what is sinful is of the devil.** Once again the present tense of the verb 'to do [what is sinful]' indicates that the author is continuing to present it as an ongoing action. So he says, those who are involved in sin in an ongoing way are of the devil. It is the secessionists whom he has in mind. They may claim to be of God while they continue in their sinful behaviour, but the truth of the matter is that they are of the devil. They are of the devil at least in the sense that they are doing what the devil does — sinning. However, it is possible that more than this is meant. When, in the Gospels of Matthew and Mark, Peter tries to dissuade Jesus from taking his appointed path to the cross, Jesus exclaims, 'Out of my sight, Satan!' (Matt 16:23; Mark 8:33). In the Fourth Gospel Jesus told his Jewish adversaries that they were of their father the devil because they wanted to carry out the desires of the devil by seeking to put him to death (John 8:44). In the Fourth Gospel, the evangelist states that the devil put it into the heart of Judas Iscariot to betray Jesus (John 13:2), and in both the Gospels of Luke and of John the evangelists say that Satan (= the devil; cp. John 13:2 and 27) entered Judas's heart when it was time to carry out the betrayal (Luke 22:3; John 13:27). In the light of all this, we should probably read the present verse to mean that the secessionists were of the devil not only because they were sinning as the devil did but also because the devil had put it into their hearts to sin in this way. Lyonnet comments:

> Just as a Christian lives under the influence of God living in him, so do sinners live under the influence of the devil and allow themselves to be seduced by him. Consequently, just as he who is born of God and in whom God dwells does what God does, or concretely, 'lives the same kind of life as Christ lived' (1 Jn 2:6), that of a son of God, so the 'chil-

dren of the devil' can only do what their 'father wants' (Jn 8:44), those very deeds which the Son of God came to undo (1 Jn 3:8).[119]

The author says that those who sin, as the secessionists do, are of the devil, **because the devil has been sinning from the beginning**. The author uses the present tense when speaking about the devil's sinning, and this shows that he is portraying it as an ongoing action which has persisted from the beginning. The devil's sinning 'from the beginning' probably refers to Genesis 1–4, where the devil tempted the first couple, and their sin spread to Cain, who murdered his brother, something which is hinted at in the Fourth Gospel, where Jesus says that the devil was a murderer 'from the beginning' (John 8:44).

To further reinforce the exhortation not to allow themselves to be deceived about the importance of doing what is right and avoiding sinful behaviour, the author adds: **The reason the Son of God appeared was to destroy the devil's work.** The devil's work is essentially trying to undo God's work by turning people aside from doing God's will, that is, causing them to sin.[120] The author does not say how Jesus destroyed the work of the devil, only that he did. He does say elsewhere that Christ appeared to take away sins (3:5), something he achieved by offering himself as an atoning sacrifice (2:2; 4:10). He also says that Jesus' blood (death) cleanses his people from all their sins (1:7, 9). We can safely infer that through his atoning death Jesus dealt with the problem of human sin and in so doing destroyed the work of the devil.[121] In the light of all this, the author urges his readers not to be led astray by those who claim that sinful behaviour does not matter. It must matter, for the Son of God appeared to destroy the work of the devil, which is to lead people into sin.

3:9   In this verse the author makes it clear not only that those who

119. Lyonnet, 'The Notion of Sin in the Johannine Writings', 44.

120. This can involve tempting people to sin (Gen 3:1-19; Job 1:6-12; 2:1-7; Matt 4:1-10; 16:23; Mark 1:13; 8:33; Luke 4:2-13; 22:31; 1 Cor 7:5; 1 Tim 3:6-7; 5:15; Rev 2:10), inciting people to sin (1 Chr 21:1; Luke 22:3; John 8:44; 13:2, 27; Acts 5:3), hindering the work of God (Matt 13:19, 38; Mark 4:15; Luke 8:12; 1 Thess 2:18), deceiving people (2 Cor 4:4; 11:14; Eph 6:11; 2 Thess 2:9; Rev 2:24; 20:10), oppressing and harming people and the church (Luke 13:16; John 8:44; Acts 10:38; 26:18; 1 Cor 5:5; 2 Cor 2:11; 12:7; Eph 6:16; 1 Tim 1:20; 1 Pet 5:8; 1 John 3:12; 5:18; Rev 12:12), and accusing people before God (Job 1:8-11; 2:3-5; Zech 3:1; Rev 12:10).

121. From broader scriptural teaching we can say that the devil's work is destroyed by the atoning sacrifice of Christ because that sacrifice dealt with human sins that provide the basis for the devil to accuse them before God and demand God's judgement. That basis is now removed, the devil's accusations no longer stand, and there is no condemnation for believers.

are born of God have been cleansed from their sins, but also that they can continue to sin no longer: **No one who is born of God will continue to sin**. This is the second of ten references to be being born of God in 1 John (2:29; 3:9 [2x]; 4:7; 5:1 [3x], 4, 18 [2x]). Nowhere in this letter does the author describe what is involved in the *process* of being 'born of God'. His interest is more practical. He is interested in the *behaviour* of those born of God: they do right (2:29), do not sin (3:9; 5:18), love one another (4:7), believe that Jesus is the Christ (5:1), and overcome the world (5:18). An understanding of the process of being born of God is best sought in the Fourth Gospel. There being born of God is equivalent to becoming a child of God, something which ultimately can be effected only by the will of God (John 1:11-12). It is also described as being born from above (John 3:3), or being born of the Spirit (John 3:5-8). Putting these things together and allowing them to inform our understanding of the present verse, we may say that to be born of God here means being brought to new spiritual life by the will of God and through the agency of his Spirit. Of such people, the author says, it is impossible for them to continue to sin. The author uses a present tense form of the verb 'to sin' *(hamartanō)*, indicating that it is sinning as an ongoing action that he has in mind here as impossible for those born of God. The possible sinless perfectionist implications of this statement are discussed below (see 'A Note on Sinless Perfectionism', pp. 126-32).

The author then explains why it is impossible for those born of God to sin in an ongoing fashion: **because God's seed** [lit. 'his seed', *sperma autou*] **remains in him**. This is a bold metaphor, using the idea of God's 'sperm' by which people are born of God, which when unpacked refers to the work of the Spirit in believers (see 'A Note on God's "Seed"', directly below).

A Note on God's 'Seed'

The word 'seed' is used in the LXX both literally (meaning plant seeds) and metaphorically (meaning male sperm, human children or descendants). It is used both literally and metaphorically in the NT also. Its metaphorical use in the NT covers a range of meanings: a person's children or physical descendants (Matt 22:24-25; Mark 12:19-22; Luke 20:28), and in particular Abraham's physical descendants (John 8:33, 37; Acts 7:6; Rom 4:18; 9:7-8; 2 Cor 11:22; Heb 11:18). It is also used metaphorically to denote Abraham's spiritual descendants (Gal 3:29) and to refer to Christ as the promised 'seed' of Abraham (Gal 3:19). However, nowhere else in the NT (or in the LXX) is it used in the expression 'God's seed', as it is here in 1 John 3:9, and not surprisingly there have been many different approaches to its interpretation.[122]

The other metaphorical uses of the word 'seed' do not help us much in seeking to understand what is meant by the expression 'God's seed' in this verse. It would make sense to take 'God's seed' to mean 'Christ', and so construe the whole verse as saying that those born of God do not continue in sin because Christ remains in them. However, the structure of the verse suggests a much bolder use of the metaphor:

a No one who is born of God
  b   will continue to sin,
    c   *because God's seed remains in him;*
  b' he cannot sin,
a' because he has been born of God.

The controlling idea in this verse is that believers are those to whom God has given birth (a, a'). As such they cannot continue in sin (b, b'), the primary reason being that God's seed remains in them (c). The author seems to be saying, within the wider context of a metaphor of God begetting, that the reason why those born of God cannot continue in sin is that God's 'sperm' remains in them; a most daring metaphor indeed. However, interpreted along these lines, it is still a metaphor, and it needs to be unpacked. What is it actually that remains in those born of God that makes it impossible for them to continue in sin? Within 1 John believers are said to have remaining in them (be indwelt by) the gospel message they heard from the beginning (2:24), the anointing/Holy Spirit (2:27), and God himself (3:24; 4:12, 15, 16). Of these three, the Holy Spirit is the most satisfactory option, in the light of the fact that the new birth is effected by God through the Spirit, and it is the Spirit who in Johannine theology remains with and in believers.[123]

---

122. J. du Preez, '"Sperma autou" in 1 John 3:9', *Neot* 9 (1975) 105-6, lists six different interpretations of *sperma autou*: children of God; the proclaimed word of God; Christ; the Holy Spirit; new life from God; and the new nature, before opting himself for the 'new life of being pure and doing right through practicing brotherly love in communion with God (Christ) and according to the example of Christ' as the best interpretation.

123. So, too, Brown, *The Epistles of John*, 411; Schnackenburg, *The Johannine Epistles*, 175. Lieu, 'What Was from the Beginning', 471, argues that 'the "seed" refers not (as usually suggested) to the word of God, or even to the Holy Spirit which protects the believer from sin; instead it recalls the theme within the Genesis narratives just explored of the seed of the woman and the "other seed" which Eve acknowledges in the birth of Seth [cf. Gen 4:25]. This means that for 1 John the believer, like Seth, either carries the "seed" of God's promise or is the "seed", in contrast to those who like Cain are the children of the devil.' However, there seems to be little in the text of 1 John 3 to alert readers to an allusion to Seth.

3:10 This verse brings to a conclusion the section 2:29–3:10, and does so by restating (cf. 3:7-8) the criterion by which the children of God may be distinguished from the children of the devil: **This is how we know** [lit. 'in this it is evident'] **who the children of God are and who the children of the devil are: Anyone who does not do what is right is not a child of God.** Therefore, doing what is right and not doing what is right (both understood as ongoing actions) become important identifying marks of the children of God and the children of the devil respectively.[124] However, these are not the only identifying marks, as the author's concluding remark in this verse makes clear: **neither is anyone who does not love his brother.** Other important identifying marks of the children of God and the children of the devil are loving and not loving fellow believers respectively. By saying this the author introduces a new element into his argument, and foreshadows the subject of the next major section of the letter, 3:11-24.

A Note on Sinless Perfectionism

Before going to the next section of the letter, we should offer some comment on the tension between 3:6-9 and 1:8-9. In 1:8-9 the author portrays authentic Christian living as that which involves honest and ongoing acknowledgement of one's sins, God's forgiveness of the same, and the cleansing of believers from all unrighteousness. This obviously stands in tension with what the author says in 3:6-9 (and 5:18) about those being born of God not sinning and in fact being unable to sin because God's 'seed' remains in them. In one place the author rejects sinless perfection, in another he assumes it.

The author's rejection of sinless perfection is reflected in six key texts in 1:6–2:10, and epitomised in 1:8:

1:6	a	If we claim
	b	to have fellowship with him
	c	yet walk in the darkness,
	d	we lie and do not live by the truth.

1:8	a	If we claim
	b	to be without sin,
	d	we deceive ourselves and the truth is not in us.

---

124. Schnackenburg, *The Johannine Epistles*, 176-77, notes that this division of people into two groups, the godly and the ungodly, was quite common (cf. *Jub.* 15:26; *Apocalypse of Abraham* 13-14; *T. Dan* 4:7; 1QS 3:20; 4:23-26.

126

1:10	a	If we claim
	b	we have not sinned,
	d	we make him out to be a liar and his word has no place in our lives.

2:4	a	The man who says,
	b	"I know him,"
	c	but does not do what he commands
	d	is a liar, and the truth is not in him.

2:6	a	Whoever claims
	b	to live in him
	e	must walk as Jesus did.

2:9	a	Anyone who claims
	b	to be in the light
	c	but hates his brother
	d	is still in the darkness.

Each text begins with an introductory formula (a), either 'if we claim' *(ean eipōmen hoti)*, or 'the man who says/whoever claims/anyone who claims' *(ho legōn)*. Each text has a statement of what is claimed (b). We then find that three of the texts (1:6; 2:4, 9) describe concomitant behaviour which is inconsistent with the claim (c), and the fourth text (2:6) describes the sort of behaviour (e) which should accompany such claims. In three texts (1:6; 2:4, 9) those who make these claims without the appropriate concomitant behaviour are said to be liars or still in darkness (d). In two texts (1:8, 10) no inappropriate concomitant behaviour is mentioned, and the claim itself is said to be inappropriate and constitutes those who make it liars (d). What all this suggests is that the author considers four out of the six claims to be appropriate, as long as the concomitant behaviour of the claimants is appropriate. It is legitimate to claim that one has fellowship with God; has come to know him; abides in him, and abides in the light. But it also suggests that the author regards two of the six claims as inappropriate altogether. It is never legitimate to claim that one has no sin/ has not sinned. In other words, the claim to intimacy with God is legitimate as long as one's behaviour does not invalidate such a claim. But the claim not to have sinned is never legitimate.

Based on these texts alone, we could conclude that the secessionists' claims to perfection included some sort of claim to be sinless. The author's understanding of perfection included intimacy with God, but involved no claim to sinlessness. To use Bogart's words, as far as the author was concerned, the opponents' claim to be perfect was both 'heretical' and 'hypocritical' — heretical as far as the claim to sinlessness was concerned, and hypocritical as far as the claim to intimacy was concerned.[125] To reinforce his own approach, the author introduces the traditional belief in Christ's atoning sacrifice for sins and expresses his understanding of perfection, that is, intimacy with God, which is based on cleansing from sin, not a complete absence of sin in the believer. This viewpoint obviously stands in tension with statements the author makes in 3:6-9.

The passage 3:6-9 is part of the treatment of the fundamental connection between knowing God and doing righteousness found in 2:29–3:10, where the author provides a basis for distinguishing between those who are the children of God and those who are the children of the devil. The connection between sin and the devil is made three times in this passage, both by explicit references to the devil (3:8, 10) and by equating sin (*hamartia*) and lawlessness (*anomia*) (3:4). *Anomia* is found only in this verse in 1 John, a letter in which the word *nomos* does not even occur, suggesting that we should not jump to the conclusion that here it denotes specifically violations of the Mosaic law.

As noted above, de la Potterie points out that in the LXX *anomia* translates about 20 different Hebrew words and becomes virtually synonymous with *hamartia*. In some places in the LXX *anomia* has Satanic associations, and in two places it is used to translate *Belial* (2 Sam 22:5; Ps 17:4 [ET Ps 18:5]). These things pave the way for the teaching in later Jewish texts that the sins of the people of Israel are brought about by the powers of wickedness — by Satan and his spirits (cf., e.g., *T. Dan* 5:4-6; 6:1-6; *T. Naph.* 4:1; 1QS 3:18-21; 4:9, 19-20, 23). People who commit sins are then called the children/men of iniquity (1QS 3:20; 5:2, 10; 10:20).[126] Among the Gospels only Matthew uses the word *anomia*, and he does so consistently in association with false prophets or others who oppose God's kingdom, and always with some association in the context with the last days or the final judgement (Matt 7:23; 13:41; 23:28; 24:21). In the Pauline corpus the singular form of *anomia* is in all cases but one used to denote a sinful power working in the world, one to which Christians must not submit themselves (Rom 6:19; 2 Cor 6:14; 2 Thess 2:3, 7). In the NT *anomia* meaning transgression of the law is completely absent.[127]

All this suggests that when the author of 1 John says that 'sin is lawlessness' he does not mean that sin is the violation of the Mosaic law, but

125. John Bogart, *Orthodox and Heretical Perfectionism in the Johannine Community as Evident in the First Epistle of John* (SBLDS 33, Missoula, MT: Scholars Press, 1977) 37.
126. De la Potterie, '"Sin Is Iniquity" (I Jn 3, 4)', 36-55.
127. De la Potterie, '"Sin Is Iniquity" (I Jn 3, 4)', 40-46.

rather that sin constitutes opposition to and rebellion against God, like the opposition and rebellion of Satan. If this is the case, then the author is really saying that those who claim to have seen God and know him, yet persist in sin, certainly do not know God, and are in fact in league with Satan. So the point the author wants to make in the passage is clear enough, and this is all summed up in 3:10: 'This is how we know who the children of God are and who the children of the devil are: Anyone who does not do what is right is not a child of God; nor is anyone who does not love his brother.'

A further problem arises because, in the process of drawing the lines between those who are the children of God and those who are the children of the devil, the author makes the following absolute statement in 3:9: 'No one who is born of God will continue to sin, because God's seed remains in him; he cannot go on sinning, because he has been born of God.' It appears that what he rejected as a heretical (and not merely hypocritical) claim when made by the secessionists, he is now claiming for the orthodox.

The traditional way of resolving the tension is to argue that 3:6-9 claims that those born of God cannot sin *habitually*, whereas 1:8-9 recognises that they do sin *occasionally*. Such a distinction is based upon the use of present tense forms of the verbs in 3:6-9 when speaking about sinning which, it is argued, denotes habitual sinning. However, the use of the present tense says nothing about the habitual or nonhabitual character of the sinning, but only shows that the author has chosen to depict the sinning as something in progress, rather than as a complete action. And, in any case, the present tense is also used in 1:8, where the author says, 'If we claim to be without sin [lit., if we say we do not have sin] we deceive ourselves'. In both cases, where sinning is said to be impossible for those born of God, and also where those who deny they have sin are said to be self-deceived, the present tense of the relevant verbs is used, depicting the sinning as something in progress.

Inman supports the traditional resolution of the problem but in a new way. He argues on the basis of a study of the distinctive Johannine vocabulary, especially the Johannine vocabulary regarding sin, that the expression *poiein hamartian* (lit. 'to do/commit sin') as it is used in the Johannine writings does denote habitual sinning. Inman draws attention to John 8:34 ('I tell you the truth, everyone who sins [*pas ho poiōn hamartian*] is a slave to sin') as one example of Johannine usage where it is clear that *poiein hamartian* denotes habitual sinning. Inman also argues that in the context of 1 John 3:8 ('He who does what is sinful is of the devil, because the devil has been sinning from the beginning') *poiein hamartian* must be understood to denote habitual sinning. In the light of these Johannine uses of *poiein hamartian* which clearly involve habitual sin, Inman argues that its use in 1 John 3:9 should be understood in the same way.[128]

Kubo argues that the affirmations of 3:6-9 must be interpreted absolutely; in other words, sinning in this context is said to be an absolute impossibility for those born of God, and to deny this is to weaken the point being made by the author. To resolve the tension between this text and 1:8-9, Kubo argues that what the author is rejecting in 1:8-9 is the claim to have no sin made *by those who walk in darkness*. He would not see it as inappropriate for Christians who walk in the light to make such a claim. And, he also argues, this does not stand in contradiction to 2:1 ('If any one does sin, we have one who speaks to the Father in our defence, Jesus Christ the righteous') either, because 3:6-9 is idealistic, whereas 2:1 is realistic.[129]

Kotzé argues that the contradictory statements about sinning are to be understood against the background of the author's eschatology. 'The believer is born of God but he is "not yet" what he will be when Christ comes again.' God and Christ dwell within believers, and therefore it is true to a certain extent to say that they cannot sin, but in their daily lives they still face the temptations of the world. Christian existence is then both secure and insecure. Kotzé concludes: 'With respect to life one can say that the believer already has it but in a sense he does "not yet" have it. In a negative sense the same must also be true with respect to sin.'[130] Schnackenburg also asserts that it is best to recognise the tension between the two passages and not try to explain it away, but instead to interpret it in terms of the eschatological tension in which believers live.[131]

Brown appears to concede that a contradiction does exist ('No other NT author contradicts himself so sharply within such a short span of writing'). He concludes: 'No matter how one modifies or relativizes the I John claims to sinlessness and impeccability, the truth in those claims comes from the divine principle that begot Christians and that remains active in them.' He argues that two types of perfectionism are reflected in 1 John, the heretical and the orthodox, and that they represent heretical and orthodox interpretations of Fourth Gospel.[132] Bogart likewise concedes that there is an unresolvable contradiction in 1 John in the matter of

---

128. Kerry Inman, 'Distinctive Johannine Vocabulary and the Interpretation of I John 3:9', *WTJ* 40 (1977-78) 136-44.

129. Sakae Kubo, 'I John 3:9: Absolute or Habitual', *AUSS* 7 (1969) 50, 55-56.

130. P. P. A. Kotzé, 'The Meaning of 1 John 3:9 with Reference to 1 John 1:8 and 10', *Neot* 13 (1979) 68-83, esp. 81.

131. Schnackenburg, *The Johannine Epistles*, 257-58.

132. Brown, *The Epistles of John*, 413, 415-16, 430.

perfectionism. He also recognises two types of perfectionism in 1 John, but he accounts for them differently. Orthodox perfectionism is to be accounted for by a development of the perfectionism implicit in the Fourth Gospel, whereas heretical perfectionism is a result of orthodox perfectionism being influenced by gnosticism.[133]

Swadling argues that the problem is more apparent than real. His suggestion is that the troublesome texts 3:6 and 3:9 are in fact quotations of heretical secessionist slogans claiming that Christians cannot sin, that is, that their spirits are unaffected by their behaviour. These slogans would have been well known to his readers. It is well known that the Fourth Gospel became popular among later Gnostics, giving rise to some of their ideas. Gnostics claimed immunity from sin by virtue of knowing God. The words 'knowing', 'being born', and 'his seed' as an indwelling principle are all gnostic commonplaces. Swadling suggests that the slogans of 3:6 and 3:9 stemmed from a 'free thinking gnostic separatist segment of the Johannine church', which was the target of the author's polemic. The reason that the author introduced these slogans was to immediately refute them by urging his readers to assess the claims involved by using the criterion that those who do right are righteous and those who do evil are of the devil.[134]

Strecker seeks to deal with the implications of this statement by saying that it is not meant to be descriptive of Christians, but functions as a prelude to an exhortation,[135] whereas Schnackenburg says that it is 'neither an apodictic statement ("cannot sin") nor is it a disguised imperative ("should not sin")', and continues, the 'categorical present tense is meant to suggest an observation and a rule . . . pointed indirectly against the gnostics and their disregard of the divine commandment.'[136] Any claims that the secessionists might make to remain in him, the author implies, are vitiated by their ongoing sinful behaviour.

It is very difficult to decide between these various options, and maybe no solution is entirely satisfactory. The habitual/occasional distinction fails because the meaning of the present tense in Greek does not support this distinction as those who advocate this view claim. The idealistic/realistic distinction which implies that believers idealistically do not sin but realistically do sin does not provide an adequate basis for distinguishing the children of God from the children of the devil on the grounds that the children of God do not sin, whereas the children of the

---

133. Bogart, *Orthodox and Heretical Perfectionism,* 90-91, 120-21.
134. Harry C. Swadling, 'Sin and Sinlessness in I John', *SJT* 35 (1982) 206-9.
135. Strecker, *The Johannine Letters,* 96.
136. Schnackenburg, *The Johannine Epistles,* 173.

devil do. The already/not yet distinction fails for the same reason. To distinguish two forms of perfectionism, the orthodox and the heretical, which acknowledge and deny the possibility of believers sinning respectively, does not provide a key to understanding the way the children of God and the children of the devil can be distinguished on the grounds of their not sinning and sinning respectively. The suggestion that the claims to sinlessness mentioned in 3:6-9 are quotations of the slogans of the secessionists, something his readers would have recognised, does not allow a distinguishing of the children of God from the children of the devil on the grounds of not sinning and sinning respectively. None of these suggestions, therefore, is satisfactory. It may be that there is no satisfactory resolution of the tension between 2:1 and 3:6-9. However, if we recognise the connection between sin and *anomia* (rebellion) in 3:1-10, we might say that the sin which distinguishes the children of the devil is the sin of the devil, rebellion or *anomia,* and it is this sin that it is impossible for believers to commit because God's 'seed' remains in them and they cannot commit it.

3:11-24 THE GOSPEL DEMAND TO LOVE ONE ANOTHER AND CONFIDENCE IN PRAYER

The previous section, which distinguished the children of God from the children of the devil on the basis that children of God are those who do what is right, concluded with the words: 'Anyone who does not do what is right is not a child of God; nor is anyone who does not love his brother'. The final clause, 'nor is anyone who does not love his brother', foreshadows what is taken up and discussed at some length in 3:11-24, that is, that genuine love for fellow believers is another mark of those who 'belong to the truth'.

3:11 The NIV translation of this verse unfortunately obscures the clear connection between what is foreshadowed in 3:10 and developed in 3:11-18 by failing to translate the conjunction *hoti* ('for') with which 3:11-18 is introduced (lit.: '*For* this is the message . . .'). This connection is established, however, not only with the conjunction, but also by the way the author picks up the notion of the person 'who does not love his brother' (3:10) when he urges his readers not to be like Cain, who 'murdered his brother' (3:12), and informs them that 'anyone who hates is brother is a murderer' (3:15).

The author begins his exposition of genuine love of fellow believers as the mark of those who belong to the truth by reminding his readers:

This is the message you heard from the beginning: We should love one another. The message to which the author appeals is described as the one they 'heard from the beginning'. This refers to the time when the readers first heard the gospel message (see 'A Note on "From the Beginning" [*ap' archēs*]', p. 57). The message they heard included the command of the Lord Jesus that those who believe in him should 'love one another'. This is the first of six references in the Letters of John to Jesus' command that his disciples should love one another (the others are found in 1 John 3:23; 4:7, 11, 12; 2 John 5). They are probably dependent on the account of the Last Supper discourses found in the Fourth Gospel (John 13:34; 15:12, 17).[137] What he means by loving one another is spelled out negatively in the next verse and positively later in this passage (vv. 16-18).

3:12 In this verse the author urges his readers not to allow themselves to fall into that category of persons who do not love fellow believers by using a negative example: **Do not be like Cain, who belonged to the evil one and murdered his brother.** The author has in mind Genesis 4:1-25, in which the account of Cain and Abel, the sons of Adam and Eve, is found. Cain was angry because his offering was not accepted by the Lord, whereas the offering of his brother Abel was accepted. In his anger Cain planned and carried out the murder of his brother Abel. It may be inferred from Gen 4:6-7 that Cain's offering was not accepted because he was an evildoer. In this text, the Lord, following his rejection of Cain's offering, and before Cain murdered his brother, says to Cain: 'Why are you angry? Why is your face downcast? If you do what is right, will you not be accepted? But if you do not do what is right, sin is crouching at your door; it desires to have you, but you must master it.'

The author's reference to Cain is the only direct reference to the OT found in this letter. His description of Cain as one 'who belonged to the evil one' has no parallel in the Genesis account, but in some Jewish texts (e.g., the second-century-B.C. *T. Benjamin* 7:1-5 and the first- or second-century-A.D. *Apocalypse of Abraham* 24:3-5) the murder of Abel by his brother Cain is regarded as an act inspired by the devil/Beliar. The evil character of Cain is universally assumed in both biblical and extrabiblical sources (see Appendix, pp. 235-42). The author, too, works on this assumption when he adds: **And why did he murder him? Because his own actions were evil and his brother's were righteous.** The text of Genesis, while implying that it was because Cain's actions were evil that his offering was not accepted by the Lord, and that it was because of Abel's righteous actions that the Lord accepted his offering, does not specify the na-

---

137. There are other allusions to Jesus' command (though not dependent on the Fourth Gospel) in Rom 13:8; 1 Thess 4:9; and 1 Pet 1:22.

ture of their respective actions. However, the writer to the Hebrews, reflecting on the text of Genesis 4, notes that: 'By faith Abel offered God a better sacrifice than Cain did. By faith he was commended as a righteous man, when God spoke well of his offerings' (Heb 11:4). As far as that writer was concerned, what differentiated Abel from Cain was the former's faith and, presumably, the latter's lack of it.[138]

3:13 Having spoken of Cain's murder of his brother, the author reminds his readers that they, too, will be the objects of hatred: **Do not be surprised, my brothers,**[139] **if the world hates you.** The expression 'do not be surprised' *(mē thaumazete)* is also used in John 5:28 (cf. 3:7) to introduce significant statements, and here it is used before a serious warning to believers of the world's hatred. This warning comes as something of a surprise, following as it does the author's stress in the previous verses on the mutual love that should exist between believers. On first reading it also appears to be out of kilter with what is taken up in the following verses: mutual love among believers as the sign of their having passed from death to life.

This association of the command to love with a warning about the world's hatred may perhaps be explained by the author's dependence on the Fourth Gospel at this point in his letter. In the Last Supper discourses, Jesus' teaching concerning the need to love one another (John 15:9-17) is followed immediately by teaching that his disciples would experience hatred from 'the world' (John 15:18-25). In the context of John 15 these two ideas function as part of Jesus' preparation of his disciples for the time following his imminent departure to the Father. They will need to adhere to one another in mutual love and be prepared to face hostility from some unbelieving Jews.

But the overall context of 1 John is different from that of the Fourth Gospel. In 1 John the conflict the readers face is from those who were once part of the Christian community, the secessionists. Why, then, remind the readers that they will be the objects of the world's hatred? And in the context of 1 John who or what is 'the world' *(kosmos)?* The word *kosmos* occurs 23 times in 1 John, and its meaning varies according to the context (see the commentary on 2:2). But here, and in several other places, it denotes the unbelieving world, that is, people who are opposed to God and believers, and who are under the power of the evil one (3:1;

---

138. In the context of Hebrews 11, faith is both trust in the promises of God and loyalty to him in the midst of afflictions, neither of which seems immediately applicable in 1 John 3:9.

139. This is the only place in the letter where the author uses the term 'brothers' *(adelphoi)* as a term of address to his readers; elsewhere he uses 'children' *(teknia)*. Modern readers should interpret 'brothers' here inclusively to mean 'brothers and sisters'.

4:5 [3x]; 5:19). However, stress on the hatred of the unbelieving world towards the readers seems out of kilter with the main thrust of the letter.

The way through this dilemma is to recognise that the author now associates the secessionists with the world. They are the 'antichrists' who 'went out from us' because none of them 'belonged to us' (2:18-19). These are the 'false prophets' who 'have gone out into the world', and they manifest 'the spirit of the antichrist' which 'even now is already in the world' (4:1-3). The secessionists 'are from the world and therefore speak from the viewpoint of the world, and the world listens to them' (4:5). But, the author assures his readers, 'you are from God and have overcome them, because greater is the one who is in you [the Spirit of truth] than the one who is in the world [the spirit of antichrist/the spirit of falsehood]' (4:4-6). The author's warning concerning the hatred of the world, then, is probably best interpreted in terms of the opposition of the secessionists towards those from whom they separated themselves, that is, the author's readers.

3:14 Following the brief digression in 3:13 with its warning that the readers will be the objects of the world's hatred, in 3:14 the author returns to the main theme of 3:11-24, that is, mutual love as a mark of true children of God. But now this theme is expressed in a different way: **We know that we have passed from death to life, because we love our brothers.** The 'mark' is the same, the love of fellow believers, but the status of those who love is described differently: they are now described as those who 'have passed from death to life'.

The expression 'we have passed from death to life' *(metabebēkamen ek tou thanatou eis tēn zōēn)* has a close parallel in the Fourth Gospel (John 5:24: 'he has passed from death to life', *metabebēken ek tou thanatou eis tēn zōēn)*, where the idea of passing from death to life is synonymous with escaping condemnation and obtaining eternal life.[140] In the Fourth Gospel, eternal life is defined as knowing God (John 17:3), who is both the source of life and the giver of life to those who come to him through Jesus Christ. The closeness of the expressions and the relationship between 1 John and the Fourth Gospel justify interpreting the statement in 1 John 3:14 in terms of its parallel in John 5:24, that is, love for fellow believers is the mark of those who have escaped condemnation because they have come to know God through Jesus Christ.

The expression 'because we love our brothers' uses a present tense form of the verb 'to love', indicating that the author is stressing that on-

---

140. Wendy E. Sproston, 'Witness to What Was *ap' archēs:* 1 John's Contribution to Our Knowledge of Tradition in the Fourth Gospel', *JSNT* 48 (1992) 50, cites 1 John 3:14/ John 5:24 (and 1 John 4:12/John 1:18) as instances where the epistle and the Gospel reproduce 'not only the same words but also often the same phrases, and sometimes even whole sentences'.

going love for fellow believers is the mark of those who have passed from death to life. Interpreted against the background of the Fourth Gospel and understood in relation to the secessionists' claims, the author of 1 John is saying that it is by their love for fellow believers that his readers may be assured that they know God and experience eternal life. It is those who have remained in the parent community, and not the secessionists, who truly know God and experience eternal life. When he adds: **Anyone who does not love**[141] **remains in death,** the author has the secessionists in mind. As far as he is concerned, the secessionists, by their ongoing lack of love for the members of the parent community, show that they have never really passed from death to life. They remain in death, they do not know God, and they do not experience the eternal life which knowledge of God entails.

What does the author of 1 John understand by 'eternal life'? He identifies it with, or says it is found in, Jesus Christ: Eternal life is promised to those who believe in him (2:25); it is found in Christ, the Son (5:11), who is the true God and eternal life (5:20); this life was with the Father from the beginning and appeared in the person of Jesus Christ to eyewitnesses (1:2); those who believe in Christ may know that they have eternal life (5:13) because they have the Son, and those who have the Son have eternal life (5:12). As far as the author is concerned, eternal life is not an unending extension of life as we know it; rather, it is 'having' the Son, Jesus Christ, for eternal life is all tied up in him.

3:15 Continuing the idea with which verse 14 ends ('Anyone who does not love remains in death'), the author adds: **Anyone who hates his brother is a murderer.** There may be an allusion to Cain's murder of his brother Abel here (something to which the author has already pointed as a negative example in 3:11). Alternatively, the author may be alluding to the teaching of Jesus that those who are angry with their fellows will be subject to judgement in the same way as those who commit murder (cf. Matt 5:21 par.). The author then continues, **and you know that no murderer has eternal life in him.** The purpose of this whole verse appears to be to heighten the force of what was said in verse 14, that is, that anyone who does not love abides in death; such a person is like a murderer, and those consumed with murderous intents clearly do not have eternal life abiding in them. In both verses 14 and 15, when describing those who do not love and those who hate, the author uses present tense forms of the verbs, indicating that it is ongoing failure to love or ongoing hatred

---

141. Some manuscripts add the words 'the brother' *(ton adelphon)* or 'his brother' *(ton adelphon autou)* here, but these additions clearly represent later attempts to conform the second part of this verse to what is found in the first part of it.

which he believes to be the mark of those who remain in death and therefore do not have eternal life in them.

3:16 The author has spoken of love as the mark of those who have passed from death to life in verse 14. Now he explains what the nature of that love is, and then stresses the obligation resting on believers to practise it. He begins: **This is how we know what love is: Jesus Christ laid down his life for us.** The readers are people who know what love is because they know that Jesus Christ laid down his life for them. The sort of love exemplified in Christ's death is love which expends itself in the interests of others. When the author speaks of Christ laying down his life for us, he is almost certainly picking up the teaching of Jesus as it is presented in the Fourth Gospel. There Jesus speaks of himself as the Good Shepherd, who lays down his life for the sheep (John 10:11, 15). He lays it down of his own accord; no one takes it from him (John 10:17, 18).

The corollary to Christ laying his life down for us is that **we ought to lay down our lives for our brothers**. This same connection is made in the Last Supper discourses of the Fourth Gospel, where Jesus says to his disciples: 'My command is this: Love each other as I have loved you. Greater love has no one than this, that he lay down his life for his friends. You are my friends . . .' (John 15:12-14). As Christ loved us and laid down his life for us, so we must do for one another. The author applies this in a very down-to-earth fashion in the following verses.

3:17-18 Applying the exhortation to the lives of his readers, the author does not speak of the extreme sort of self-giving involved in actually laying down their lives for fellow believers, but of something far more down to earth. He asks: **If anyone has material possessions** [lit. 'worldly goods', *ton bion*[142] *tou kosmou*] **and sees his brother in need, but has no pity** [lit. 'closes his heart or affections'] **on him, how can the love of God be in him?**[143] In the light of Christ's self-giving love for them, the author says, they should not close their hearts toward fellow believers in material need.[144] In fact, they cannot close their hearts to them and still rightly claim that the love of God remains in them.

---

142. The word *bios* has a range of meanings, including 'life', 'livelihood', 'living', 'property', and 'possessions'. It occurs 10 times in the NT. It is also found 6 times in the Synoptics with the meaning material possessions (Mark 12:44; Luke 8:14, [43]; 15:12, 30; 21:4). It is found 2 times in 1 Timothy, in both places meaning one's life (1 Tim 2:2, 4). It is found 2 times in 1 John, in the first case (2:16) probably meaning material possessions, and here in 3:17 the context indicating clearly that it means property or possessions, which is the predominant meaning of *bios* in the NT.

143. A third-class conditional sentence is used (*ean* + subjunctive in the protasis) by which the author projects a hypothetical situation.

144. Mark 10:21 and Luke 10:25-37 contain positive examples of what is here intended.

It is difficult to know how to construe 'the love of God' in this verse. It could mean' love for God'. If so, it would be in line with what the author says later: 'If anyone says, "I love God," yet hates his brother, he is a liar. For anyone who does not love his brother, whom he has seen, cannot love God, whom he has not seen' (4:20). There it is emphasised that love for God and love for fellow believers go hand in hand. Alternatively it could mean the 'love that comes from God', and the verse would then say that love coming from God is not found in a person who shows no pity to those in need. While it is difficult to say which shade of meaning the author intended here, both represent genuine aspects of the author's understanding of the love of God. In Johannine terms the love which comes from God both creates believers' love for fellow believers (4:19) and expresses itself in love for them (4:20).

Deuteronomy 15:7-9 may provide the background to the idea of closing one's heart towards others in need. The passage reads:

> If there is a poor man among your brothers in any of the towns of the land that the LORD your God is giving you, do not be hardhearted or tightfisted toward your poor brother. Rather be openhanded and freely lend him whatever he needs. Be careful not to harbor this wicked thought: "The seventh year, the year for canceling debts, is near," so that you do not show ill will toward your needy brother and give him nothing. He may then appeal to the LORD against you, and you will be found guilty of sin.

In this passage the Israelites were cautioned against allowing a calculating meanness to cause them to close their hearts when confronted with a poor and needy person. They were to be generous and lend to the poor even if the seventh year (when all debts would be cancelled) was near. It is perhaps with this passage in mind that the author reminds his readers that the love of God and meanness of spirit cannot coexist.

Rather than to be mean-spirited, the author urges his readers to be generous and practical in their love: **Dear children, let us not love with words or tongue but with actions and in truth.** They must not just talk about love, but must practise it, and in this context that means using their own resources to relieve the needs of others. To love 'in truth' here means to love truly,[145] as distinct from loving in word only. It is synonymous with loving in action in this context. An illustration of what it can mean to 'love with words or tongue' but not 'with actions and in truth' may be

---

145. Contra Strecker, *The Johannine Letters*, 119, who says that 'love must be associated with . . . eschatological truth' and that 'eschatological truth that is believed should become concrete action'.

found in Jas 2:15-16: 'Suppose a brother or sister is without clothes and daily food. If one of you says to him, "Go, I wish you well; keep warm and well fed," but does nothing about his physical needs, what good is it?'[146]

3:19-22 On first reading, these verses appear to be a digression from the theme of loving one another that runs through 3:11-18 and is picked up again in 3:23-24. They seem to speak about the believer's assurance before God in a way that is unrelated to the topic of loving one another which is the main theme of 3:11-24.

Understood as a digression, the passage has been interpreted in two ways: (i) In a positive way: if our hearts (read consciences) condemn us, God is greater (read 'kinder') than our hearts, knowing everything, and if our hearts do not condemn us, then we may have confidence that our prayers will be heard.[147] (ii) In a rigorous way: if our hearts (read 'consciences') condemn us, God is more rigorous in his condemnation than our hearts are because he knows everything, but if hearts do not condemn us, then we may have confidence that our prayers will be heard.[148] Both of these approaches to verses 19-22 run into difficulties.

First, they treat the word 'heart' (*kardia*) as a synonym for conscience (*syneidēsis*), and there is no precedent for doing so elsewhere in the NT. (The word *kardia* is found 156 times in the NT, including four times in 1 John [all in 3:19-21]. In no place outside 1 John does *kardia* function as a synonym for *syneidēsis* [conscience], and therefore there is no good reason to interpret it in that way here.)[149]

---

146. C. René Padilla, 'A Reflection on 1 John 3:16-18', *Transformation* 6 (1989) 15-18, offers three suggestions on the application of 3:16-18 to Christians today: (i) the place to begin acting is the church (cf. Acts 2:45; 4:32-37); (ii) we must make sure that our evangelism takes the whole gospel and the whole person seriously — not merely an offer of benefits won by Christ, but a call to repentance as well (remember the rich young ruler); (iii) we must do all we can to foster justice in society, locally, nationally, and internationally.

147. So, e.g., Strecker, *The Johannine Letters*, 122-23; Brown, *The Epistles of John*, 460.

148. As Brown, *The Epistles of John*, 459, notes, this is the interpretation adopted by early church fathers, Augustine, Calvin, and the teachers of the Counter-Reformation.

149. Joachim Kügler, '"Wenn das Herz uns auch verurteilt . . .": Ägyptische Anthropologie in 1Joh 3,19-21?', *BibNotiz* 66 (1993) 13-14, draws attention to parallels to the notion of the human heart as an autonomous arbiter (1 John 3:20) that occur in Egyptian texts and in *T. Gad* 5:3. *T. Gad* 5:2-3 reads: 'I tell you this, my children, from experience, so that you might escape hatred and cling to love of the Lord. Righteousness expels hatred; humility kills envy. For the person who is just and humble is ashamed to commit an injustice, not because someone else will pass judgment on him but out of his own heart, because the Lord considers his inner deliberations' (*OTP*, 815). While there is precedent for the use of *kardia* in a way that implies an arbitrary function in Egyptian texts and in the *T. Gad*, the fact that no such use is found anywhere else in the NT makes it most unlikely that such a meaning should be given to *kardia* in 1 John 3:19-21.

Second, these approaches interpret the Greek word *peithō* as the NIV does, to 'set at rest' or 'reassure'.[150] The word *peithō* is found 52 times in the NT, including this one time in 1 John. In every other place *peithō* bears the meaning 'to persuade, convince' (42x), or the related meanings 'to trust' (6x) or 'to obey' (3x), but it never bears the meaning 'to reassure' or 'to set at rest'. If 3:19 can be satisfactorily interpreted when *peithō* is given the normal meaning it bears in the NT ('to persuade, convince'), then it would be better to do so.

Third, these approaches ignore the grammatical connection between 3:19ff. and what precedes, a connection made explicit by the opening words of verse 19: 'This then . . .' [lit. 'And by this . . .', *kai en toutō*]. The author uses the expression *en toutō* in this explanatory way 13 times in 1 John, and in every other case it points forward to what follows (2:3, 5; 3:10, 16, 19, 24; 4:2, 9, 10, 13, 17; 5:2), but it does so in a way that carries forward the preceding discussion. Therefore, we might also expect verses 19-22, introduced by the expression *kai en toutō*, to pick up the preceding discussion and carry it forward. Accordingly, verses 19-22 should not be read as a digression or as the beginning of a new section, but rather as an integral part of the exhortation to love one another which runs through 3:11-24.

Bearing these three things in mind, and taking note of Deuteronomy 15:7-9 as the probable background to this passage, Court says that the interpretation offered by Sir Edwin Hoskyns ought to be explored once more.[151] Court argues:[152]

> The demand for sacrificial charity has been made towards 'a poor man, one of your brethren' (Deut xv.7, cf. 1 John iii.17); but a base thought arises in the heart of a Christian which condemns the sacrifice demanded as unnecessary, and suggests that it can be avoided and that love can be maintained apart from a definite surrender of life or goods. The writer of the letter insists that this impulse, however natural, must be eradicated. The heart must be reasoned with and persuaded in the presence of God to make the sacrifice willingly. The demand of God is greater than the base and ignorant impulse of the human heart (cf. iv.4). Moreover, His knowledge is infinite, and no motion of the heart escapes His notice.

150. So also, e.g., Schnackenburg, *The Johannine Epistles*, 185.
151. Sir Edwin Hoskyns, in *A New Commentary on Holy Scripture*, ed. Charles Gore, Henry Leighton Goudge, and Alfred Guillaume, first published in 1928, cited in J. M. Court, 'Blessed Assurance?' *JTS* 33 (1982) 512.
152. 'Court, 'Blessed Assurance?', 512.

This approach provides a satisfactory resolution to the difficulties presented to the reader by verses 19-22, and makes way for an interpretation which takes full account of the integral nature of the whole section 3:11-24, and the place of verses 19-22 within it. The comments on verses 19-22 which follow reflect this approach.

3:19-20 When the author says, **This then is how we know**[153] **that we belong to the truth,** he is reinforcing the exhortation to his readers not to close their hearts towards their fellow believers in need: they will know they belong to the truth when their love finds practical expression in helping those in need. So that they may know that they belong to the truth, the readers must 'persuade their hearts in the presence of God' (not **and set our hearts at rest in his presence,** as the NIV has), so that they do not succumb to the meanness in their hearts and refuse to offer material assistance. This persuasion is to be undertaken **whenever our hearts condemn us,** that is, whenever their hearts object to legitimate calls upon their generosity when they are in fact in a position to respond. To assist his readers to persist in the necessary process of self-persuasion, the author provides them with a compelling reason for doing so: **For God is greater than our hearts, and he knows everything.** While the NIV does not translate it as such, this verse is actually a conditional sentence (lit. 'because, if our heart condemn us, God is greater than our heart and knows all things'),[154] by which the author says, should it happen that our hearts condemn us, God is greater than our hearts. The statement 'God is greater than our hearts' in this context seems to mean that God does not share in the meanness that is so often found in human hearts. His generosity is far greater, his compassion towards the needy much greater, than theirs. This fact should function as a reason for them to overcome the meanness of their own hearts and to seek to be like their God. When the author continues, 'and he knows everything', he is reminding his readers that any meanness of heart on their part will not go unnoticed by an omniscient God. As was the case in Deuteronomy 15:7-9, so too here, God knows what his people do, and judges them accordingly.

In summary, verses 19-20 function as a stern warning against that meanness of heart which objects to our expending material resources to meet the needs of fellow believers, and provide a foil for the positive reinforcement of generosity offered in verses 21-22.

3:21-22 To encourage generosity of heart in his readers, the author

153. The best-attested reading here is the future tense, 'we shall know' (*gnōsometha*), though its meaning here is probably gnomic, i.e., it has a present meaning.

154. A third-class conditional sentence is used (*ean* + subjunctive in the protasis) by which the author projects a hypothetical situation.

addresses them as **dear friends**, so drawing attention to his affection for them, and then asserts, **if our hearts do not condemn us,**[155] **we have confidence before God**. Following the line of interpretation adopted for this passage, this conditional statement is interpreted to mean that, if the readers' hearts do not object to their responding to calls on their generosity so that they actually provide the material assistance needed by their fellow believers, then they will experience confidence *(parrēsia)* in their relationship with God.[156] The sort of confidence the author has in mind here is disclosed in the following clause: **and receive from him anything we ask**. When they do not succumb to meanness of heart they will experience confidence before God when they approach him in prayer; a confidence that God will hear them when they pray and will grant their requests. The reason why believers have this confidence before God, the author adds, is **because we obey his commands and do what pleases him**. The author uses present tense forms of the verbs 'to obey' and 'to do' here, indicating that the action he has in mind is ongoing. Doing what God commands and so pleasing him is what engenders confidence when believers pray. And the command we obey when we respond to fellow believers in need is the dominical command to love one another, as the following verses make clear. Acting generously means not only obeying the dominical command, but also doing what pleases God. God is greater than our meanness and is himself generous, and it pleases him to see his people acting generously and so being like him.

3:23 In verses 19-22 the author warned his readers against succumbing to meanness of heart and encouraged them to practise generosity in face of the material needs of fellow believers. When they did this, he said, they would be obeying God's command and doing what pleases him. In verse 23 the author makes explicit what God's command is: **And this is his command: to believe in the name of his Son, Jesus Christ, and to love one another as he commanded us**. God's fundamental command to human beings is 'to believe in the name of his Son, Jesus Christ' (cf. John 6:29). To believe in the name is the same as believing in the person (see the commentary on 2:12). To believe in the name of Jesus Christ involves total commitment and obedience to him (cf. John 8:31; Matt

155. Other manuscripts omit 'our' and 'us', thus giving the reading, 'if the heart condemn'. However, the passage indicates that whether or not these omissions are taken as original, the sense remains the same.

156. The word *parrēsia* is found 4 times in 1 John (2:28; 3:21; 4:17; 5:14), and in each case it denotes the confidence believers enjoy before God. They have this confidence because they 'continue in him' (2:28), because their 'hearts do not condemn' them (3:21), and because 'love is made complete' among them (4:17), and this leads to confidence in prayer (3:21; 5:14).

7:21/Luke 6:46),[157] and this always involves doing what he commanded, 'to love one another'. There can be no obedience of God's commands if there is no love for one another, there can be no love for one another if people close their hearts to those in need, and there can be no confidence when approaching God in prayer when people close their hearts to fellow believers in need.

3:24 The main point of the extended section 3:11-24 is summed up in the words: **Those who obey his commands live in him, and he in them.** Those who believe in God's Son and love one another as he commanded them are those who truly live in God and God in them. Thus the author comes back to his main purpose in this letter: to enable his readers to distinguish those who claim to live in God but do not (the secessionists) from those who do (those who like the author and his readers remain faithful to the message they heard from the beginning). What it means to live in God is not easy to define. The concept is found in ten places in the letter (2:5, 6, 27, 28; 3:6, 24; 4:13, 15, 16; 5:20), including places, as here, where it is part of a broader concept: the mutual indwelling of believers in God and God in believers (3:24; 4:13, 15, 16). In two of the four places where this mutual indwelling is mentioned, the author says that believers can be assured of it because of the Spirit whom God has given to them (3:24; 4:13). This suggests that when the author speaks about believers living in God and God living in believers, as he does here, it involves something more than keeping God's commands. It is the new and very real spiritual existence that believers enjoy, and this is effected through the agency of the Spirit. This becomes quite clear in the second part of v. 24.

And this is how we know that he lives in us: We know it by the Spirit he gave us. This is the first of several references to the Holy Spirit in 1 John (other references are found in 4:2, 6, 13; 5:6, 8), and the Spirit is introduced here in connection with believers' assurance: it is by their experience of the Spirit whom God gave to them that the readers may know that God lives in them. What role of the Spirit does the author have in mind here? Is it something similar to what the apostle Paul spoke about in Rom 8:15-16: 'For you did not receive a spirit that makes you a slave again to fear, but you received the Spirit of sonship. And by him we cry, "Abba, Father." The Spirit himself testifies with our spirit that we are God's children'? Attractive as this suggestion might first seem, it does not fit with the way the role of the Spirit is portrayed in 1 John (see 'A

---

157. The verb 'to believe' (*pisteuō*), used to denote belief in Jesus Christ, is found in three different constructions: (i) with *hoti* — believing that Jesus is the Christ, etc.; (ii) with the dative of (the name of) Jesus; (iii) with the preposition *eis*. There seems to be little difference in 1 John between *pisteuō* + the dative and *pisteuō* followed by *eis*.

Note on the Role of the Spirit', pp. 151-55). In 1 John the Spirit's primary role is to bear witness to the truth about Jesus, and this is what the passage which immediately follows (4:1-6) emphasises. We should probably see 3:24 as transitional, its meaning being that we know God lives in us because we have believed the testimony of the Spirit (whom God gave us) concerning his Son Jesus Christ.

4:1-6 TESTING THE 'SPIRITS'

4:1 In 3:11-24 the author explained to his readers that they may know that they have passed from death to life and that they dwell in God and God in them when they show love towards fellow believers. And in 3:24 he added that they may also know that God dwells in them because of the Spirit he gave them. However, it is not only those who, like the author, remain faithful to the message heard from the beginning and who love fellow believers who claim an experience of the Spirit. There are many others who claim to be indwelt by God, to have received his Spirit, and to speak in his name. Included among such people, and no doubt to the forefront in the author's thinking as he wrote, were the secessionists. In 4:1-6 he warns his readers to exercise discernment when they encounter people claiming to speak in the name of God: **Dear friends, do not believe every spirit, but test the spirits to see whether they are from God**. Here he addresses his readers as 'dear friends' *(agapētoi)* both to express again something of the affection in which he holds them and to gain their attention for the important statement which is to follow (as he does elsewhere in the letter; cf. 2:7; 3:2; 4:7, 11). The important statement here is the exhortation *not* to believe every spirit. Believing every spirit would connote a certain gullibility. Not everyone claiming to speak in the name of God actually does so. For this reason his readers must 'test the spirits to see whether they are from God'. 'To test the spirits' means to evaluate the utterances of such people 'to see whether they are from God', and the criteria to be used in testing the spirits are spelled out in the following verses.[158]

---

158. The 'testing of the spirits' referred to here is different from what Paul had in mind when he spoke of testing everything in 1 Thess 5:19-21 and of discerning the spirits in 1 Cor 12:10; 14:1, where the use of spiritual gifts in the congregation was the subject. Probably the closest parallel in Paul's writings is 1 Cor 12:3, where he reminds his readers that no one speaking by the Spirit says, 'Jesus be cursed'. That discerning true and false prophets continued to be a problem in the early church is evident from the *Didache*, which also provides tests for making the distinction (*Did.* 11:7-9). There, too, it is what the prophet teaches that determines his *bona fides* or otherwise.

Before explaining these criteria, however, the author explains why testing the spirits is so important: **because many false prophets have gone out into the world**. Warnings about false prophets operating within the Christian community are found in several places in the NT (Matt 7:15; 24:11, 24; Mark 13:22; 2 Pet 2:1; 1 John 4:1). By their very nature false prophets *appear* to be genuine (cf. Matt 7:15: 'They come to you in sheep's clothing, but inwardly they are ferocious wolves'), and by their false teaching they lead people away from the truth (cf. 2 Pet 2:1: 'They will secretly introduce destructive heresies, even denying the sovereign Lord who bought them'). The false prophets are here said to '*have gone out* into the world' (as distinct from false prophets who remain within the Christian community). In the context of 1 John this is yet another allusion to those who seceded from the author's community and were yet seeking to deceive those who remained within it (cf. 2:18-27). By saying that these people 'have gone out *into the world*' the author alludes not only to the fact that they had seceded from his community, but also to their affinity with the unbelieving world (something he develops further in 4:5).

4:2-3a Having warned his readers of the need to 'test the spirits' in 4:1, the author now provides them with a doctrinal test that they can use to distinguish those who are from God from those who are not. The criterion to be used in testing people's claims is first stated positively (to be used to identify those who are of God): **This is how you can recognize the Spirit of God: Every spirit that acknowledges that Jesus Christ has come in the flesh is from God,**[159] and then negatively (to be used to identify those who are not of God): **but every spirit that does not acknowledge Jesus is not from God.**[160] The Spirit of God is recognised as the one

159. The affirmation that Christ came in the flesh is part of the mystery of godliness in 1 Tim 3:16: 'He appeared in a body [lit. 'in the flesh', *en sarki*], was vindicated by the Spirit, was seen by angels, was preached among the nations, was believed on in the world, was taken up in glory.'

160. Strecker, *The Johannine Letters,* 135-36, adopts the majority reading represented by the NIV text ('every spirit that does not acknowledge [*homologei*] Jesus is not from God'). Brown, *The Epistles of John,* 494, 496, and Schnackenburg, *The Johannine Epistles,* 201-2, adopt the minority reading ('every spirit who negates [*lyei*] Jesus'). Bart E. Ehrman, '1 Joh 4 3 and the Orthodox Corruption of Scripture', ZNW 79 (1988) 242, sums up the case for retaining the majority reading in this verse: 'We can now restate our reasons for concluding that the original text of 1 Joh 4 3 must have read *pan pneuma ho mē homologei ton Iēsoun ek tou theou ouk estin*, "every spirit that does not confess Jesus is not from God." The absolute domination of the Greek MS tradition by this grammatically incongruous [*mē* with the indicative *homologei*] reading cannot be explained adequately if it is not genuine. Furthermore, the alternate reading *pan pneuma ho lyei to Iēsoun ek tou Theou ouk estin* must have originally meant "every spirit that looses (separates or divides) Jesus is not from God", a meaning that does not fit well into the context of the Johannine community of the first century. On the contrary, this reading opposes a different kind of

teaching human beings ('every spirit') when they acknowledge that Jesus Christ 'has come in the flesh'. When humans beings ('every spirit') do not acknowledge this they show they are not of God (not taught by the Spirit of God). The negative expression of the criterion does not mirror fully its positive form, for it omits the reference to Jesus Christ 'come in the flesh'. The expression 'to acknowledge Jesus Christ' is but a shortened version of the expression 'to acknowledge that Jesus Christ has come in the flesh'.[161] It is important to note that both here and in 4:6 the Spirit's role is that of witness to the truth about Jesus Christ.

When in 4:2 the author refers to the confession 'that Jesus Christ has come in the flesh', he uses a perfect form of the verb 'to come', indicating that it is Christ's status as one come in the flesh,[162] rather than simply the

---

docetism from that otherwise evident in the later stages of the community: while the author of 1 John seems to have been confronted with a "phantasmal" kind of docetism, not unlike that later attacked by Ignatius [Ign. *Smyrn.* 1.1-2; 2.2; 3.2-3; 4.2; 5.2; Ign. *Trall.* 9.1-2; 10.1], the docetism that is rejected by this variant reading is the kind that posits a differentiation between the man Jesus and the heavenly Christ [as Ehrman points out earlier in his article, either the docetism of Cerinthus: Christ was manifested at the beginning of Jesus' ministry when he entered him at baptism, but left him prior to the crucifixion; or the docetism of Basilides, who taught that Simon of Cyrene, who was forced to bear Jesus' cross, was miraculously transformed into Jesus' likeness and so was mistakenly crucified while the Christ looked on. Hence Christ only appeared to suffer]. . . . The variant did not originate, as did many others, from a simple scribal error. It did not originate, in fact, as a variant reading at all, but as an interpretative paraphrase of 1 Joh 4 3 in the context of orthodox Christological polemics. Its earliest datable occurrence is in Irenaeus' opposition to Valentinian Gnosticism. This indeed may have been its originating context.'

161. This partial mirroring suggests that there were longer and shorter ways of signaling what was at issue between the author and the secessionists. Bringing together the various expressions of what was at issue that are found in the letter, we may say that, stated fully, it concerned the confession of Jesus as the Christ, the Son of God, come in the flesh and the reality of his atoning death. However, it appears that the author could signal the whole matter at issue by referring to just one or another aspect of it. So, e.g., in 2:22 the antichrist denies that 'Jesus is the Christ'; in 4:2 it is those who acknowledge that 'Jesus Christ has come in the flesh' who are of God; in 4:3 it is those who do not 'acknowledge Jesus' who are of the antichrist; in 4:15 it is those who confess that 'Jesus is the Son of God' who are indwelt by God; in 5:1 it is those who believe that 'Jesus is the Christ' who are born of God; in 5:5 it is those who believe that 'Jesus is the Son of God' who overcome the world; and in 5:6 allusion is made to those who deny that 'Jesus Christ came through water and blood', 'coming by blood' being a reference to the physical reality of Jesus' death upon the cross.

162. Most commentators agree that the reference here to Jesus Christ come in the flesh is an affirmation of Jesus' true humanity. However, Martinus C. de Boer, 'The Death of Jesus Christ and His Coming in the Flesh (1 John 4:2)', *NovT* 33 (1991) 330, 345-46, argues that it is primarily a reference to Jesus' death, and only secondarily to his humanity. De Boer appeals to 5:6 in support of this view. For the secessionists Jesus came in water only, i.e., acted salvifically only through baptizing people, but the author insists he acted salvifically not only in water but in blood, which in 1 John refers to his salvific death. De

historic act of his coming that he had in mind.[163] And it was Christ's status as one come in the flesh in the person of Jesus that the secessionists denied, that is, they denied the reality of his humanity (and the significance of the atoning work he did in the flesh).[164] (For a fuller discussion of what this involved, and possible parallels in early Christian heresies, see the discussion of 'the opponents' and their teaching in the Introduction, pp. 15-27.) Those remaining in the author's community were to recognise that the secessionists, who denied these things, could no longer claim to be from God.

It is noteworthy that the test which the author gives to his readers relates to what the secessionists taught. In this respect it parallels warnings about false prophets in both Deuteronomy and the *Didache*. In Deut. 13:2-6 a prophet who predicts the future or performs miraculous signs while urging people to go after other gods must not be heeded. In *Didache* 11:7-8 the true prophet is known by behaviour consistent with that of the Lord, and his teaching of the truth. In both places, the content of the prophet's teaching is a determining factor, as it is here in 4:2-3.

4:3b The secessionists' denial also indicates that the spirit by which they were speaking was not the Spirit of God (cf. 4:2), but, as the author says: **This is the spirit of antichrist, which you have heard is coming and even now is already in the world**. In the commentary on 2:18 the teaching on the antichrist found in several early Christian traditions was set forth. A distinction was made between the great antichrist figure who will appear near the very end of the age and lesser antichrist figures whose influence is already being felt. This reflects the already/not

---

Boer points out that 5:6 is the only place in 1 John, apart from 4:2, where the verb *erchesthai* is used with the preposition *en* following, and this suggests to de Boer that the thought in both verses is similar, i.e., that 'to come in flesh' (4:2) means the same as 'to come by blood' (5:6). De Boer appeals to 3:11-24 (esp. v. 16) and 4:1-7 for contextual support for his view. However, there is little support for his view within the immediate context (4:1-6), and therefore I have not adopted his suggestion in this commentary. Paul S. Minear, 'The Idea of Incarnation in First John', *Int* 24 (1970) 292, adopts quite a different approach, arguing that in 4:2 the author's statement about Jesus come in the flesh is not a reference to his incarnation or his humanity, but to the indwelling of Christ in the believer. He appeals to the wider context (3:23–4:9), and to 4:4 with its reference to 'the one who is in you' in particular, in support of his view. The argumentation, in the opinion of this commentator at least, is unconvincing.

163. Cf. Hans-Josef Klauck, 'Bekenntnis zu Jesus und Zeugnis Gottes: Die christologische Linienführung im Ersten Johannesbrief', in *Anfänge der Christologie. Festschrift für Ferdinand Hahn zum 65. Geburtstag*, ed. Cilliers Breytenbach and Henning Paulsen (Göttingen: Vandenhoeck & Ruprecht, 1991) 299-300.

164. Brown, *The Epistles of John*, 505, says that it was not Christ's real humanity that the secessionists denied, but that his being in the flesh was of salvific significance. So, too, Schnackenburg, *The Johannine Epistles*, 201.

yet tension of primitive Christian eschatology. In 2:18ff. the secessionists were identified as antichrists who had already gone out into the world. Here in 4:3 the secessionists are said to be activated by 'the spirit of the antichrist', of whose coming the readers had already heard (as part of common early Christian teaching to which the author has already referred in 2:18). The spirit of antichrist, the author says, is 'even now in the world', and active in people like the secessionists who are now part of 'the world', that is, those people who are motivated by those desires which are not of God (cf. 2:15-17). The aim of the antichrist is to deceive people by denying the truth about Jesus Christ, and in particular, within the context of 1 John, by denying the true humanity of Christ (that Jesus is the Christ come in the flesh). As Strecker notes, evil reveals itself in false teaching.[165]

4:4 In the face of the threat posed by the spirit of antichrist active through the secessionists, the author seeks to encourage his readers by reminding them: **You, dear children, are from God**. The author addresses his readers as 'dear children' *(teknia)* seven times in this letter (2:1, 12, 28; 3:7, 18; 4:4; 5:21), and in each case this direct form of address introduces something which he wants to impress upon them. Here he wants them to know that by their confession of Jesus come in the flesh they show that they 'are from God'. To say that people are 'from God' means that they are children of God (3:10), or born of God ((3:9; 4:7; 5:1, 4, 18). The author also wants them to know that they are people who **have overcome them**. In John 16:33 Jesus says: 'In this world you will have trouble. But take heart! I have overcome the world'. Here in 4:4 the readers are told that they have 'overcome them', that is, the secessionists, and what is meant is that they have overcome them by rejecting their heretical teaching that denies Christ come in the flesh.

The author recognises that his readers have overcome them, not by their own unaided efforts, but **because the one who is in you is greater than the one who is in the world**. According to 1 John, believers are not only 'from God' as this verse indicates, but also indwelt by God (4:12, 13, 15), an indwelling effected by the Spirit (4:13). The Spirit of God who indwells the believers is certainly greater than the spirit of antichrist which operates in the secessionists. The author speaks of the spirit of antichrist operating in the secessionists as 'the one who is in the world', suggesting an identification with 'the prince of this world' mentioned in the Fourth Gospel (John 12:31; 14:30; 16:11). The secessionists, having gone out from the community of believers, are now part of the world. They have joined that part of humanity which hates the author's community and is subject

165. Strecker, *The Johannine Letters*, 137.

to the control of the evil one (cf. 3:13; 5:19). True believers overcome the secessionists because God is at work in them through his Spirit so that they reject their erroneous teaching.

The author knew that the spiritual security of his readers depended ultimately upon God's work within them by his Spirit, and that there is no power greater than the Spirit of God that would be able to destroy that work. In the present day and age also, our own spiritual security depends on the Spirit of God and his work within us, and this is a firm basis of Christian assurance.

4:5 In 4:4 the author told his readers that they 'have overcome them'. In this verse he says of 'them': **They are from the world and therefore speak from the viewpoint of the world, and the world listens to them.** Those he has in mind are the secessionists. They left the author's community and went out into the world; that part of humanity which is opposed to the gospel (cf. the commentary on 2:1; 4:1-3). Now the secessionists may be said to be 'from the world' *(ek tou kosmou),* for by rejecting the message heard from the beginning they have to all intents and purposes thrown their lot in with the world. When they speak, they 'speak from the viewpoint of the world' *(ek tou kosmou),* because their teaching about the person of Christ is shaped, not by the original gospel message, but by worldly (albeit religious and philosophical) categories. And 'the world listens to them',[166] because their teaching is shaped by worldly categories and is therefore acceptable to those of the world.

4:6 In stark contrast to what he has just written about the secessionists, the author, now adopting the first person plural, says to his readers: **We are from God, and whoever knows God listens to us**. While the secessionists are from the world and listened to by the world, the author and his community are from God *(ek tou theou),* and those who truly know God will listen to them, and not to the secessionists. The opposite is also true, as the author observes: **but whoever is not from God does not listen to us**. He and his readers must not be surprised if they cannot get a hearing for the original gospel from the secessionists, or from others who are not from God. A persistent acceptance of the gospel proclaimed by the author and his community marks those who are from God, and a persistent rejection of their gospel marks those who are not from God.

In 4:6b the author finishes the section 4:1-6 as he began it: **This is how we recognize the Spirit of truth and the spirit of falsehood** (cf. 4:1-

166. Schnackenburg, *The Johannine Epistles,* 204, suggests that the statement 'the world listens to them' is evidence that the secessionists had experienced considerable success in propagating their teaching; but Strecker, *The Johannine Letters,* 139, contends that this is overestimating the possibility of obtaining historical information from the text.

2). This reference to the two spirits is reminiscent of teaching about 'the spirits of truth and falsehood' in the Qumran literature (1QS 3:18-19, 25), indicating that the author was using a well-known concept here. The whole section is concerned with testing the spirits 'to see whether they are of God' (4:1), and two related tests are put forward. The first concerns the confession of Jesus Christ come in the flesh (4:2-3) and the second concerns giving heed to those who make that confession. The author tells his readers that they may, by the application of these two related tests, distinguish the Spirit of truth from the spirit of falsehood. In the context of 1 John this means that they will be able to recognise that the secessionists are not speaking by the Spirit of God (the Spirit of truth), but by the spirit of antichrist (the spirit of falsehood). It is important to note that here, as in 4:2, it is implied that the role of the Spirit is to bear witness to the truth about Jesus Christ.

In the commentary on 4:6 above, the 'we' and the 'us' have been interpreted inclusively, and so taken to denote the author and his community (including his readers). However, the 'we' and the 'us' could be interpreted exclusively to denote the author and some of his associates to the exclusion of his community as a whole, and to the exclusion of his readers as well. This would leave the way open to see in this text a reference to official teachers of the church. In this case what would distinguish those who know God from those who do not know God would be the acceptance or rejection respectively of the teaching authority of the church.[167]

It is difficult to decide between these two approaches because the use of first person plural forms ('we'/'us') in 1 John is varied. The author uses first person plural forms exclusively when he groups himself with other eyewitnesses and writes about the message they heard from the lips of Christ, or their having seen him and touched him (1:1-3, 5; 3:11; 4:14). He uses it inclusively when he speaks in general terms about Christian experience (so, e.g., 1:6, 7-10; 2:1-3, 5, 28; 3:1-2, 14, 16, 18-19, 21-24; 4:9-13, 16-17, 19; 5:2-3, 14-15, 18-20). In a couple of places (2:19; 4:6) it is

---

167. Cf. de la Potterie, 'The Truth in Saint John', in *The Interpretation of John*, 60, who comments: 'In 4:1-6 he no longer speaks of anything except faith: he wants to show that the Spirit causes us to adopt the attitudes of faith in the community and that these are the criteria of his action within us. These criteria are first the believers' confession of faith (vv. 2-3) and their readiness to accept the teaching authority (v. 6b). This is only a development of the theme underlined in 3:24: the Spirit as the source of our faith. But it will be observed that this faith is considered from within the Church, in opposition to the heretics. So the bearing of the concluding verse is plain: if the Spirit is called the Spirit of truth it is because he causes us to confess our faith in Jesus Christ and to submit ourselves to the Church. If this is how we act, says John, we can be sure that the Spirit of truth abides in us.'

difficult to determine whether the usage is inclusive or exclusive, and 4:6 is one of these. However, while 4:6a may be ambiguous, 4:6b is clear enough. It reads: 'This is how we recognize the Spirit of truth and the spirit of falsehood'. In this sentence, the 'we' is clearly inclusive of the readers, because the purpose of the whole passage, 4:1-6, is to provide the readers with the means to test the spirits (4:2). If the 'we' of 4:6b is inclusive, then most likely the 'we' and the 'us' of 4:6a are also inclusive. This would mean that the author is saying that the second mark of those who know God mentioned in this passage (4:1-6) is that they listen to the author, his community, and his readers rather than saying they listen to the teaching authority of the church. This is the approach adopted in the commentary on 4:6 above.

A Note on the Role of the Spirit

The Spirit plays an important role in the teaching of 1 John, and in a number of ways that teaching picks up important elements of the teaching about the Spirit found in the Fourth Gospel. Before we focus on the role of the Spirit in 1 John, it might be helpful to review the data in the Fourth Gospel concerning the Spirit.

The Role of the Spirit in the Fourth Gospel

Jesus is proclaimed by the Baptist as the one upon whom the Spirit descended and remained (John 1:32-33), possibly distinguishing Jesus from the prophets who might be regarded as those whom the Spirit sporadically inspired to prophesy. Unlike John who only baptises in water, Jesus is presented as the one who baptises in the Spirit (John 1:33). Jesus himself speaks the words of God, and his testimony may be regarded as trustworthy because God has given him the Spirit 'without measure' (John 3:34), possibly again distinguishing Jesus from the prophets to whom the Spirit may be said to have been 'measured'. Jesus' glorification (= death) was the necessary precursor to the bestowal of the Spirit upon his followers (John 7:39).

The Fourth Gospel makes it very clear that only those who are born from above by the mysterious work of the Spirit can see/enter the kingdom of God (John 3:5-8). The words of Jesus, which are spirit and life, mediate the birth from above (John 6:63). Jesus offers living water which wells up to eternal life within those who believe (John 4:13-14); rivers of living water that shall flow from within believers (John 7:37-39). These two metaphors refer to the effect of the Holy Spirit in the lives of believers. Jesus, when speaking to the Samaritan woman, foreshadowed a time when people would worship God in Spirit (no longer at sacred sites like Gerizim or Jerusalem but in the Spirit which Jesus would give) and truth (according to the revelation which Jesus brought and embodied) (John 4:21-23).

In the Last Supper discourses Jesus spoke again of the Spirit, promising his disciples another Paraclete after his departure, one who would be with them forever (John 14:16). The Paraclete is identified as 'the Spirit of truth' (John 14:17), whose role has reference to both the internal life of the community (teaching the disciples all they need to know; guiding them into the truth) (John 14:25-26; 16:12-13) and the witness of the community to the world (bearing witness to Christ in a hostile world) (John 15:26-27; 16:7-9). Finally, in his appearance to the disciples in the upper room following his resurrection, Jesus breathed out and said to his disciples, 'Receive the Holy Spirit' (John 20:22).[168]

Summing up, we can say that in the Fourth Gospel the Spirit is introduced to highlight the significance of Jesus as the Spirit-endowed revealer, the one whose word is Spirit and life, the inaugurator of the new worship ('in spirit and in truth'), and the one who will send the Spirit/Paraclete to his disciples. The Spirit is the advocate for Jesus in a hostile world, the one who strengthens the disciples for their witness in the same hostile world, and the one who teaches them everything and guides them into the truth.

The Role of the Spirit in 1 John

The background to the Letters of John is different from that of the Fourth Gospel. The background to the Gospel is the hostility of unbelieving Jews to Christ and his followers; something which possibly also reflects the

---

168. There have been various ways of interpreting this difficult passage. Burge notes the following: (i) it is a pre-Pentecost anointing, which although important is not the fulfillment of the promise of the Paraclete (Dodd distinguishes the rather impersonal insufflation from the personal characteristics of the promised Paraclete; (ii) it is a symbolic bestowing of the Spirit upon the disciples, which was actually experienced at Pentecost; (iii) it is an ordination gift — John is distinguishing between the anointing of the disciples/the Twelve for ministry (John 20:22) and the anointing of the whole community which took place at Pentecost; (iv) it is the power of life (an impersonal force) as distinct from the Spirit experienced (personally) as the Paraclete at Pentecost; (v) it is an embryonic bestowal of the Spirit, which after Jesus' departure was to be experienced as the Paraclete; (vi) it is the Johannine Pentecost — the evangelist, who was not going to produce a second work as Luke did, telescoping Jesus' post-Easter appearances, Ascension and Pentecost. See Gary M. Burge, *The Anointed Community: The Holy Spirit in the Johannine Tradition* (Grand Rapids: Eerdmans, 1987) 117-31.

tension between the Christian community and local Jewish synagogues at the time of the writing of the Gospel. The background to 1 John is the hostility existing between the secessionists and those believers who have remained faithful to the message of the gospel as it was proclaimed at the beginning. The role of the Spirit in 1 John is related to the problems addressed by 1 John, but, as we will see, it builds upon the teaching about the Spirit found in the Fourth Gospel. There are several important passages related to the Spirit in 1 John, which are discussed in turn below.

In 1 John 2:18-27 the author urges his readers to allow the message they heard from the beginning, when they first became believers, to remain in them. They need to do this because already there are many antichrists in the world, and the antichrists will try to deceive them. Surprisingly, these antichrists are identified as people who were once members of the author's own Christian community, but they have seceded from it. Facing this threat, the believers are to remember that they also have an anointing from the Holy One. This means that all of them have knowledge (2:20) and therefore do not need anyone (i.e., the secessionists) to teach them, seeing that the anointing teaches them about all things (2:27). As argued in the commentary on this passage, the 'anointing' is best understood as the Holy Spirit who has been given to believers.

The concomitant of having this anointing is that the believers know 'all things' (see commentary *ad loc.* for a discussion of the variant reading involved here). Because they know 'all things', they do not need the author to teach them (2:21), and certainly not the secessionists (2:26-27a). The reference to knowing 'all things' here needs to be understood in the context, where the subject under discussion is the denial that Jesus is the Christ, God's Son come in the flesh. Nothing they need to know about these matters has to be learned from the secessionists. Everything they need to know has been taught them by the Spirit they have received. There is a close parallel between this teaching and that found in the Fourth Gospel, where Jesus promises his disciples that the Paraclete would teach them everything (John 14:26) and guide them into the truth (John 16:13). It appears that the author of 1 John has taken up this teaching and applied it to the new situation faced by his readers following the secession.[169]

The next text to be discussed, 1 John 3:9, does not contain the word Spirit *(pneuma)*, but speaks of the seed *(sperma)* of God, which remains in believers and renders them incapable of sinning. This text is part of a longer passage (2:29–3:10) in which the readers are given instruction on the way to distinguish those who are born of God from those who are not;

---

169. Cf. discussion in J. C. Coetzee, 'The Holy Spirit in 1 John', *Neot* 13 (1979) 53-55.

those who are the children of God from those who are the children of the devil. The criterion is doing or not doing righteousness; sinning or not sinning. Sin itself in this context is defined as *anomia,* a word which is never used in the NT in relation to violations of the Mosaic law, but has connotations of eschatological rebellion. What the author says in this passage, then, is that those who truly know God can never be a part of the rebellion, and in the context of 1 John this means that they can never take sides with the secessionists, who have shown themselves to be antichrists.

What is significant for our present purposes is that it is the 'seed of God' *(sperma theou)* which renders believers incapable of rebellion. As we have argued in the commentary on 1 John 3:9, this is a very bold metaphor which, when unpacked, refers to the Holy Spirit who effects spiritual birth in those who believe. If this is a legitimate interpretation of 1 John 3:9, we have here a description of the role of the Spirit which is different from all the others in 1 John. Here the Spirit's role is the means by which God brings his spiritual children to birth, and by which he renders them incapable of apostasy. The Spirit's role in effecting new birth is of course a major theme in the Fourth Gospel, and the author of 1 John has introduced it here as part of his explanation to his readers about how they can distinguish the children of God from the children of the devil.

In 1 John 3:11-24 the author explained to his readers that they may know that they have passed from death to life and that they dwell in God and God in them when they show love towards fellow believers. And in 3:24 he added that they may also know that God dwells in them because of the Spirit he gave them. However, it is not only those who, like the author, remain faithful to the message heard from the beginning and who love fellow believers who can claim an experience of the Spirit. Many others, to be sure, claim to be indwelt by God and to have received his Spirit and speak in his name. Included among such people, and no doubt to the forefront of the author's thinking as he wrote, were the secessionists. The thrust of 3:24b–4:6 is a warning to the readers to exercise discernment when they encounter people claiming to speak in the name of God. It is in this context that the author makes more comments which reveal his understanding of the role of the Spirit. First, in 1 John 4:2 the readers are told: 'By this you know the Spirit of God: every spirit that confesses that Jesus Christ has come in the flesh is from God'. Here, as in the Fourth Gospel, the role of the Spirit is to bear true witness to the person of Jesus. Second, in 1 John 4:6 the Spirit's role as witness to the truth about Jesus is reinforced indirectly when the author tells his readers that they may distinguish between the Spirit of truth and the spirit of error by taking note of who listens and who does not listen to us (as we bear witness to Jesus Christ come in the flesh).[170]

1 John 4:13-16 is one of those passages in which the author seeks to bolster the assurance of his readers by telling how they may know that they abide in God: 'By this we know that we abide in him and he in us, because he has given us of his Spirit'. This passage is part of a larger section, 4:7-21, in which the love of fellow believers in the light of God's love for us is the evidence that we know God and dwell in him, and he in us. This might lead to the conclusion that the author's point is that the presence of the Spirit leads believers to love one another and therefore they may know they abide in God because he has given them his Spirit and the Spirit produces that love. However, the immediate context of the statement about the Spirit leads to a different conclusion, for the author proceeds immediately to speak of the Father sending the Son as the Saviour of the world. Thus, once again, the role of the Spirit that is emphasised in this letter is his role as true witness to Jesus, something which is a prominent theme in the Fourth Gospel.[171]

In 1 John 5:6-8 the author speaks of three witnesses, the Spirit, the water, and the blood. Concerning the Spirit, he says: 'And the Spirit is the one who testifies, for the Spirit is the truth'. Here the Spirit is brought in to support the truth that Jesus 'did not come by water only, but by water and blood'. The meaning of this text is discussed in the commentary on this passage. Here it is sufficient to say that once again the Spirit's role is that of witness to Jesus Christ as he is in the Fourth Gospel. Like the Beloved Disciple in John 19:34-35, the Spirit bears witness to the reality of Jesus' death.[172]

In conclusion, we may say that this survey of the Spirit texts of 1 John indicates that the author has portrayed the role of the Spirit primarily as testimony to the tradition, not as a source of new revelation. In all probability he did this because the secessionists were claiming the Spirit as the source of their new and heretical doctrines concerning Christ. The author, therefore, felt that it was necessary to hold together the word and the Spirit, or, put in other words, he felt that it was necessary to stress the Spirit's role as witness to the truth of the gospel concerning Jesus as it was proclaimed from the beginning.

---

170. Coetzee, 'The Holy Spirit in 1 John', 52-53.
171. Coetzee, 'The Holy Spirit in 1 John', 56-61.
172. Coetzee, 'The Holy Spirit in 1 John', 44-51.

4:7–5:4A CLAIMS TO LOVE GOD TESTED BY LOVE FOR FELLOW BELIEVERS

Following 4:1-6, in which the author provided criteria that his readers could use to 'test the spirits', he returns to the theme of loving one another expounded in 3:11-24 and develops it further in 4:7-21. The structure of this passage and the progression of thought within it are difficult to explain, even though the smaller units which make it up are easy to identify: (i) 4:7a: the exhortation to love one another; (ii) 4:7b-8: the assertion that those who practise love know God, while those who do not practise love do not know God; (iii) 4:9-11: the demonstration of God's love in the sending of his Son as an atoning sacrifice, and the resulting obligation on the part of believers to love one another; (iv) 4:12-13: love for fellow believers is evidence that people dwell in (the unseen) God and God in them; (v) 4:14-15: belief in Jesus as the Son of God and Saviour is also evidence of this mutual indwelling; (vi) 4:16: believers know the love God has for them, and dwelling in love themselves is evidence that they dwell in God and God in them; (vii) 4:17-18: believers who are perfected in love have confidence and experience no fear as they face the day of judgement; (viii) 4:19-20: we love God because he loved us, but to say that we love God without loving one another means we are liars; (ix) 4:21: a reiteration of the obligation that those who say they love God should love one another also.[173]

4:7a   Returning to the theme he was addressing before the digression concerning testing the spirits (4:1-6), the author now says, **Dear friends, let us love one another.** He addresses his readers as 'dear friends' (*agapētoi*), expressing something of his affection for them and introducing a matter for which he wants their special attention, as he frequently does in this letter (2:7; 3:2, 21; 4:1, 7, 11).[174] The author not only exhorts his readers

---

173. David M. Scholer, '1 John 4:7-21', *RevExp* 87 (1990) 310-11, suggests the following five-part structure for 4:7-21: (i) 4:7a: the statement of the theme for this whole unit (1 John 4:7-21): 'Beloved, let us love one another'; (ii) 4:7b-11: the command to love one another is rooted in the character of God as love and in God's love toward believers demonstrated in the sending of the Son as expiation for sin; (iii) 4:12-16: obedience to the command to love one another brings assurance of mutual abiding between God and the believer, even though no one has ever seen God; (iv) 4:17-18: as a result of obedience to the command to love one another, love is perfected, and perfect love delivers one from the fear of judgement and punishment; (v) 4:19-21: a summary of the passage, opening with the affirmation of the practice expected of the members of the community: 'We love,' which is again rooted in God's love, followed by the great challenge ('if . . .'); finally, the command is reiterated as a closing to the whole unit.

174. The author of 3 John uses the same expression four times in his brief letter (vv. 1, 2, 5, 11), one hint that 3 John was written by the same person who wrote 1 John.

to love one another, but he also provides a reason for them to do so: **for love comes from God**. The significance of this statement is teased out in 4:9-10, where the historical expression of God's love is explained.

4:7b-8   Before the author explains the nature of the love that comes from God (vv. 9-10), he draws an important conclusion from the fact of that love: **Everyone who loves has been born of God and knows God.** His point is that love for one another is evidence that a person 'has been born of God and knows God' because such love comes from God. The converse is also true: **Whoever does not love does not know God, because God is love.** The point here is that the absence of love for one another is evidence that a person does not know God, because God is love, and there can be no real knowledge of God which is not expressed in love for fellow believers.

As indicated in the commentary on 2:29 above, the meaning of the expression 'born of God' is best explained by reference to the Fourth Gospel. John 1:12-13 emphasises that people become children of God, not by natural birth, but by being born of God. In John 3 Jesus tells Nicodemus that he must be born 'from above', and this is equivalent to being 'born of the Spirit'. Being born of God, then, is quite distinct from natural human procreation. It is brought about by God through his Spirit, in conjunction with faith in Christ on the part of those concerned.

When the author says that 'God is love', he is not making an ontological statement describing what God is in his essence; rather, he is, as the following verses (4:9-10) reveal, speaking about the loving nature of God revealed in saving action on behalf of humankind.[175] Verse 9 speaks of God showing his love by sending his Son so that people might have life through him, and verse 10 explains that this involved sending his Son as an atoning sacrifice for people's sins.

4:9   This is the first of the two verses in which the author spells out what he means by saying that 'love comes from God' and that 'God is love'. He does so here by recounting how God revealed his love to humankind: **This is how God showed his love among us: He sent his one and only Son into the world that we might live through him.** The showing of God's love was a public affair, carried out among human beings ('among us', as the text says) so as to be seen by them and appreciated by them.[176] The love of God was shown to humankind when God 'sent his

175. Cf. C. Spicq, 'Notes d'exégèse johannique: la charité est amour manifeste', *RB* 65 (1958) 363-64. Strecker, *The Johannine Letters*, 149, observes: 'The text has no intention of describing an inner-trinitarian relationship. What is important is, rather, that God has appeared as one who loves.'

176. This is reminiscent of John 1:14, where the evangelist says, 'The Word became flesh and made his dwelling among us.'

one and only Son into the world'. The one sent is described as God's 'one and only' *(ton monogenē)* Son', describing his uniqueness (see 'A Note on *Monogenēs*,' directly below). God had only one Son, and he sent him into the world because of his love for the world (cf. John 3:16). The purpose of the sending of the Son was 'that we might live through him'. The 'we' in this context refers to the believing community, those who respond positively to the demonstration of God's love by believing in the Son.

The demonstration of God's love was not a mere sending of his one and only Son into the world, it was the sending of his Son into the world 'that we might live through him'. The author uses the verb 'to live' *(zaō)* only here. Elsewhere in his letter he frequently uses the expressions 'life' *(zōē)* and 'eternal life' *(zōē aiōnios)*, and this life is always identified with, or said to be found in, Jesus Christ.[177] In the Fourth Gospel Jesus gives the following definition: 'This is eternal life: that they may know you, the only true God, and Jesus Christ, whom you have sent' (John 17:3). Life involves 'knowing' or 'having' Jesus Christ himself, for life is all tied up in him. Hence the author's statement that God's purpose in sending his one and only Son into the world was that we might live 'through him'. However, the possibility that people 'might live through him' by 'knowing' or 'having' Jesus Christ depended on much more than a revelation of God's love in sending his Son into the world. A far greater demonstration of his love was needed, as the next verse (4:10) makes clear.

A Note on *Monogenēs*

The word *(monogenēs)*, translated 'one and only' here in the NIV, is in some other translations rendered 'only begotten'. That the word is correctly translated as 'one and only' in the NIV is confirmed by an examination of its usage elsewhere in the NT, where it is found a total of nine times. It is found three times in the Gospel of Luke: once to describe the widow of Nain's 'one and only son' (Luke 7:12); once to describe the 'one and only daughter' of Jairus (Luke 8:42); and once to describe the 'one and only son' of the man who sought Jesus' help with his demon-possessed boy (Luke 9:38). It is found once in Hebrews, where Isaac, whom Abraham was about to sacrifice, is described as his 'one and only' son (Heb 11:17). In each of these cases the expression is used to add poi-

---

177. Eternal life is found in Jesus Christ, God's Son (5:11). He, in fact, is eternal life (5:20), and that eternal life was with the Father from the beginning (1:2). Those who believe in the Son have eternal life (5:13). Those who acknowledge Jesus Christ have the Son (and the Father) (2:23), and those who have the Son have eternal life (5:12).

gnancy to a story by highlighting that it was the person's 'one and only' child who was in dire need, threatened, or had died. The stress is not on the fact that the person was begotten of the father or mother concerned, but on the fact that the father or mother had only one child, and that child was the one who was so sadly affected.[178]

In the Fourth Gospel *monogenēs* is used four times, and in each case it is used in relation to Jesus as God's Son. In John 1:14 we read that the Word (later identified as Jesus Christ) became flesh, and 'we have seen his glory, the glory of the One and only *(hōs monogenous)'*. In John 1:18 we are told that 'No one has ever seen God, but God the One and Only *(monogenēs)*, who is at the Father's side, has made him known.' And in John 3:16 we find: 'For God so loved the world that he gave his one and only *(ton monogenē)* Son, that whoever believes in him shall not perish but have eternal life'. Finally, in John 3:18 we read: 'whoever does not believe stands condemned already because he has not believed in the name of God's one and only *(monogenous)* Son'. In each case *monogenēs* denotes, not that the Son was 'begotten' of the Father, but rather his uniqueness as God's 'one and only' Son. Thus, in John 1:14, 18 the emphasis is upon Jesus' unique role as the bearer and revealer of the glory of God, and in John 3:16, 18 the emphasis falls upon the sacrifice made by the Father in giving his only Son for the salvation of all who believe, and the seriousness of not believing in the 'one and only' Son whom God gave.

The use of *monogenēs* in 1 John 4:9 fits into the same category as its use in John 3:16, for here in 4:9 the author also emphasises the fact that the one whom God sent into the world was his 'one and only' Son. Once again the emphasis is not that Jesus was 'begotten' of God, but that God had only one Son, and this 'one and only' Son he sent into the world so that 'we might live through him'.

A Note on the Son's Preexistence

The question has been raised whether the author's reference here to God sending his Son into the world assumes the preexistence of the Son (i.e., that he was sent from heaven into this world), or whether something less is implied (i.e., a prophetic sending without any assumptions of preexistence). In the Fourth Gospel Jesus says to his Father, 'As you sent me into the world, I have sent them [his disciples] into the world' (John

---

178. In the LXX *monogenēs* translates *yāḥîd*, which means 'uniquely beloved', a word also translated in the LXX by *agapētos* ('beloved'). Cf. Strecker, *The Johannine Letters*, 151; Schnackenburg, *The Johannine Epistles*, 208; Brown, *The Epistles of John*, 515-17.

17:18), and to his disciples he says, 'As the Father has sent me, I am sending you' (John 20:21). Here the sending of the disciples by Jesus is likened to the sending of Jesus by the Father, and clearly the sending of the disciples does not presuppose any preexistence on their part. So, clearly, reference to Jesus being sent into the world does not necessarily imply preexistence, nor does it exclude it.

However, another text in the Fourth Gospel speaks of Jesus coming into the world in a way that must be read in terms of preexistence in heaven prior to his coming into the world. John 16:28 reads: 'I came from the Father and entered the world; now I am leaving the world and going back to the Father.' In addition to this, there are a number of references in the Fourth Gospel to Jesus having come 'down from heaven' (John 3:13; 6:33, 41, 42, 50, 51). All of these references suggest that the author understood Jesus' coming into the world in a way that assumed his preexistence. Therefore, while we cannot be sure that the author's statement about the Son being sent into the world here in 4:9 must be understood as implying his preexistence, nor can it be read as if it does not.[179]

4:10 In this verse the author spells out further what he means by saying 'love comes from God' and 'God is love'. He does so by explaining what God did for us: **This is love: not that we loved**[180] **God, but that he loved us and sent his Son as an atoning sacrifice for our sins.** The author begins negatively by pointing out that love is not to be understood in terms of our love for God: 'This is love: not that we loved God'. Having made that clear, he states positively that love is to be understood in terms of God's love for us: 'This is love . . . that he loved us and sent his Son as an atoning sacrifice for our sins'. The combined effect of verses 9-10, then, is that the expression 'God is love' is to be understood, not as an ontological statement about God's essential being, but in terms of the love of God expressed historically in the sending of his one and only Son into the world as an atoning sacrifice for our sins.

The word translated here as 'atoning sacrifice' *(hilasmos)* is found in

179. Eduard Schweizer, 'Zum religionsgeschichtlichen Hintergrund der "Sendungsformel" Gal 4 4f. Rm 8 3f. Joh 3 16f. I John 4 9', *ZNW* 57 (1966) 207, notes that in the cases of both Paul and John references to the sending of the Son have as their background a Christology which involves preexistence, in the case of Paul preexistent Wisdom and in the case of John the preexistent Logos. Brown, *The Epistles of John*, 517, believes that this sending 'into the world' constitutes an incarnation formula.

180. Some manuscripts have the perfect tense *(ēgapēkamen)* of the verb 'to love', while others have the aorist *(ēgapēsamen)*. While the external support for the two readings is about even, the aorist reading probably represents an assimilation of an original perfect tense to the aorists which follow *(ēgapēsen, apesteilen)*.

only two places in the NT, both of them in this letter (here and 2:2, see 'A Note on *Hilasmos*', pp. 75-76). *Hilasmos* occurs six times in the LXX (Lev 25:9; Num 5:8; Ps 129:4 [= 130:4 ET]; Ezek 44:27; Amos 8:14), and in every case except Amos 8:14 it relates to the removal of guilt because of sin, and in most places (Ps 129:4 and Amos 8:14 are the only exceptions) it relates to the removal of sin through sacrifice. There can be little doubt, then, that when the author uses the term *hilasmos* here he is emphasising that God sent Jesus Christ to be the atoning sacrifice to remove the guilt we had incurred because of our sins so that we might have eternal life. This was the great expression of God's love, and on this basis the author can say, 'God is love'.[181]

4:11   The author's purpose in explaining the nature of God's love expressed in the sending of his one and only Son as the atoning sacrifice for our sins (4:9-10) is very practical, and is related to the central purpose of the letter, that is, to reassure his readers that they are in the truth, and to furnish them with criteria by which to evaluate the false claims of the secessionists. The author is not giving a lesson about the love of God for its own sake, but to show that God's love for us must cause us to love one another. Accordingly, he writes: **Dear friends, since God so loved us, we also ought to love one another.** Since God so loved 'us', there is an obligation resting upon 'us' to love one another.

4:12   In this context, the author is not interested in the obligation to love one another for its own sake, but because it is the sign that God lives in us. Thus, he says: **No one has ever seen God; but if we love one another, God lives in us.** The invisibility of God is an important theme in the Fourth Gospel ('No one has ever seen God, but God the One and Only, who is at the Father's side, has made him known' [John 1:18]; 'And the Father who sent me has himself testified concerning me. You have never heard his voice nor seen his form' [John 5:37]; 'No one has seen the Father except the one who is from God; only he has seen the Father' [John 6:46]). The author's statement about the invisibility of God reproduces

181. Stanislaus Lyonnet, 'The Terminology of "Expiation" in the NT', in Stanislaus Lyonnet and Léopold Sabourin, *Sin, Redemption, and Sacrifice: A Biblical and Patristic Study* (Rome: Biblical Institute Press, 1970) 154, comments: 'Christ is called *hilasmos* in 1 Jn 4:10 in the same sense as in 2:2, namely, inasmuch as through Christ and in Christ (through his death, i.e., through his supreme act of love which, together with his resurrection, constitutes one unique mystery of salvation) God the Father fulfils and executes the plan of his love. This he does by showing himself propitious, by forgiving sins (by removing and destroying them according to the OT notions of sin and expiation), by establishing his reign, instead of that of Satan, over mankind, by communicating his own life to men, so that they no longer are "in the power of the evil one" but "in the power of the true one, in his son Jesus Christ" who is "the true God and eternal life" (1 Jn 5:19f), no longer "children of the devil" but "children of God" (1 Jn 3:10)'.

the statement found in John 1:18, with only minor variations.[182] The author's point, then, is that while no one can claim to have seen God (apart from God's one and only Son) believers who love one another demonstrate that the unseen God lives in them.[183] This teaching is meant to reassure the readers that they do really know God, despite what the secessionists might say to the contrary.

However, even more can be said about believers who love one another, so the author adds: **and his love is made complete in us**. This is the second of four references the author makes to completeness of love in this letter. The first is found in 2:5, where completeness of love for God is expressed in obedience to his word. The third and fourth references are found in 4:17, 18, where God's love is said to have completed its work in believers when they can face the day of judgement without fear. Here in 4:12 God's love[184] is made complete in believers when they love one another. To put it in other words, the circuit of God's love is completed when we love one another.

4:13   It is difficult to know whether this verse should be read with

182. John 1:18 has *theon oudeis heōraken pōpote,* and 1 John 4:12 has *theon oudeis pōpote tetheatai.* The differences are: (i) *pōpote* is the last word in John 1:18 and the second to the last in 1 John 4:12; (ii) 1 John 4:12 has *tetheatai* instead of *heōraken.* All three references to the unseen God in the Fourth Gospel (John 1:18; 5:37; 6:46) use *horaō,* which suggests that the author of 1 John may have deliberately changed the verb when reproducing this tradition in his letter. This is a little surprising because in 1 John 1:1-3, where he includes himself among those who have seen the Word of life, he uses *horaō.* It is probably just a stylistic variation because there is little known difference between the meanings of *theaomai* and *horaō.*

P. W. van der Horst, 'A Wordplay in 1 Joh 4 12?' *ZNW* 63 (1972) 280, argues that this modification of the formula might have its origin in an etymological wordplay. The etymological connection between *theos* and *theasthai* was already known in the second century B.C., and it is possible that the author of 1 John knew this etymology and, as, e.g., Plotinus does so often, played with it in the formula *theon oudeis pōpote tetheatai.*

Sproston, 'Witnesses to What Was *ap' archēs',* 50, cites 1 John 4:12/John 1:18 (and 1 John 3:14/John 5:24) as instances where the epistle and the Gospel reproduce 'not only the same words but also often the same phrases, and sometimes even whole sentences'. She says, 'If we compare the sentence *theon oudeis heōraken pōpote* in Jn 1.18 with *theon oudeis pōpote tetheatai* in 1 Jn 4.12 the correspondence is obvious. But what is equally obvious is that beyond this point all correspondence ceases. For the Evangelist the application of the statement is christological: he uses it as a basis to speak of Jesus as the sole exegete of the Father. This is not the case in 1 Jn 4.12. There the same sentence has been put in the context of the command to love one another and when, in 4.20, the theme of God's invisibility returns, the interest centers on loving one's brother whom one *has* seen.'

183. Strecker, *The Johannine Letters,* 157, says: 'Since God, as the invisible one, is unapproachable, escape into a direct vision of God is closed to the Christian community. The encounter with God that is promised to them takes place, instead, here and now in the love for one another.'

184. Construing *hē agapē autou* as a subjective genitive.

what precedes or what follows it. The author writes: **We know that we live in him and he in us, because he has given us of his Spirit.** Here he speaks about the assurance believers have that they live in God and God in them, and this theme is found in both what precedes (4:12) and what follows (4:14-15). The difference between what precedes and what follows is that the former (4:12) emphasises love for fellow believers, and the latter (4:14-15) the testimony born by the eyewitnesses that God's love was expressed in sending Jesus to be the Saviour of the world. The question we are left with is: When the author introduces the giving of the Spirit as the ground of assurance in 4:13, is he implying: (a) that the Spirit motivates love for fellow believers and the objective practice of love is the basis of their assurance; or (b) that the Spirit teaches the truth about God's sending Jesus as the Saviour of the world and knowing this provides believers with the basis of assurance; or (c) that the very presence of the Spirit himself in believers creates the sense of assurance?

Of these three alternatives, the second option is best. In 3:24b a similar statement is found ('And this is how we know that he lives in us: We know it by the Spirit he gave us'), which leads immediately into a discussion of the way the Spirit of Truth can be distinguished from the spirit of error, namely, that the Spirit of truth acknowledges that Jesus Christ has come in the flesh and the spirit of error does not. Within this letter the role of the Spirit is always related to the truth about Jesus Christ (see 'A Note on the Role of the Spirit', pp. 151-55). If we take note of the role of the Spirit in the rest of the letter, we have to conclude that it is neither the very presence of the Spirit nor the activity of the Spirit producing love for fellow believers that the author has in mind here, but rather the Spirit as witness to the truth about Jesus proclaimed by the eyewitnesses (cf. 2:18-27; 3:24b–4:6; 5:6-8 and commentary *ad loc.*). This being the case, we would have to say that although 4:13 is transitional it is more closely connected with what follows than with what precedes. What the author is implying in 4:13, then, is that because the Spirit teaches believers about the love of God expressed in the sending of the Son to be the Saviour of the world (4:14), and because they believe that teaching, they may be assured that they dwell in God and God in them.

4:14 The author introduces the testimony of the eyewitnesses with the words, **And we**[185] **have seen and testify.** These words echo 1:1-4 and

---

185. Brown, *The Epistles of John*, 523, holds that the 'we' here denotes 'the members of the Johannine community faithful to the author'. Judith Lieu, *The Second and Third Epistles of John: History and Background* (Edinburgh: T. & T. Clark, 1986) 144, argues: 'The language of witness can be used of the whole community, rooted in their experience of God's love and gifts, although presumably only possible because some did physically see and believe. . . . With whatever authority the writer may speak, it allows him to say

recall the author's place among the eyewitnesses. The content of this testimony is **that the Father has sent his Son to be the Saviour of the world**. This is a very significant expression of the orthodox belief about Jesus because it does not focus upon Jesus having come in the flesh, that is, the reality of his incarnation, that we find in other places in the letter, but upon Jesus having been sent to 'be the Saviour of the world'.

A Note on the Saviour of the World

The expression 'Saviour of the world' (*sōtēr tou kosmou*) is found only twice in the NT, here and in John 4:42. In John 4:42 it forms part of the Samaritan villagers' response to the woman who encountered Jesus at the well of Sychar. When they heard her testimony they came and met Jesus themselves, and then the evangelist says: 'They said to the woman, "We no longer believe just because of what you said; now we have heard for ourselves, and we know that this man really is the Saviour of the world"'. In this context the expression 'Saviour of the world' carries the sense that Jesus is the Saviour of Samaritans as well as Jews. It is as Saviour *of the world* that he is recognised. This is in line with the purpose of the Fourth Evangelist to acquaint his readers with the true identity of Jesus so that, believing in him, they might enjoy life in his name.

However, the concerns of 1 John are different from those of the Fourth Gospel. The background of 1 John was strife within the Christian community. The question of whether Jesus is the Saviour *of the world* was not the issue. What was in question was whether Jesus needed to be recognised as Saviour at all. In particular, it was whether belief in Jesus' death as an atoning sacrifice for sin was necessary. Those who had seceded from the author's community denied that they had sinned (cf. 1:6–2:2 and commentary *ad loc.*) and argued that Jesus' atoning death was unnecessary and did not take place (cf. 5:6-8 and commentary *ad loc.*). Those who, with the author, acknowledged their sins, confessed the importance of Jesus' atoning sacrifice which provided cleansing from their sins. They confessed that the Father 'sent his Son to be the Saviour of the world'.

---

little that cannot equally be said of or for his readers, who have the authority given by belief and life within the community; indeed, given the probable stress on the Gospel message or tradition of the community as that which was "from the beginning" in the opening verses of the letter, it is likely that the authority with which the writer speaks as "we" in those verses is ultimately the authority of that tradition and community life.' See 'A Note on the Language of Sense Perception', pp. 53-56, for a critique of this sort of approach.

4:15 Following the statement of the content of the testimony of the eyewitnesses (4:14), the author now applies it to bring assurance to his readers: **If anyone acknowledges that Jesus is the Son of God, God lives in him and he in God.** It is puzzling at first why the author does not stay with the content of the testimony as he stated it in the previous verse. He speaks here about acknowledging that Jesus is the Son of God, and not about God sending his Son to be the Saviour of the world. The reason probably is that the full orthodox confession to be maintained in face of the secessionist denials was that Jesus was the Christ, the Son of God, who came in the flesh as the Saviour of the world and gave himself as an atoning sacrifice for the sins of the whole world. However, the author did not need to state this fully every time he alluded to the secessionists' teaching. He could call his readers' attention to all that the secessionists denied, and to all that his readers should affirm, by referring to but one aspect of it, as he does in verses 14 and 15. What the author affirms in verse 15 is that those who do acknowledge Jesus in this way are those in whom God lives and who live in God.

What 'God lives in him and he in God' means is not easy to define. The concept of the mutual indwelling of believers in God and God in believers occurs in four places in this letter (3:24; 4:13, 15, 16). Assurance of this mutual indwelling is related in two cases to the presence of the Spirit, who bears witness to Jesus (3:24; 4:13; see commentary *ad loc.*). In the other cases it is related to the confession of Christ (4:15) and abiding in love (4:16).

4:16a The author concludes this brief section (4:13-16a) with the words, **And so we know and rely on the love God has for us.**[186] He is concluding that the testimony of the eyewitnesses (4:14: 'the Father sent the Son to be the Saviour of the world') is an affirmation of the demonstration of the love of God, and based on that testimony believers may know and rely on the love God has for them. The expression 'know and rely on' *(egnōkamen kai pepisteukamen)* appears to be a hendiadys, that is, the use of two words to express essentially one idea. A similar expression is found in John 6:69 ('We believe and know [*pepisteukamen kai egnōkamen*]

---

186. Edward Malatesta, *'Tēn agapēn en [sic] echei ho theos en hēmin*: A Note on 1 John 4:16a', in *The New Testament Age: Essays in Honor of Bo Reicke*, vol. II, ed. William C. Weinrich (Macon, GA: Mercer University Press, 1984) 310, argues that 'the use of *en, echein* and *agapē* in 1 John; the immediate context and literary structure of 4:14-16; the Johannine theology of love and Christian interiority' all justify translating 4:16a as 'We know and believe the love God authors and sustains within us'. However, the stress on God's love demonstrated in sending his Son to be the Savior of the world in this section (4:13-16a; cf. 4:14) militates against the view that the love of God here is to be understood as something 'God authors and sustains within us'.

that you are the Holy One of God'). The same connection between God's love for believers and the sending of his Son is made in 4:10 ('This is love: not that we loved God, but that he loved us and sent his Son as an atoning sacrifice for our sins').

4:16b Following on from the appeal to the testimony about God's love in sending his Son as the basis of believers' assurance, the author states that **God is love**. This is the second statement of this kind in this letter. Like the first (4:8), this is not intended to be an ontological statement describing what God is in his essence, but rather a statement about the loving nature of God revealed in his saving action on behalf of humankind. This has already been teased out in verses 10 and 14, where God's love has been explained in terms of his sending his Son as the atoning sacrifice for the our sins (v. 10); as the Saviour of the world (4:14).

Because 'God is love', the author can assure his readers that **Whoever lives in love lives in God, and God in him.** Here the author returns to the overarching theme of 4:7-21, that is, that loving one another is the mark of those who truly know God. The statement here in 4:16b is intended to bolster the confidence of the readers. They, unlike the secessionists, do love each other, and the author wants them to recognise that this is evidence that God does live in them and they in God, despite the assertions of the secessionists to the contrary. As we noted above (see the commentary on 4:15), assurance of this mutual indwelling is related to the presence of the Spirit who bears witness to Jesus (3:24; 4:13), the confession of Christ (4:15), and abiding in love (4:16).

4:17-18 These verses contain the third and fourth references to the completeness of love found in 1 John. The first is found in 2:5, where completeness of love for God is said to be expressed in obedience to his word. The second is found in 4:12, where God's love is said to be made complete in believers when they love one another. Here in 4:17-18 love is said to have completed its work in believers when they can face the day of judgement without fear.

The author begins: **In this way, love is made complete among us so that we will have confidence on the day of judgement.** The type of love the author has in mind when he says 'love is made complete among us' (lit. 'with us', *meth' hēmōn*)[187] here would seem to be God's love that is with us, which completes its work so that our fear as we face the day of judgement is removed.

What the author means by having 'confidence *(parrēsian)* on the day

---

187. 2 John 3 uses a similar construction when the elder invokes blessings upon his readers: 'Grace, mercy and peace from God the Father and from Jesus Christ, the Father's Son, will be with us [*meth' hēmōn*] in truth and love'.

of judgement' can be deduced from a parallel passage found in 2:28: 'And now, dear children, continue in him, so that when he appears we may be confident *(echōmen parrēsian)* and unashamed before him at his coming.' Here confidence is equated with being unashamed before Christ at his coming, and in the context of 2:28 that confidence arises out believers' obedience to God's word. The confidence to which the author refers here in 4:17-18, then, can be understood in terms of believers being unashamed before the Son of God on the day of judgement. This confidence, as we have seen, arises within the love relationship believers have with God.

The author then explains further why believers will have confidence on that day: **because in this world we are like him** *(hoti kathōs ekeinos estin kai hēmeis esmen en tō kosmō toutō,* lit. 'because as he is, we are also in this world'). Unfortunately, this explanation is very hard for us to understand, and therefore we need to try to unpack its meaning step by step. First, it may be noted that while in 1 John the word 'world' often relates to the world of humanity in its alienation from God (cf. 2:15-16), the expression 'in this world' in 4:17 almost certainly relates to the natural world in which believers now live (as distinct from being in the heavenly world in which God dwells).[188] If we interpret 'in this world' in 4:17 in this way, then the author is explaining that we may have confidence because as he is, so are we in this present world.

Second, we need to ask who is the 'he' with whom believers are compared. The answer is that 'he' is the one before whom we may have confidence on the day of judgement (4:17a), that is, Jesus Christ. Two considerations support the view that the author has Christ in mind: (a) the parallel text (2:28) speaks of believers being unashamed before Christ at his coming, thus implying that Christ is the judge before whom believers must stand; (b) in the Fourth Gospel, when the agent of divine judgement is mentioned, Jesus Christ is always that agent (5:22, 27, 30; 8:16; 12:31-33). God has delegated to him the responsibility of judging the world.

Third, then, we need to ask what the author means by 'as he is' *(kathōs ekeinos estin)* when he says, 'as he is, we are also in this world'. There are a number of ways of explaining this: (i) Christ has retained in heaven the characteristics he had on earth, and, as Schnackenburg says, 'he is still, even in the moral sense, what he was on earth, a pattern for those in union with him, with those who are still "in the World"'.[189] (ii) Believers are now children of God just as Christ is the Son of God, and

188. The same idea is found in the Fourth Gospel, where Jesus repeatedly speaks of being 'in this world' and of his leaving 'this world' to go to the Father (John 9:5; 13:1; 17:11, 13), and of his disciples being for the present 'in this world' (John 12:25; 13:1; 16:33; 17:11).

189. Schnackenburg, *The Johannine Epistles,* 223.

167

in that sense they are in the world, just as he is.[190] But there is a more straightforward explanation: (iii) Bearing in mind that the present tense of the Greek verb on its own does not designate action in the present, but action presented as ongoing by the writer, whether in the past or the present, we are justified in translating this text so as to read: 'we are in the world in the same way as he was'.

Fourth, we need to ask how the statement 'we are in the world in the same way as he was' would function as a basis for believers having confidence on the day of judgement. One way forward is to recognise that 4:17b falls within a section (4:7-21) whose overall theme is love for one another as the mark of those who live in God. Knowing this, we could say that believers who love one another in this world, in the same way as Christ loved his disciples (John 13:1, 34; 15:9, 12) when he was in the world, show that they live in God, and therefore they need have no fear as they face the day of judgement.

In 4:18a the author explains why love produces this confidence: **There is no fear in love. But perfect love drives out fear.** What the author means by perfect love here is God's love for them which dispels their fear. But God's love for believers cannot be separated from their love for God. Brown states the matter comprehensively when he says: 'There is probably continuity with the theme of love that has run through the unit: an outgoing love that comes from God, is manifested in Jesus, gives us life, and remains in us actively manifesting itself in love of others and of God.'[191] When believers love God because he first loved them (4:19), then their fear of God is driven out. Love for God and fear of God cannot coexist (cf. Rom 8:15). The type of fear the author is speaking about is revealed in 4:18b when the author explains why there is no fear in love: **because fear has to do with punishment**. The type of fear meant here is fear of punishment. The word translated 'punishment' *(kolasis)* is found in only one other place in the NT, Matthew 25:46: 'Then they will go away to eternal punishment, but the righteous to eternal life' — the words with which Jesus concludes the parable of the sheep and the goats. Punishment there is what God metes out to the unrighteous on the day of judgement. Punishment here in 1 John is also the punishment to be meted out to the unrighteous, and it is fear of this punishment that is driven out by love. People cannot love God and fear his punishment at the same time.

When people fear God's punishment, it is a sign that they have not yet been perfected in love: **The one who fears is not made perfect in love.** Perfection in love here involves a love for God which is based upon

190. Brown, *The Epistles of John*, 529.
191. Brown, *The Epistles of John*, 530.

our sense of God's love for us, and this love relationship is what removes our fear as we face the day of judgement. The author has already underlined the greatness of God's love for believers in several places in this letter. In 3:1 he wrote: 'How great is the love the Father has lavished on us, that we should be called children of God! And that is what we are!'; in 3:16: 'This is how we know what love is: Jesus Christ laid down his life for us'; and in 4:16: 'And so we know and rely on the love God has for us. God is love.' When the realisation of God's love for us in Christ penetrates our minds and spirits, then we are perfected in love so that fear of God's judgement is removed.

4:19-20   As so often in this letter, in these verses the author underscores the connection between our love for God and our love for fellow believers. He begins by reminding his readers that **we love**[192] **because he first loved us.** God showed his love for us first by sending his Son as an atoning sacrifice for our sins, as the author has already made clear (4:10). Those who are the beneficiaries of that love, love God in return. However, the love relationship believers have with God, if it is real, will manifest itself in their love for Christian brothers and sisters. Because there is such a necessary connection between love for God and love for fellow believers, the author goes on: **If anyone says, "I love God," yet hates his brother, he is a liar.** This theme, which recurs repeatedly throughout the letter (2:9-11; 3:11-24; 4:7-21; 5:2), needed to be stressed in the situation in which this letter was written; a situation in which the secessionists had set themselves against those believers who, with the author, remained faithful to the original message of the gospel. By stressing this theme in his letter the author sought to achieve two ends: to reassure his readers that they really knew God, and to show them that the claims of the secessionists were false.

The necessary connection between loving God and loving fellow believers is explained by the author when he adds: **For** *(gar)* **anyone who does not love his brother, whom he has seen, cannot love**[193] **God, whom**

---

192. Some manuscripts have 'we love God' or 'we love him', but these variants must be regarded as early scribal attempts to improve upon the original by providing the verb 'love' here with an object. The reading without the object which is adopted in the NIV has significant support in the Greek manuscripts (A B 322 323 945 1241 1243 1739 1852 1881 2464 vg[ww, st] geo slav Augustine[6/10]). However, the way the author develops his argument in vv. 19-21 indicates that these early scribal additions did in fact express more explicitly what the author had in mind, i.e., that believers love God because he first loved them. *Agapōmen* may be construed as either indicative ('we love'), as in the NIV, or subjunctive ('let us love'), as in 4:7. The context here, which is not hortatory, suggests that the former is preferable.

193. This renders the variant, *ou dynatai agapan*. The alternate reading is *pōs dynatai agapan*. The former is much better supported by reliable witnesses, the latter probably being an attempt to improve the style.

he has not seen. This is an *a fortiori* statement, arguing from the lesser to the greater. If people cannot carry out the lesser requirement (to love their fellow believers whom they have seen), they cannot carry out the greater requirement (to love God whom they have not seen). As explained in the commentary on 4:12, when the author speaks of God as the one whom we have not seen, he is picking up an important theme from the Fourth Gospel, where the invisibility of God is mentioned again and again (John 1:18; 5:37; 6:46). Here the author repeats the point he made in 4:12, that claims to know the 'unseen' God must be validated by love for fellow believers who can be seen. The nature of the true experience of God is such that it cannot exist without manifesting itself in love for God's people. Already in 4:7-8 the author has shown that God is loving, that all those who are born of God are loving as well, and that those who do not love, therefore, do not know God.

4:21 The connection between love for God and love for Christian brothers and sisters which was explained in 4:20 in terms of the nature of the experience of the unseen God is now shown to be the subject of the command of God as well: **And he has given us this command: Whoever loves God must also love his brother.** Here the author picks up a major theme from the Last Supper discourse in the Fourth Gospel, where Jesus stresses that his disciples' love for him must express itself in obedience to his command, and that his command is that they should love one another (cf., e.g., John 13:34: 'A new command I give you: Love one another. As I have loved you, so you must love one another'; John 14:15: 'If you love me, you will obey what I command'; John 15:12: 'My command is this: Love each other as I have loved you'; John 15:17: 'This is my command: Love each other'). The author's purpose in picking up this theme here is to reassure his readers who did love their fellow believers that they really knew God, and to show them that the claims of the secessionists to know him were false.

5:1 This verse begins: **Everyone who believes that Jesus is the Christ is born of God.** Here the author reintroduces a theme he developed earlier in the letter, reminding his readers that only those who believe that Jesus is the Christ are born of God. This is something the secessionists denied (see 2:22-23 and commentary *ad loc.*), but true believers acknowledge. The secessionists' aberrant Christology is reflected in various allusions the author makes to their beliefs in the letter. When one puts them all together, it becomes clear that their Christology involved a denial that Jesus Christ is the Messiah, God's Son, come in the flesh and whose death was both real and necessary (4:2-3, 15; 5:1, 6-8). However, at different places in the letter, the author refers to the whole by mentioning one part. Accordingly, in the present context, where the author says that those who believe that Jesus is the Christ are born of God, he is stressing the content of the true Christian confession over against the denials of the secessionists.

We discussed the meaning of the concept 'born of God' in the commentary on 2:29, where we noted that the best explanation of what it means, as far as members of the author's community were concerned, is to be found in two places in the Fourth Gospel (John 1:12-13; John 3). Both places make very clear that being born of God is quite different from natural birth. It is something initiated by God and effected through his Spirit, and it takes place in conjunction with faith in Christ.

Having stated that it is those who believe that Jesus is the Christ who are born of God, the author then adds: **and everyone who loves the father loves his child as well**[194] (lit. 'Everyone who loves the one who begets also loves the one begotten of him'). This is a metaphor drawn from natural experience, in which a person who loves and respects a father will also love and respect his child. On first reading it might appear that the sense of this clause is that those who love God will love his Son, Jesus Christ, also. However, a closer reading of the text (cf. 5:2) indicates that the one said to be born of God in this verse is not Jesus himself, but the one who believes that Jesus is the Christ.[195] So when the author adds, 'everyone who loves the father loves his child as well', he is saying, in effect, that all those who love God will be marked by their love for the children of God, that is, their fellow believers. This is in line with the major theme running right through 4:7–5:4a, and in particular what is stated, albeit negatively, in 4:20 ('If anyone says, "I love God," yet hates his brother, he is a liar. For anyone who does not love his brother, whom he has seen, cannot love God, whom he has not seen').

5:2 Having made the point in 5:1 that those who love God also love the children of God, the author now explains how people may know that they love the children of God: **This is how we know that we love the children of God: by loving God and carrying out**[196] **his commands.** By so saying, the author appears to be reversing the approach he uses else-

---

194. The word *(kai)* translated 'as well' here in the NIV is omitted in some manuscripts, and the support in the witnesses is fairly evenly divided. The sense of the verse is not changed much, no matter which variant is adopted.

195. While Jesus is referred to as the 'one and only' *(monogenēs)* Son of the Father, he is never said to be born of God in either the Fourth Gospel or 1, 2, and 3 John. In these books those said to be born of God are always believers (John 1:13; 3:3, 5, 8; 1 John 2:29; 3:9; 4:7; 5:1, 4). The one possible exception to this is 1 John 5:18.

196. 'Carrying out his commands' translates *tas entolas autou poiōmen,* a very rare expression in the NT. There is a variant reading, 'keeping his commands' *(tas entolas autou tērōmen),* which is far more common. The former has probably been changed to the latter to conform to the use of the common expression also found in 5:3.

where in the letter. His usual approach is to say that people's claims to love God are to be tested by the presence or absence of love for fellow believers. But here he does the reverse. He states that whether or not people love the children of God can be determined by the presence or absence of love for God and obedience to God's commands. The author's thought appears to go in a circle. This is perhaps because the two things involved, as far as he is concerned, cannot exist apart from one another. One cannot love God and keep his commands without loving the children of God, and one cannot love the children of God without loving God and keeping his commands (cf. 2:7-8; 3:22-24; 4:21).

5:3a   In this verse, the author reverts to the more usual way of juxtaposing love for God and love for fellow believers. He says: **This is love for God: to obey his commands**. Once again he speaks of the observable mark of love for God, namely, obedience to God's commands; and as already noted, in 1 John these commands nearly always include love for one's fellow believers (cf. 3:23).

5:3b-4a   In these verses the author brings the long section 4:7–5:4a to a close by affirming: **And his commands are not burdensome, for everyone born of God overcomes the world.** The command to love one another does not prove burdensome[197] for those who know God because they have been born of God, and love for others who have also been born of God is a natural outworking of that. This is so, the author adds, 'for everyone born of God overcomes the world'.

What it means to be 'born of God' was discussed in the commentary on 2:29 and 5:1 above. There we noted that it means something quite distinct from natural human procreation; rather, it was something effected by God himself through his Spirit, in conjunction with faith in Jesus Christ on the part of those concerned.

We listed the various meanings that the word 'world' carries in 1 John in the commentary on 2:10 above. There can be no doubting that in the present context it means 'worldly attitudes or values that are opposed to God'. In 2:15-17 the author explained how love for the 'world', understood in this negative way, and love for God were mutually exclusive. In that context the author also gave a definition of 'everything' that is 'in the world'. That definition included three elements. The first was a general category: the 'cravings of sinful man', and the second and third elements were subcategories: 'the lust of his eyes' (lit. 'the desire of the eyes'), that is, those sinful cravings which are activated by what people see, and

---

197. In Deut 30:11 the commands of God are described as 'not too difficult for you or beyond your reach', and in Matt 11:30 Jesus tells his disciples that his yoke is easy and his burden is light.

which lead to covetousness and 'pride in possessions' (lit. 'pride of life' [*alazoneia tou biou*]), that is, being puffed up in pride because of one's material possessions. In the light of all this it becomes clear why it is not burdensome for believers to obey God's commands and love one another, and how that relates to their having been born of God and overcoming the world: those who have been born of God have overcome the worldly tendency to satisfy their own sinful cravings, and as a result they are free to show love to others and so fulfil God's command.

5:4B-12 ACCEPTING GOD'S TESTIMONY AND ETERNAL LIFE

The long section (4:7–5:4a) dealing with claims to love God tested by love for fellow believers concludes at 5:4a. A new section (5:4b-12) begins at 5:4b, in which there is no further mention of the love imperative. Here the focus of attention shifts to the 'faith' which overcomes the world and leads to eternal life. It is true that the idea of overcoming the world is found in 5:4a, but there its primary reference appears to be overcoming those desires which militate against the love of God (cf. 2:15-17), whereas in 5:4b-5 its primary reference appears to be overcoming the false teaching about Christ propagated by the secessionists (cf. 5:6-10).

In this passage the author speaks of the faith which overcomes the 'world', a faith in Jesus as the Son of God who 'came by water and blood'. To the testimony of the water and the blood is added the testimony of the Spirit and of God himself. All who accept the testimony of God concerning his Son have eternal life, while those who do not accept it do not have eternal life.

5:4b-5 By saying, **this is the victory that has overcome the world, even our faith,**[198] the author defines what it is that enables those born of God to overcome the world. It is their faith. This is the only place in the Johannine writings where the noun 'faith' (*pistis*) is found. Elsewhere the author prefers to use the verb (*pisteuō*) and portray faith dynamically. The nature of the faith that overcomes the world is made clear in the following rhetorical question and answer: **Who is it that overcomes the world? Only he who believes that Jesus is the Son of God.** It is faith in Jesus as

198. Brown, *The Epistles of John,* 569, translates this clause as 'Now this is the conquering power that has conquered the world' to bring out the connection between the cognate noun 'victory' (*nikē*) and the participle 'has overcome' (*nikēsasa*).

the Son of God which enables believers to overcome the world. In this context the influence of the 'world' comes primarily through the secessionists and their false teaching (cf. 5:9-10).[199] To overcome the world, the readers must persist in their faith in him despite the propaganda of the secessionists. In 1 John 'the Son of God' is virtually equivalent to 'Christ' (cf. 2:22, 23; 5:1, 5). It was only those who held the belief that Jesus is the Son of God who could be said to have overcome the world. The secessionists who denied these things were, as far as the author was concerned, still part of the world (2:18-19; 4:1-3; cf. 2 John 7) and subject to the power of the evil one (5:19).

The author uses two different tenses of the verb 'to overcome' *(nikaō)* in 5:4b-5. He uses the aorist participle *(nikēsasa)* in 5:4b, and then the present participle *(nikōn)* in 5:5. This does not reflect any time difference, as if the first represents a victory in the past and the second a victory in the present. Rather, it is stylistic, indicating the author's choice to portray the victory of faith as a complete action in the first case and as an ongoing process in the second (both without necessary time reference).

5:6a Following his description in 5:5 of those who overcome the world as those who believe that Jesus is the Son of God, here the author describes the Jesus in whom he believes: **This is the one who came by water and blood** *(di' hydatos kai haimatos)*[200] — **Jesus Christ**. His belief is different from the belief of the secessionists, and in 5:6b the author indicates the difference between his view and theirs: **He did not come by water** *(en tō hydati)* **only, but by water and blood** *(en tō hydati kai en tō haimati)*.[201] This text indicates two things: what was not in dispute (Jesus came 'by water'), and what was in dispute (Jesus came 'by water and blood').

---

199. The elements of the secessionist Christology are reflected in various allusions the author makes to their beliefs in this letter. When one puts all the elements together, it becomes clear that their Christology involves a denial that Jesus Christ is the Messiah, God's Son, come in the flesh, whose death was real and vicarious (4:2-3, 15; 5:1, 6-8). However, at different places in the letter, the author refers to the whole by mentioning one part.

200. Some manuscripts read 'by water and Spirit' or 'by water and blood and Spirit' or 'by water and Spirit and blood', but these other readings are poorly attested, and the reading adopted in the NIV is certainly the original.

201. The two different expressions translated 'by water' here *(di' hydatos* and *en tō hydati)* are not significant. They probably represent only a stylistic variation. Contra Strecker, *The Johannine Letters*, 183, who says that the change from *di' hydatos kai haimatos* to *en tō hydati kai en tō haimati* represents a shift in the author's focus from the baptism and death of Jesus to the 'two community sacraments of Baptism and the Lord's Supper'.

This is a very difficult text to interpret. The first thing to ascertain is the meaning of what was not in dispute between the author and the secessionists, that is, what both parties understood Jesus' coming 'by water' *(en hydati)* to mean. There are a number of ways to interpret this statement. First, in the Fourth Gospel the expression 'by water' *(en hydati)* is used three times, each time in relation to the ministry of John the Baptist (John 1:26, 31, 33). Taking this as a clue, we could say that both the author and the secessionists agreed that Jesus underwent John's baptism, and, we might add, that Jesus was endowed with the Spirit at that time (cf. John 1:33, where the Baptist says: 'I would not have known him, except that the one who sent me to baptize with water told me, "The man on whom you see the Spirit come down and remain is he who will baptize with the Holy Spirit"'). Understood in this way, the statement that Jesus came 'by water' recalls his baptism in water by John and the concomitant endowment with the Spirit that he experienced.[202] His coming by water would then mark the beginning of his ministry, as his coming by blood (i.e., his death) marked its end.

Second, it is possible that the previous interpretation misreads the significance of the uses of 'by water' *(en hydati)* in the Fourth Gospel. It is true that all these uses are connected with the ministry of the Baptist, but that is the point: they are connected with the *ministry* (active) of the Baptist, not the *experience* (passive) of Jesus when he received baptism at his hands. If the uses of *en hydati* in the Fourth Gospel all relate to John's practice of water baptism, then it is possible that the reference in 1 John 5:6 to Jesus coming *en hydati* refers to Jesus' ministry of baptism, not to his experience of baptism. There are a number of references to Jesus' baptising ministry in the Fourth Gospel (John 3:22, 26; 4:1), although he clearly entrusted the actual baptising of people to his disciples (John 4:2). However, while the Fourth Gospel mentions Jesus' ministry of baptism (with water), it places greater emphasis upon his future ministry of baptism with the Spirit. As already noted above, in John 1:33 the Baptist says of Jesus: 'I would not have known him, except that the one who sent me to baptize with water told me, "The man on whom you see the Spirit come down and remain is he who will baptize with the Holy Spirit."' When the author of 1 John and the secessionists agreed that Jesus came *en hydati*, therefore, they agreed that Jesus had a baptising ministry. Jesus once baptised with water but now baptises with the Spirit, and it has been suggested that those in the author's community understood that Jesus now

202. Schnackenburg, *The Johannine Epistles,* 232-33, interprets Jesus' coming by water as his revelation as Messiah to Israel at the time of his baptism; his revelation to Israel as the one who possesses the Spirit.

baptised people with the Spirit when they baptised them with water in Jesus' name.[203]

Third, it has been argued that coming 'by water' is a reference to natural birth, water being an allusion either to male semen or amniotic fluid. Witherington lists Prov 5:15-18 and Song of Songs 4:12-15 as OT texts where water relates to birth (semen in one place, amniotic fluid in the other) as well as a number of texts from other Jewish and ancient Near Eastern literature.[204] If it is correct to interpret Jesus' coming 'by water' as a reference to his natural birth, then the author and the secessionists would have agreed that Jesus' humanity was real. However, it is quite clear that this was not something about which they agreed (4:2; cf. 2 John 7). Further, when the author wants to emphasise the reality of Jesus' humanity elsewhere in 1 John, he does not speak of Jesus coming 'by water' *(en hydati),* but coming 'in the flesh' *(en sarki)* (4:2; cf. 2 John 7). For this reason it is unlikely that the reference to Jesus coming *en hydati* here constitutes an affirmation of his real humanity.

Fourth, there is a view that Jesus' coming 'by water' and his coming 'by blood' must be taken together. It is argued that 5:6 reflects the view found in ancient Jewish sources that the human body is composed of two elements, water and blood. The whole statement that Jesus came 'by water and blood' is then seen as analogous to the author's reference in 4:2 to Jesus' coming 'in the flesh' *(en sarki),* both of which function as affirmations of his real humanity. Thus to say that he came 'by water' only would be to deny his real humanity.[205] Adopting this view, we would have to say that Jesus' coming *en hydati* was not something agreed upon by the author and the secessionists, but that it represented the secessionists' denial of the real humanity of Jesus — a denial that the author strenuously opposed.

---

203. Martinus C. de Boer, 'Jesus the Baptizer: 1 John 5:5-8 and the Gospel of John', *JBL* 107 (1988) 93-100, reaches similar conclusions, but begins his discussion with a consideration of Jesus' coming 'by blood' *(en haimati),* which he interprets in the light of 1 John 1:7. There the blood of Jesus, which cleanses people from sins, is 'the instrument with which Jesus Christ . . . accomplishes God's salvific purposes'. Thus if Jesus' coming 'by blood' has active connotations, he argues, so must Jesus' coming 'by water'. Therefore it refers, not to something done to Jesus, e.g., his baptism at the hands of the Baptist, but to something which Jesus does, i.e., to his work as the baptizer. De Boer adds that 'unlike the baptism of that other baptizer, John, his baptism "with water" was also baptism "with the holy spirit".'

204. Ben Witherington, III, 'The Waters of Birth: John 3.5 and 1 John 5.6-8', *NTS* 35 (1989) 155-58.

205. Cf. G. Richter, 'Blut und Wasser aus der durchbohrten Seite Jesu (Joh 19,34b)', in *Studien zum Johannesevangelium* (Regensburg: Pustet, 1977) 129-30, 134-35, 138 (cited by de Boer, 'Jesus the Baptizer', 91).

Fifth, it has been suggested that Jesus' coming 'by water' is an allusion to the sacrament of baptism (and Jesus' coming 'by blood' is an allusion to the sacrament of the Eucharist).[206] But, as Venetz points out, no matter how attractive this might seem to later readers of the letter, it hardly does justice to the intention of the original author, who was not discussing sacramental theology but dealing with a christological heresy.[207] In addition, it does not do justice to the aorist participle, 'the one who came' *(ho elthōn)*, which presents the action as complete, not ongoing as one would expect if the reference was to the sacrament.

Of these various suggested interpretations of Jesus' coming 'by water', it is the second, that is, that it refers to Jesus' baptising ministry, which has the most to commend it. It takes note of the way the expression 'by water' *(en hydati)* is used in the Fourth Gospel, and it allows the expression to function actively and so in line with the way the complementary expression, 'by blood', also appears to function. It is this latter expression which we must explore now.

If there was no dispute between the author and the secessionists concerning the fact that Jesus came 'by water', the same cannot be said about Jesus' coming 'by blood', for the author insists: 'He did not come by water only, but by water and blood.' The question we must now ask is, What is it that the author affirmed by saying that Jesus came 'by blood', and therefore what was it that the secessionists denied by rejecting that affirmation? A couple of interpretations have been suggested.

First, there is the interpretation already mentioned above that Jesus' coming 'by water' and his coming 'by blood' must be taken together as a single affirmation of his real humanity, something the secessionists denied and the author asserted. The weaknesses of this interpretation have already been explained above.

Second, there is the more usual and far more likely interpretation which explains Jesus' coming 'by blood' in terms of his death on the cross. The only other reference to Jesus' 'blood' in this letter (apart from references here in 5:6-8) is located in 1:7: 'But if we walk in the light, as he is in the light, we have fellowship with one another, and the blood of Jesus, his Son, purifies us from all sin'. Here the 'blood' denotes Jesus' death by which he made atoning sacrifice for the sins of his people. Thus the reference to his 'blood' refers, not to something done to Jesus, but to something Jesus did. The author did not see Jesus as a passive victim

---

206. Cf. Schnackenburg, *The Johannine Epistles*, 233-34.

207. Hermann-Josef Venetz, '"Durch Wasser und Blut gekommen": Exegetische Überlegungen zu 1 Joh 5,6', in *Die Mitte des Neuen Testaments: Einheit und vielfalt neutestamentlicher Theologie. Festschrift für Eduard Schweizer zum siebsigsten Geburtstag*, ed. Ulrich Luz and Hans Weder (Göttingen: Vandenhoeck & Ruprecht, 1983) 357-58.

when he came to the cross, but as the active party: 'Jesus Christ laid down his life for us' (3:16). The Fourth Gospel repeatedly emphasises the same active role of Jesus in laying down his life for his people (cf. John 10:11, 15, 17, 18; 15:13).

Thus, we may say that Jesus' coming 'by water' and his coming 'by blood' both refer to things Jesus did. His coming 'by water' refers to his baptising ministry. His coming 'by blood' refers to his laying down his life as an atoning sacrifice in order to provide cleansing for the sins of his people. It was the reality and atoning significance of Jesus' death that the secessionists denied, and that the author felt compelled to assert.

The author's purpose, then, in 5:6a is to deny the limited view of the secessionists that Jesus came by water only, that is, that his ministry was essentially a baptising one. The secessionists may have connected baptism in Jesus' name with the anointing with the Spirit. (That they stressed the importance of this anointing may be inferred from 2:20-21, 27-28, where the author reminds his readers that they, too, have received the anointing of God's Spirit. This he does presumably to reassure them in the face of exclusive claims by the secessionists.) However, the author's purpose in 5:6a was not just to deny what the secessionists taught, but also to state what he believed to be the truth about Jesus' ministry; that he came 'by water and blood',[208] that is, he was not only the baptizer but the Saviour who made the atoning sacrifice for sins.

5:6b Having made the point that those who truly believe that Jesus is the Son of God also believe that he is the one who came 'by water and blood', the author now indicates that the Spirit himself testifies to this truth: **And it is the Spirit who testifies, because the Spirit is the truth.** In 4:6 the author described the Spirit as 'the Spirit of truth', and in the upper room discourse in the Fourth Gospel Jesus describes the Spirit in a similar way three times (John 14:17; 15:26; 16:13). Both here in 1 John 5:6 and in the Fourth Gospel (John 15:26) the role of the Spirit is to bear witness to the truth about Jesus. In the Fourth Gospel the Spirit's testifying role is mainly bearing witness to Jesus against the world. In 1 John the Spirit's testifying role is mainly bearing witness to believers concerning the truth of the message about Jesus that they heard from the beginning (cf. 2:24-27). The author invokes the Spirit as a witness to the truth of the fact that Jesus came 'by water and blood' because, he says, 'the Spirit is the truth'. At a minimum this constitutes

---

208. De Boer, 'Jesus the Baptizer', 89, notes that 'the preposition *dia* governs both nouns in v 6a: Jesus Christ is "the one who came through water-and-blood." We may surmise that, in using the preposition *dia* and causing it to govern both nouns, the author expresses his own distinctive views with respect to the coming of Jesus Christ'.

a guarantee of the truthfulness of the Spirit as witness to Jesus, but it may also imply that, as truth is personified in God elsewhere in 1 John (5:20) and in Jesus in the Fourth Gospel (John 14:6), so also it is personified in the Spirit in this verse.

5:7-8   For there are three that testify: the Spirit, the water and the blood. In both the OT and the NT important issues were decided with the testimony of two or three witnesses (Deut 17:6; 19:15; Matt 18:6; John 8:17; 2 Cor 13:1; 1 Tim 5:19; Heb 10:28). Here in this context the author cites three witnesses, the Spirit, the water, and the blood,[209] to the truth he affirms. What it means here for the Spirit to testify seems reasonably clear. The Spirit confirms to believers the truth of the message about Jesus that they heard from the beginning (cf. 2:24-27). It is more difficult to say how the water and the blood make up the second and third witnesses. Normally witness is given by one *person* concerning another. However, in the Fourth Gospel, when people will not accept Jesus' own testimony about himself, he points them to his works, for these, too, bear witness, albeit silent witness, to the truth about him (cf. John 5:36; 10:25). It may be, then, that in this verse the author is suggesting that alongside the Spirit's witness concerning Jesus there stands the silent witness of Jesus' work as the baptizer and the one who made atoning sacrifice — the witness of the 'water' and the 'blood'.[210]

The author then adds: **and the three are in agreement.** In judicial cases it is vital that the testimony of different witnesses should agree. The author builds his case here by showing that his three witnesses, the Spirit, the water, and the blood, concur in their testimony. The secessionists denied that Jesus came by water and blood, focussing only upon his coming by water, which they probably associated with their experience of the Spirit. The author insists that Jesus came by water and blood, and that to

---

209. While in the Greek language 'Spirit', 'water', and 'blood' are all neuter nouns, the author chooses masculine (not neuter) plural forms when he says 'there are three that testify' *(treis eisin hoi martyrountes)*, indicating, perhaps, a realisation on the author's part of the personal dimensions of the subjects.

210. Brown, *The Epistles of John,* 596-99, argues that the author here alludes to John 19:34, the flow of water and blood from Jesus' side at the crucifixion: 'The true salvific coming in water was not John's baptizing with water, but water flowing from the side of Jesus. For the Christian the life-giving moment of the Spirit was not simply the descent of the Spirit upon Jesus in the form of a dove, but the Spirit flowing from within Jesus after his death' (597). The temptation to make some connection between the water and blood coming from Jesus' side when he was pierced by the soldier's spear and the statement in 5:7-8 that the water and the blood bear their witness alongside the Spirit is very tempting. But if our interpretation of Jesus' coming by water in terms of his own baptising ministry is correct, then there is not a lot to be gained by calling upon this incident to help in the interpretation of 5:7-8.

this the Spirit also bore witness. It is only in the concurrence of these three witnesses that the truth about Jesus is to be found.[211]

In verses 9-12 the author continues to work with the theme of witness *(martyria)*, reflecting the fact that 5:9-12 forms a subsection of 5:6-12. However, he expands the scope of the witness theme to include the gift of eternal life that God gives those who believe his testimony concerning his Son (cf. vv. 11-12).

5:9 The NIV renders 5:9a as follows: **We accept man's testimony, but God's testimony is greater because it is the testimony of God, which he has given about his Son.** However, the NIV here obscures the meaning of the original text, which opens with an incomplete conditional sentence (providing the protasis but expecting the reader to supply the apodosis). Rendered literally (and supplying the apodosis), the verse would read: 'If we accept the testimony of men [then we should accept the testimony of God]'.

The first part of the verse is an argument from the lesser to the greater: if we accept human testimony, then we should certainly accept God's testimony. What is the human testimony that the author alludes to here? It can hardly be a reference to the threefold testimony of Spirit, water, and blood. Is it an allusion to the witness of John the Baptist? In the Fourth Gospel Jesus refers to the Baptist's testimony as 'human testimony' and indicates that it is much less important than God's testimony (John 5:33-36). Does it refer to the testimony of the eyewitnesses to the Word of life (1:1), which, though trustworthy, is not of the same order as God's own testimony. Or is it merely a general statement indicating that God's testimony is always more important than human testimony. Probably the last is the best alternative, for the first two suggestions create new problems. There are no other allusions to the Baptist's ministry in 1 John, and the author would not want to downplay the testimony of the eyewitnesses because he believes that to be a true report of the truth of God.

The next question that needs to be addressed is what the author means by 'God's testimony'. Is it to be identified with the testimony of

---

211. There is a longer version of 5:7-8 which reads: 'For there are three that testify in heaven, the Father, the Word and the Holy Spirit, and these three are one; and there are three that testify on earth, the Spirit, the water and the blood, and these three are one'. This longer version, known as the Johannine Comma ('comma' meaning 'sentence'), is preserved in only a few later Greek manuscripts (dating from the tenth to the eighteenth centuries). It is thought that the Johannine Comma found its way into the Greek manuscripts via the Latin manuscripts of the ninth century. The Johannine Comma is found in no early Greek manuscripts and is not found in the Old Latin versions before the seventh century, nor in the Vulgate before the eighth century. It is correctly omitted from all modern translations of the NT. For a full discussion of the textual tradition see Brown, *The Epistles of John*, 775-87; Strecker, *The Johannine Letters*, 188-91.

the three witnesses, the Spirit, the water, and the blood?[212] Is his testimony to be heard through the Spirit/anointing which believers have received, and through the baptising and atoning work of Jesus? In this letter, as in the Fourth Gospel, the Spirit bears witness to Jesus, and in the Fourth Gospel the works of Jesus do bear testimony to who he is. Or is the testimony of God additional to the testimony of the three witnesses, so that the author has provided an ascending order of witnesses, the water, the blood, the Spirit, and finally God himself? In support of this view Brown cites John 5:31-40, where Jesus speaks of an ascending order of witnesses. These include the Baptist's testimony, the testimony of Jesus' own works, and finally the testimony of God himself. This last testimony, Jesus implies, is the voice of God which he hears but which his opponents have never heard ('you have never heard his voice nor seen his form', John 5:37).[213] Or is it to be identified with the testimony of the eyewitnesses, God speaking through them. This last alternative is preferable because the content of God's testimony described in 5:11 is that God has given us eternal life in his Son, which is the central feature of the testimony of the eyewitnesses alluded to in 1:1-4.

5:10 In this verse the author explains that the divine testimony is appropriated internally by those who believe in Christ: **Anyone who believes in the Son of God has this testimony in his heart** (lit. 'in himself').[214] The testimony referred to here is God's testimony to his Son made known through the testimony of the eyewitnesses.

There are two ways of interpreting this statement. First, in the light of verse 6 we might say that it refers to the inner witness of the Spirit. And it cannot be denied that the role of the Spirit in this letter and in the Fourth Gospel is to testify to Jesus. But this verse does not actually say that believers have 'the inner testimony of the Spirit in their hearts'; it simply states that they have 'the testimony' in themselves. The second and more likely interpretation is that the testimony believers have in themselves is the true testimony concerning Jesus Christ which they heard from the eyewitnesses and have accepted and internalised.[215]

This is not the case with those who reject God's testimony: **Anyone**

212. So Strecker, *The Johannine Letters,* 192-93.

213. Brown, *The Epistles of John,* 587.

214. Translating *en heautō.* Some manuscripts have *en autō,* but if this were the original it would have probably carried a reflexive sense.

215. Cf. Klauck, 'Bekenntnis zu Jesus und Zeugnis Gottes: Die christologische Linienführung im Ersten Johannesbrief', in *Anfänge der Christologie,* 303-4. Schnackenburg, *The Johannine Epistles,* 239, notes that 'in the Johannine writings *martyrein* [to bear witness] and *martyria* [testimony] always refer to external testimony, as they do in the preceding vv. 6c and 7f.'

who does not believe God[216] **has made him out to be a liar.** The author uses the present tense here when depicting those who do not believe, thereby portraying their unbelief as a process. Such people are not accepting the true testimony concerning Jesus Christ.[217] The author has the secessionists in mind. As far as he is concerned, they are the ones who do not believe God's testimony concerning his Son. They deny that Jesus is the Christ come in the flesh. They deny that he came by water and blood. By so doing, the author says, they make God out to be a liar.

This is the fifth time in the letter that the author accuses his opponents of either being liars or making God out to be a liar (1:10; 2:4, 22; 4:20; 5:10). In 5:10 such people are said to make God out to be a liar **because he has not believed the testimony God has given about his Son**. If we ask when the author thought the secessionists heard and then rejected God's testimony, his answer would be that they did so when they heard and then turned away from the original message of the gospel; the message proclaimed by those who at the beginning had seen and handled the Word of life (cf. 1:1-4). For the author, the testimony of God is the same as the message proclaimed from the beginning. It is this message to which God bears witness by his Spirit, and to which believers must remain committed (cf. 2:23-24, 27). The secessionists, of course, did not see it that way. They claimed to be enlightened by the Spirit (cf. 2:20, 27), but their 'enlightenment' led them to deny the truth about Jesus Christ to whom God himself bore witness.

5:11 Amplifying now the nature of the witness which God gave, the author adds, **And this is the testimony: God has given us eternal life, and this life is in his Son.** Up to this point the author has emphasised God's witness concerning the person (came in the flesh) and work (came by water and blood) of the historical Jesus, but here he emphasises God's testimony concerning the benefit made available to believers through him. Simply put, what is stressed here is God's testimony concerning the eternal life he gives people 'in his Son'. In 1 John eternal life is not an unending extension of life as we know it; rather, it is 'having' Jesus Christ himself. Eternal life is identified with Jesus Christ. He, in fact, is eternal life (5:20); the eternal life that was with the Father from the beginning (1:2).

5:12 Because God's gift of eternal life is given 'in his Son', it fol-

---

216. Other manuscripts have, instead of 'God', either 'the Son' or 'the Son of God', but the reading 'God' is best attested; the other readings may be explained as attempts to conform the latter part of this verse to the earlier part, which speaks of belief in 'the Son of God'.

217. An example of the opposite response is found in John 3:33: 'The man who has accepted it has certified that God is truthful'.

lows that **he who has the Son has life**. What it means to 'have the Son' is closely related to believing in the Son, as the next verse (5:13) indicates. Believing in the Son is closely connected with accepting the proclamation. But the question remains: Is the expression 'having the Son' a synonym for 'believing in the Son'? Or does 'having' the Son involve something more than this? We get some help from the 'abiding' language of Fourth Gospel (John 6:56; 14:23; 15:4-7). As far as it relates to believers abiding in Christ, it denotes continuing loyalty and obedience to Christ, but it is not exhausted by this. There is an ontological dimension to it as well. As far as it relates to Christ abiding in believers, it clearly has ontological significance.

Allowing ourselves to be guided by the relevant material in the Fourth Gospel, we may say that to 'have the Son' means to be indwelt by the Son, something which, when viewed from the human perspective, takes place when people believe in him. To have the Son is to have eternal life because the Son himself is the eternal life that was with the Father. He has eternal life in himself, and he gives eternal life to those who believe in him. (See 'A Note on Eternal Life', pp. 184-87.)

While those who believe in and are indwelt by the Son have eternal life, the opposite is the case for those who do not believe in him and so are not indwelt by him: **he who does not have the Son of God does not have life**. If having the Son involves believing in him, and if believing in him involves accepting the message that was proclaimed at the beginning by the eyewitnesses, then, as far as the author is concerned, the secessionists do not have eternal life because they do not 'have the Son' in this sense.

A Note on Witness

The verb 'to witness' (*martyreō*) and the noun 'witness' (*martyria*) are found a total of 113 times in the NT. Of these, 47 are found in the Fourth Gospel and 17 in the Letters of John. This means that more than half of the NT occurrences of these two words are found in the Gospel and Letters of John.

Witness is a major theme in the Fourth Gospel, and all but three of the 47 uses of the witness terminology involve testimony to Jesus (given by the Baptist, other humans, Jesus himself, Jesus' works, God the Father, the Scriptures, and the Holy Spirit) or Jesus' own testimony to the truth. In many but not all cases the witness motif is found in contexts where God, incarnate in Jesus Christ, has a controversy with the 'world', incarnate in 'the Jews'. The witness motif in the Fourth Gospel contributes to its overall purpose of setting forth Jesus as the Christ, so that people might believe in him and so enjoy eternal life.

In the Letters of John the witness terminology is used in the following ways: (i) in relation to the eyewitness testimony concerning the eternal life which was with the Father and appeared to them (1 John 1:2) and their testimony concerning the Father's sending the Son to be the Saviour of the world (1 John 4:14); (ii) in relation to the testimony God gave concerning his Son — he gives eternal life to those who believe in him; a testimony that is internalised in the hearts of those who believe (1 John 5:9-11); (iii) in relation to the testimony of the Spirit, the water, and the blood — the Spirit confirms the truth of the witness to Jesus, and the water and the blood add their silent testimony as well (1 John 5:6-8; see commentary *ad loc.*); (iv) in relation to the testimony given by believers concerning the faithfulness of other believers (3 John 3, 6, 12).

However, the purpose of the inclusion of the witness motif in the Letters of John differs from the purpose of its inclusion in the Fourth Gospel. In the letters it serves the purpose of distinguishing the errors of the secessionists from the truth of the message of the gospel as it was heard from the beginning. It is also used in recommending faithful missionaries to other Christian communities, and to describe the reports of those missionaries to their home churches concerning the hospitality they had received from those to whom they had been recommended.[218]

A Note on Eternal Life

The First Letter of John begins and ends on the note of eternal life (1:1-2; 5:20), and the theme of eternal life pervades throughout. At one point the author describes the purpose of his letter to be that his readers might know that they have eternal life (5:13). The expressions 'life' and 'eternal life' are used interchangeably. In 1 John eternal life almost always refers to a present experience as far as believers are concerned. (Eternal life as a future experience that may be lost may possibly be implied in 1 John 5:16-17.)

Strecker documents possible parallels to the Johannine idea of (eternal) life in Greek mythology, Gnosticism, and Hellenistic Judaism.[219] However, our best chance of understanding what the author meant is to examine what is found in 1 John itself, and what further light is thrown on the subject by the Fourth Gospel.

218. Cf. Allison A. Trites, *The New Testament Concept of Witness* (SNTSMS 31, Cambridge: Cambridge University Press, 1977) 124-27.
219. Strecker, *The Johannine Letters*, 17-18.

Eternal life was with the Father and is revealed in Christ. In the opening paragraph of 1 John, where the author reminds his readers of what it is that he proclaims (the Word of life), he also tells them that 'this life was revealed, and we have seen it and testify to it, and declare to you the eternal life that was with the Father' (1:2). This reference to the eternal life 'that was with the Father' *(hētis ēn pros ton patera)* is almost certainly an allusion to the Fourth Gospel, where the Logos is described as the one who 'was with God' *(houtos ēn . . . pros ton theon)* (1:1-2). In the light of this allusion, we can say that 'eternal life' here does not denote an impersonal quality of life that was with the Father, but refers to the Word of life, the Son of God, who was with the Father prior to his incarnation and revealed to us (the eyewitnesses). That this is what the author of 1 John intends is confirmed in 5:20, where he says, Jesus Christ 'is the true God and eternal life'.

The following passages from the Fourth Gospel further illustrate what the author means when he asserts that Jesus is the eternal life that was with the Father:

John 5:26: "For just as the Father has life in himself, so he has granted the Son also to have life in himself." (NRSV)

John 1:4: in him was life, and the life was the light of all people. (NRSV)

John 11:25: Jesus said to her, "I am the resurrection and the life. Those who believe in me, even though they die, will live." (NRSV)

John 14:6: Jesus said to him, "I am the way, and the truth, and the life. No one comes to the Father except through me." (NRSV)

John 17:2: "since you have given him authority over all people, to give eternal life to all whom you have given him." (NRSV)

What these passages reveal is that Jesus Christ is eternal life because, just as God the Father has life in himself, so he has given the incarnate Son to have life in himself.

Those who have the Son have eternal life. In 1 John the author reminds his readers that God has promised them eternal life (2:25) and also explains that this gift of eternal life is tied up with God's Son. The key text is 1 John 5:11-13:

And this is the testimony: God gave us eternal life, and this life is in his Son. Whoever has the Son has life; whoever does not have the Son of God does not have life. I write these things to you who believe in the

185

name of the Son of God, so that you may know that you have eternal
life.

Consistent with the opening statement of the letter, where the author
points out that the eternal life which was with God has been revealed to
us in the incarnate Son, he now makes clear that God's promise of eternal
life for those who believe is intimately connected with God's Son. When
God gives eternal life to human beings, he gives it with his Son. To have
the Son is to have life; not to have the Son is not to have life. What it
means to 'have the Son' is closely related to believing in the Son, as the
passage just cited indicates. And believing in the Son is closely connected
with accepting the proclamation.

But the question remains: Is the expression 'having the Son' a synonym for 'believing in the Son'? Or does 'having' the Son involve something more than this? We get some help in answering this question from
the 'abiding' texts in the Fourth Gospel:

John 6:56:   "Those who eat my flesh and drink my blood abide
             in me, and I in them." (NRSV)
John 14:23: Jesus answered him, "Those who love me will keep
             my word, and my Father will love them, and we will
             come to them and make our home with them."
             (NRSV)
John 15:4:   "Abide in me as I abide in you. Just as the branch
             cannot bear fruit by itself unless it abides in the vine,
             neither can you unless you abide in me." (NRSV)
John 15:5-7 "I am the vine; you are the branches. Those who
             abide in me and I in them bear much fruit, because
             apart from me you can do nothing. Whoever does not
             abide in me is thrown away like a branch and with-
             ers; such branches are gathered, thrown into the fire,
             and burned. If you abide in me, and my words abide
             in you, ask for whatever you wish, and it will be
             done for you." (NRSV)

It is apparent that the 'abiding' language of John's Gospel, as far as it relates to believers abiding in Christ, denotes continuing loyalty and obedience to Christ, but it is not exhausted by this. There is an ontological dimension to it as well. As far as it relates to Christ abiding in believers
(which is closer to the notion of 'having the Son'), the abiding language
definitely has ontological significance. In the light of the latter, we could
say that in 1 John to 'have the Son' means to be indwelt by the Son, some-

thing which viewed from the human perspective is initiated when people believe in him. To 'have the Son' is to have eternal life because the Son himself is the eternal life that was with the Father.

What does it mean to have eternal life? The author of 1 John does provide one clue concerning what it means to have eternal life. In 3:14 he speaks of believers passing from death to life, indicating that the experience of eternal life expressed negatively is escaping death. The same idea is found in the Fourth Gospel where, again and again, eternal life is expressed in terms of escaping death and judgement. Not to have eternal life is to perish (John 3:16; 10:28); to endure God's wrath (John 3:36); to come under God's judgement (John 5:24); and to experience the resurrection to condemnation (John 5:29).

First John gives us virtually no clues as to what is involved positively in having eternal life. However, there are a number of clues in the Fourth Gospel: to have eternal life means to have one's spiritual hunger and thirst satisfied (John 4:14; 6:35); to be raised up on the last day and to live forever (John 6:40, 51, 54); to have the light of life so that one does not walk in darkness (John 8:12); to have abundant life (John 10:10); to know the only true God, and Jesus Christ whom he sent (John 17:3); and that, though we die, we will live (John 11:25).

Eternal life and being born of God. 1 John makes it clear that those who believe in the Son have eternal life, and viewed from a human perspective, belief is the means by which a person receives eternal life. However, the extensive use of the 'begetting' language in 1 John suggests that, viewed from God's perspective, believers have eternal life because they have been 'born of God' (2:29; 3:9; 4:7; 5:1, 4, 18).

Evidences of eternal life. The begetting texts mentioned above also reveal what the author of 1 John believed to be the evidences of eternal life: belief that Jesus is the Christ (5:1), avoidance of sin and doing what is right (2:29; 3:9; 5:18), overcoming the 'world' (5:4), and love of fellow believers (4:7). The author places heavy emphasis upon the fact that eternal life manifests itself in love for fellow believers (see esp. 3:11-17). This is no surprise once we recognise that to have eternal life means to have the Son, that is, to have Christ indwelling us. To have Christ indwelling us means that we will love fellow believers. Therefore, to say that we have eternal life while we hate fellow believers is a contradiction in terms. To shut our hearts against fellow believers in need is evidence that we do not have eternal life.

5:13-21 CONCLUDING REASSURANCES AND EXHORTATIONS

With this section, 5:13-21, the author brings his letter to its conclusion. In doing so, he picks up several of the themes already developed within the letter. This concluding section comprises four subsections: (a) 5:13-15: the author indicates that his purpose in writing was to reassure his readers concerning their possession of eternal life, and explains what that means as far as prayer in general is concerned; (b) 5:16-17: he amplifies the theme of prayer, urging his readers to pray for those overtaken by sins that do not lead to death, while indicating that he is not asking them to pray for those whose sins do lead to death; (c) 5:18-20: the author further reassures his readers by reminding them that they are no longer under the power of the evil one, being kept safe by Jesus Christ himself, and that they have been given knowledge of the truth and eternal life in Jesus Christ; (d) 5:21: the concluding exhortation, 'Dear children, keep yourselves from idols', with which the letter ends.

5:13   In this verse the author states explicitly for the first time his purpose in writing the letter: **I write these things to you who believe in the name of the Son of God so that you may know that you have eternal life.** 'These things' refer to the contents of this letter which is now being brought to its conclusion. Those 'who believe' are those who, along with the author, continue in the teaching about Jesus Christ that they heard from the beginning. To believe 'in the name' (an expression found also in 3:23) means the same as believing 'in the person' who bears the name. Texts from the Fourth Gospel, such as John 1:12 ('Yet to all who received him, to those who believed in his name, he gave the right to become children of God') and John 3:18 ('Whoever believes in him is not condemned, but whoever does not believe stands condemned already because he has not believed in the name of God's one and only Son'), confirm this by placing the idea of believing in his name and believing in his person in parallel.

The author's purpose in writing, he says, is that 'you may know that you have eternal life'. His readers had been disturbed by the denials and claims of the secessionists. These people denied important elements of the message the readers had embraced at the beginning. They also claimed to be recipients of special revelation through the Spirit to which the readers were not privy. The readers' assurance had been shaken by these denials and claims, and the author's primary reason for writing the letter was to bolster their assurance by counteracting the false teaching of the secessionists. The author sought to do this by pointing out that it was his readers who had truly received eternal life, who truly knew God, not the secessionists. It was his readers who manifested the authentic marks of those who have eternal life: they were the ones who continued in the teaching first proclaimed by the eyewitnesses; they were the ones who continued to obey the commands of the Lord; and they were the ones who loved the children of God, which is the essential mark of those who have eternal life.

There is a remarkable similarity between the way the author states his purpose in writing this letter ('I write these things to you who believe in the name of the Son of God so that you may know that you have eternal life') and the way the Fourth Evangelist states the purpose of his Gospel (John 20:31: 'But these are written that you may believe that Jesus is the Christ, the Son of God, and that by believing you may have life in his name'). In both cases the purpose includes reference to what has been written, belief in Jesus Christ as the Son of God, and the possession of eternal life. The difference reflects the different purposes of the letter and the Gospel. The Gospel has an evangelistic purpose (that you may believe that Jesus is the Christ and so have eternal life), whereas the purpose of the letter is to reassure those who are already believers (that you may know that you have eternal life). That the letter and the Gospel both end (and begin) on the same note (life) is noteworthy, and is one more piece of evidence suggesting a common authorship, or at the least that the author of 1 John was intimately acquainted with the Gospel and deeply influenced by its theology; a theology he adapted to the new situation that his letter addresses.

5:14-15 These verses are linked with 5:13 by the conjunction *kai* ('and'), which is unfortunately omitted in the NIV translation. The presence of the conjunction suggests that the author wants to say that, along with assurance of eternal life, believers also experience confidence in their relationship with God and, in particular, confidence in prayer: **[and] this is the confidence** *(parrēsia)* **we have in approaching God** *(pros auton):* **that if we ask anything according to his will, he hears us.** The NIV translates *pros auton* as 'in approaching God'. It is better translated 'in his [God's] presence' (cf. John 1:1: 'In the beginning was the Word, and the Word was with God [*pros ton theon*])'. The author is speaking about the confidence believers have 'in the presence of God', something which is further described as the knowledge that 'if we ask anything according to his will, he hears us'. This statement recalls the promise of answered prayer made by Jesus to his disciples in the upper room (John 16:23-26).

This is the second place in the letter where the author speaks about believers' confidence *(parrēsia)* in prayer. In the first place (3:22-23), he linked confidence in prayer to pleasing God by doing what he commanded (believing in the name of his Son and loving fellow believers).[220] In the present context believers' confidence in prayer arises out of their assurance of eternal life and is linked to their asking according to his will (v. 14a). When they pray in this way, the author assures them, God will 'hear' the requests they make according to his will. In this context, 'to hear' *(akouō)* carries the sense of 'giving heed to' what is asked, that is, responding positively to the request. That this is the case is confirmed in 5:15: **And if we know that he hears** *(akouei)* **us — whatever we ask — we know that we have what we asked of him.** When believers ask God for anything according to his will, he gives heed to their requests, and they receive what they ask of him.[221]

5:16a In 5:16-17 the author amplifies the theme of prayer by applying the general statements of 5:14-15 to the particular need of prayer for believers who fall into sin: **If anyone sees his brother commit a sin that does not lead to death, he should pray and God** [lit. 'he'] **will give him life**. When his readers see fellow believers ('a brother') committing a sin, the author says they are to pray for them. The fact that the readers may 'see' a fellow believer fall into sin indicates that the sin is observable, not some internal attitude. In his exhortation the author uses a future form of the verb 'to pray', but here it carries the sense of command. In response to such prayer, the author adds, '*he* will give him life'. Thus it is not absolutely clear whether the author is saying that it is God who will give life to the repentant believer, or that the believer who prays for him will give life to him through his prayers. Either way, it is God ultimately who gives the life in answer to prayer.[222]

This promise of life for those who sin is restricted to the case where the person involved is a 'brother' (a believer) who has committed 'a sin that does not lead to death', something the author reiterates when he

---

220. Cf. 3:21-22, where the author speaks about believers being confronted by a brother or sister having a genuine need that they could meet. In this situation believers should persuade their reluctant hearts to be generous, so that their hearts do not condemn them for their generosity. If their hearts do not condemn them, then they will have confidence *(parrēsia)* before God, and receive what they ask of him, because they have obeyed his commands (to love one another).

221. Schnackenburg, *The Johannine Epistles*, 248, comments: 'We cannot fail to notice how certain the Johannine Christ is of being heard by his Father (John 11:41f.). This provides the supreme example of the power of prayer. Christians share in this power to the same degree or distance that their own fellowship with God approximates to the intimacy of the Father and the Son or fails to do so.'

222. Schnackenburg, *The Johannine Epistles*, 248-49, notes that in later Judaism the prayer of exceptionally holy people was regarded as efficacious, e.g., the prayers of the patriarchs, Moses, the prophets, and martyrs. Brown, *The Epistles of John*, 635-36, notes that in the NT the prayers of ordinary Christians are efficacious.

adds: **I refer to those whose sin does not lead to death.** The 'sin that does not lead to death' is the sin believers commit and for which forgiveness has been secured by the atoning sacrifice of Christ (cf. 1:9; 2:1-2) (see 'A Note on Sins That Do and Do Not Lead to Death', pp. 193-94). For this reason, the author is quite confident that prayer for the restoration of a repentant believer will be answered, 'and God will give him life'. It is difficult to explain what the author means by saying that, in answer to prayer for a believer who sins, 'God will give him life'. In this letter believers already have eternal life (cf. 3:14; 5:11, 12, 13). How can it be said, then, that in answer to prayer God will give them life? There are three possibilities: In answer to prayer (a) God will give repentant believers reconfirmation of their transfer from the realm of death to the realm of life;[223] (b) God will grant forgiveness to the repentant believer, and receiving forgiveness means having life with God;[224] (c) God will give the promised resurrection life to sinning believers who repent.

The first interpretation runs into difficulties because it speaks of reconfirmation of life for repentant believers, whereas the text speaks of the gift of life. The second interpretation runs into difficulties because it virtually equates life with forgiveness, something which this letter does not do. The third interpretation is preferable. It receives support from the fact that, in one other place at least in this letter (see the commentary on 2:25), eternal life is portrayed as something promised for the future.[225] Interpreted along these lines, the promise of 5:16a is that the repentant believer will, in answer to prayer, be granted life on the last day along with other believers. This interpretation gives the future verb 'he will give' (*dōsei*) a prospective sense which the context seems to demand. The promise to those who pray, then, is that, in answer to their prayers, God will give the promised resurrection life to those for whom they pray. They will not miss out on what has been promised to them.

5:16b In 5:16a the author speaks confidently of prayer being answered for a person whose sin does not lead to death. But in 5:16b he says, **there is a sin that leads to death,** and he does not advise believers

223. David M. Scholer, 'Sins Within and Sins Without: An Interpretation of 1 John 5:16-17', in *Current Issues in Biblical and Patristic Interpretation: Studies in Honor of Merrill C. Tenney Presented by His Former Students,* ed. Gerald F. Hawthorne (Grand Rapids: Eerdmans, 1975) 246.

224. Cf. Marianne Meye Thompson, 'Intercession in the Johannine Community: 1 John 5.16 in the Context of the Gospel and Epistles of John', in *Worship, Theology and Ministry in the Early Church: Essays in Honor of Ralph P. Martin,* ed. Michael J. Wilkins and Terence Paige (JSNTSup 87, Sheffield: Sheffield Academic Press, 1992) 244.

225. Even though, for the most part, the letter depicts eternal life as a present possession of believers.

to pray for those who commit this sin. There has been a lot of debate concerning the nature of the sin that leads to death (usually called mortal sin). Traditionally it has been defined in terms of sins for which there was thought to be no forgiveness (murder, idolatry, apostasy, adultery, etc.). Sometimes it has been assumed that believers are also in danger of committing mortal sins and so losing the eternal life that God has given them. However, as far as the author is concerned, believers cannot commit sins which lead to death. Unlike other writers of the NT (e.g., the author of Hebrews), he does not contemplate the possibility of apostasy on the part of true believers.[226]

When the author speaks of a sin that 'leads to death' (*pros thanaton*), he is referring to the outcome of such sin. Outside of 5:16-17, there is only one other place in the NT where the expression *pros thanaton* is found, and that is in John 11:4, where Jesus responds to news of the sickness of his friend Lazarus: 'Jesus said, "This sickness will not end in death (*ouk estin pros thanaton*). No, it is for God's glory so that God's Son may be glorified through it."' Lazarus, of course, did die, but that was not the end of it because Jesus restored him to life. His sickness was not *pros thanaton* in the sense that its ultimate outcome was not physical death because Jesus restored him to life. However, when speaking about 'sin that leads to death' the author of 1 John does not have physical death in mind, for all sinners are susceptible to physical death because of sin. What he has in mind is spiritual death, that failure to experience eternal life which is the privilege of those who believe in the Son of God.

When the author speaks of 'sin that leads to death', it is very likely that he has the sin of the secessionists in mind. They are people who deny that Jesus is the Christ come in the flesh, and also deny the significance of his atoning death. This would mean that they place themselves outside the sphere of forgiveness, and their sins become sins unto death. (See 'A Note on Sins That Do and Do Not Lead to Death', pp. 193-94.)

Concerning this sin, the author tells his readers, **I am not saying that he should pray**[227] **about that**. The author speaks in a roundabout fashion here. Elsewhere in the letter (2:1a) when he urges people to re-

---

226. Cf. Scholer, 'Sins Within and Sins Without', 241-42, who draws particular attention to 1 John 2:19 to argue that the author does not contemplate the possibility of believers committing apostasy. This verse makes clear that the author's opponents, though once members of the Christian community, were in fact never really members, for if they had been they would never have left it. Their leaving the community showed that they were never really part of it, but merely pretenders.

227. The verb (*erōtaō*), translated 'pray' here, is different from the verb (*aiteō*) translated 'pray' in 5:14, 15. However, the two verbs have a very similar range of meanings, and the variation is probably stylistic.

frain from doing something he uses a more direct form of speech: 'I write this to you so that you will not sin' *(tauta graphō hymin hina mē hamartēte)*, and if it was his intention to give clear directions here we would expect a similar direct form, and not the ambiguous form we find in this verse, 'I am not saying that he should pray about that' *(ou peri ekeinēs legō hina erōtēsē)*. For this reason, it is difficult to know whether the author is sidestepping the issue because it is not one he wishes to address, or whether he is ambivalent about it, or whether this is in fact an implied command that his readers desist from praying for people who persist in unrepentance.

If what the author writes here is an implied prohibition, saying that his readers should not pray for such people, there is precedent for it in the OT. The word of the Lord came repeatedly to the prophet Jeremiah, ordering him not to pray for Israel because her sins were so repugnant (Jer 7:16-18; 11:14; 14:11).[228] There is also a precedent for it in the Fourth Gospel, where Jesus refrains from praying for the 'world' (John 17:9).

5:17 In this verse the author restates and reinforces the distinction he made in 5:16 between sins that do and do not 'lead to death': **All wrongdoing** *(adikia)* **is sin, and there is sin that does not**[229] **lead to death**. The reinforcement here of the distinction between the sins that lead to death and those that do not seems to function as an assurance to his readers that, though they may fall into sin from time to time, their sins do not lead to death. Back in 1:9 the author had already told his readers that God forgives those who confess their sins and cleanses them from all unrighteousness, or wrongdoing *(adikia)*.

A Note on Sins That Do and Do Not Lead to Death

The distinction between sins that do and do not lead to death has been explained in numerous ways. One approach is to explain it in terms of the OT distinction between sins committed unintentionally and sins commit-

228. Thompson, 'Intercession in the Johannine Community', 237-42, provides a helpful discussion of the role of intercession in the OT, Apocrypha, Pseudepigrapha, and Qumran literature. She concludes: 'The intercessory prayer of the righteous person secures forgiveness of sin and often preserves the life of the sinner. It can even be said that such intercession makes atonement. . . . But in all cases it is assumed that the sinner has confessed and repented of his or her transgression. . . . Moreover, in some instances of deliberate and continued sinning, intercession is expressly forbidden. In these cases it is clear that the very prohibition of intercessory prayer for the sinner is a part of God's judgment.'

229. Some manuscripts omit the negative particle 'not' *(ou)*, but its inclusion is very well attested.

ted defiantly (Lev 4:2; Num 15:22-25, 30-31; cf. 1QS 8:21–9:2). However, there is no hint in 1 John that this is the distinction the author has in mind. Another approach involves identifying the sin that leads to death with blasphemy against the Holy Spirit (Mark 3:28-30). This identification is most unlikely because it fails to note the explanation given by Mark concerning the nature of this sin, that is, that it involves ascribing the miracles of Jesus to the work of the devil. There is no hint of this in 1 John. A third approach identifies the sin that leads to death with what are regarded as particularly heinous offences, for example, adultery, murder, idolatry, and apostasy. This is also an unlikely explanation because there is little supporting evidence for it in 1 John itself. A fourth approach holds that the sin that leads to death is deliberate and persistent rejection of the truth. Such a sin would lead to death, but it is not clear that this is the line along which the author's thought proceeds here in 1 John.

A better approach is to examine who it is in 1 John that the author sees committing sins which do and do not lead to death. It is the 'brother' whose sin is not unto death for whom the readers are urged to pray. This suggests that the sin that does not lead to death is the sin of the believer. If this is the case, then the sin that does lead to death is most likely that of the unbeliever. Within the overall context of 1 John, where the secessionists are now regarded as unbelievers, even antichrists, the sin that leads to death is probably the sin of the secessionists, in particular their denial that Jesus is the Christ come in the flesh and that his death is necessary for salvation.[230] This explanation has the advantage of relating the matter of sins that lead and do not lead to death to the central issues being addressed by the letter.[231]

In 5:18-20 the author further reassures his readers by reminding them of their privileged position in Christ. This desire to reassure is reflected in the fact that each of these three verses begins with the words 'we know', as the author includes his readers with himself, reminding them of all that they have in Christ.

5:18　In the first place he reiterates something written earlier in the letter (cf. 3:9): **We know that anyone born of God does not continue to**

230. Tim Ward, 'Sin "Not unto Death" and Sin "Unto Death" in 1 John 5:16', *Churchman* 109 (1995), 236, writes: 'the distinction between the two sins must be found in the fact that sin "unto death" is the Christ-rejecting behavior evidenced by those who also deny their own sinfulness, their need for atonement, and Christ's ability to provide that atonement. Their sin is deadly because in the context of their current fundamental attitude towards Christ they have no hope of atonement'.

231. For a detailed discussion of the sin that leads to death, see Brown, *The Epistles of John*, 612-19.

sin. His readers, unlike the secessionists, have been born of God, and therefore they will not continue in sin.[232] By the use of a present tense form of the verb 'to sin', the author portrays the sinning here (as also in 3:9) as an ongoing process. In 3:9 the basis for the readers not continuing to sin was that they were born of God and God's 'seed' remained in them. Here in 5:18 the basis of their not sinning is put differently: **the one who was born of God keeps him**[233] **safe, and the evil one cannot harm him.** In 1 John most references to being born of God relate to believers (2:29; 3:9 [2x]; 4:7; 5:1, 4, 18 [1x]). However, the reference here in 5:18 to 'the one born of God' is best interpreted as a reference to Jesus himself.[234] That this is an appropriate interpretation is supported by the fact that in the Fourth Gospel Jesus is portrayed as the one who keeps his disciples safe. In Jesus' prayer in John 17 he speaks of having kept safe all those whom God had given him (except Judas, who was doomed to destruction), and prays, not that God will take them out of the world, but that he will 'protect them from the evil one' (John 17:12-15).[235]

This letter contains a number of references to 'the evil one'. In 2:13-14 the author twice refers to the 'young men' as those who have 'overcome the evil one', in 3:12 he warns readers not to be 'like Cain, who belonged to the evil one', and in 5:19 he speaks of the whole world being 'under the control of the evil one'. The author uses the term 'the evil one' interchangeably with the term 'the devil' (cf. 3:8, 10). The author's assurance that Jesus Christ will keep his readers safe from the harm that the evil one would inflict upon them is best understood, in the whole context of 1 John, as an assurance that Jesus Christ will keep them from being led astray by the false teaching of the secessionists.

5:19 Continuing to reassure his readers, the author, using the

232. See 'A Note on Sinless Perfectionism', pp. 126-32, for a full discussion of the nature of the 'sinlessness' of the believer.

233. Some manuscripts read 'himself' *(heauton)* instead of 'him' *(auton)*. A decision between these variants depends to a large extent upon whether 'the one born of God' is interpreted as the believer or as Christ. In this commentary 'the one born of God' is understood to refer to Christ, hence, with the NIV, we have adopted 'him', not 'himself'.

234. So, too, Strecker, *The Johannine Letters*, 208-9. Brown, *The Epistles of John*, 620-22, lists a number of possible interpretations of this verse, including those which identify 'the one born of God' with believers themselves, as well as one which interprets it as a reference to Christ. Brown himself favors the view that it is a reference to believers, but prefers to translate what follows as 'is protected' (rather than 'keeps him safe') so that the question of who protects whom (God protects the believer or the believer protects him/herself) is left open.

235. The problem with this interpretation is that nowhere else in the Johannine writings is Jesus described as 'born of God', unless one interprets 5:1 along those lines, an option already rejected in the commentary on that verse. However, the close parallel between John 17:12-15 and 1 John 5:18 is, perhaps, enough to enable us to ignore this fact.

second of his 'we know' expressions in 5:18-20, contrasts their position with that of the rest of the world: **We know that we are children of God, and that the whole world is under the control of the evil one.** The NIV has rather unnecessarily added the word 'children' in its translation of the first clause (literally translated it would read: 'we know that we are of God'). The contrast between true believers and those of the rest of the world is that the former belong to God, while the latter are under the control of (lit. 'lie in') the evil one. In the light of the previous verse, believers are no longer under the control of the evil one because Jesus Christ keeps them safe so that the evil one cannot harm them. The teaching that the rest of the world is under the control of the evil one has its counterpart in the Gospel of John, where three times (John 12:31; 14:30; 16:11) the evangelist mentions the prince (ruler) of this world *(ho archōn tou kosmou)*. In the context of 1 John, those in the world include the secessionists, whom the author now regards as belonging to the world (cf. 2:18-19 and 4:1-5).

5:20 The author's reassurance continues into this verse. Using now the third of his 'we know' expressions, he reminds his readers: **We know also that the Son of God has come and has given us understanding.** Two elements of the work of the Son of God are alluded to here, his coming as the historical Jesus, and his giving understanding to people when they became believers. The word translated 'understanding' *(dianoia)* is found only here in the Johannine writings, but the context makes its meaning clear enough: he has given us understanding **so that we may know him who is true.**[236] The understanding which the Son of God gives is knowledge of God the Father himself. In John 17:3 Jesus addresses his Father as 'the only true God'. That the author of 1 John refers to the God and Father of Jesus Christ when he uses the expression 'the one who is true' is made abundantly clear in the following sentence: **And we are in him who is true — even in his Son Jesus Christ.** The one who is true is the one whose Son is Jesus Christ. However, what the author wants to stress is that those who believe are actually 'in him who is true', that is, in God the Father, because they are 'in his Son Jesus Christ'.

What it means to be 'in him who is true — even in his Son Jesus Christ' is not easy to define. The general concept of believers dwelling in God/in his Son is found in nine other passages in the letter (2:5, 6, 24, 28; 3:6, 24; 4:13, 15, 16). Sometimes it is part of a broader concept: the mutual indwelling of believers in God and God in believers (3:24; 4:13, 15, 16). In

---

236. Some manuscripts have 'what is true' *(to alēthinon)* instead of 'who is true' *(ton alēthinon)*; however, the latter has the best attestation.

two of the four places where this mutual indwelling is mentioned, the author maintains that believers can be assured of it because of the Spirit whom God has given to them (3:24; 4:13). All this suggests that the expression 'in him who is true — even in his Son Jesus Christ' denotes a new and real spiritual existence that believers enjoy, which is effected through the agency of the Spirit.

The author reminds his readers that 'we are in him who is true' to reassure them of their standing as believers so as to counteract any doubts they may have because of the claims the secessionists were making. It is those who hold to the message passed on by the ones who heard it from Christ himself in the beginning who are 'in him who is true' because they are 'in his Son Jesus Christ'. There is no being in God without being in his Son Jesus Christ. Here the author is not only reassuring his readers but making plain that the secessionists' claims to be in God are invalid because they do not believe in God's Son.

Verse 20 concludes with the words: **He is the true God and eternal life.** It is difficult to know whether 'he' refers to God ('the one who is true') or to 'his Son Jesus Christ'. In the first case, the author would be emphasising that the Father of our Lord Jesus Christ is the true God and the source of eternal life, a noncontroversial statement (cf. John 17:3; 1 Thess 1:9, other texts which speak of 'the true God'). In the second case, the author would be saying that Jesus Christ himself is 'the true God and eternal life'. In preceding verses the author has already stressed that eternal life is to be found in Jesus Christ, so to say that Jesus Christ is 'eternal life' would come as no surprise. However, to maintain that Jesus Christ is the true God is striking. There is no other statement like it in 1 John, though there is such a statement in the Fourth Gospel (John 1:1: 'In the beginning was the Word, and the Word was with God, and the Word was God'). Supporting such an interpretation is the fact that 'Jesus Christ' is the closest antecedent for 'he' in the context. If it is right to interpret this text in this way, Schnackenburg's comment would be entirely appropriate:

> For here the full identity of Jesus with God is recognized without reserve (note the article with *theos*, God). This seems to occur intentionally at the end of the letter, at the climax of the triumphant expression of faith. It is hardly an accident that it is precisely at the beginning (1:1, 18) and the end (20:28) of the Gospel of John that the light of Jesus' divinity shines forth most fully. The climactic christological confession becomes visible here in all its clarity.[237]

237. Schnackenburg, *The Johannine Epistles*, 263.

Brown also understands the statement 'He is the true God and eternal life' to refer to Jesus Christ, and so constitutes a very strong affirmation of his divinity,[238] but later adds, 'Jesus may be God but he is not the Father'.[239]

A Note on the Bases of Assurance

The author of 1 John seeks to bolster the assurance of his readers, whose confidence in the message they had heard from the beginning had been shaken by the teaching of the secessionists. He does this by showing:

(i) *Assurance is based on God's testimony to his Son.* This note is sounded most clearly in 5:9-13, where the believer's assurance of eternal life is based on the testimony of God in their hearts. This is not the sort of 'testimony' of which Paul writes in Rom 8:16 ('The Spirit himself testifies with our spirit that we are God's children') but God's own witness concerning his Son. Those who believe that testimony may know that they have eternal life.

(ii) *Assurance in the day of judgement is based on righteous living.* In 1 John 2:28 we find one of four passages in which the author uses the Greek word *parrēsia* ('confidence' or 'boldness'). He urges his readers to abide in Christ 'so that when he is revealed we may have confidence [*parrēsia*] and not be put to shame before him at his coming', adding that 'if you know that he is righteous, you may be sure that everyone who does right has been born of him'. Here confidence is the opposite to being ashamed. Those who abide in Christ will have boldness when they stand face to face with him at his appearing, and not shrink back in shame. The abiding which forms the basis of this assurance is here associated with doing right and purifying oneself as Christ is pure, and showing oneself to be the child of God by doing what is right (see 3:4-11). The basis of assurance, then, in this text is righteous living.

(iii) *Assurance in prayer is based on loving action and concern.* In 3:21-22, the second of the passages in which the author uses the Greek word *parrēsia* ('confidence' or 'boldness'), he declares: 'Beloved, if our hearts do not condemn us, we have boldness [*parrēsia*] before God; and we receive from him whatever we ask, because we obey his commandments and do what pleases him'. In the commentary on

238. Brown, *The Epistles of John,* 626.
239. Brown, *The Epistles of John,* 640.

this verse we argued that 3:16-22 depicts a situation in which believers, when confronted by a brother or sister in genuine need that they are in a position to meet, do not shut their hearts against that brother or sister. Rather, they persuade their hearts to be generous, knowing that God sees all. If they persuade their hearts to be generous so that their hearts do not condemn them for their response to the need of the brother or sister, then the author says: 'we have confidence before God and receive from him anything we ask, because we obey his commands and do what pleases him' (3:21-22). In this case, assurance/boldness before God in prayer is based on loving response to those in need.

(iv) *Assurance on the day of judgement is based on loving action.* In 1 John 4:17, the third of the passages in which the author uses the Greek word *parrēsia* ('confidence' or 'boldness'), he writes: 'Love has been perfected among us in this: that we may have boldness [*parrēsia*] on the day of judgement'. The wider context of this passage (4:7-21) indicates that perfection of love involves genuine love for fellow believers. Those who love their brothers and sisters are those in whom love has been perfected (in action), and this results in confidence on the day of judgement.

(v) *Assurance in prayer is experienced when we ask according to his will.* In 5:14, the last of the passages in which the Greek word *parrēsia* ('confidence' or 'boldness') is found, the author asserts: 'And this is the boldness [*parrēsia*] we have in him, that if we ask anything according to his will, he hears us'. Here boldness is associated with prayer 'according to his will', and the sort of prayer the author has in mind is a request for the restoration of fellow believers who commit sins that are not 'mortal'.

(vi) *Assurance is based on obedience to the love command.* This is a fairly pervasive theme in 1 John. It is found in passages like 2:3-6, which in its context indicates that when God's love is fulfilled in us in acts of love towards fellow believers we keep his command and this results in our being sure that we know him. A similar statement is made in 3:14, where the author says that the believer's assurance arises out of his/her obedience to the love command.

(vii) *Assurance is based on the Spirit's testimony to Christ.* Two passages link assurance to the work of the Spirit in believers. But in both of these passages the Spirit's work in them is to confirm the orthodox confession of Christ. In the first of these, 3:24–4:3, the author says: 'And this is how we know that he lives in us: We know it by the Spirit he gave us' (3:24); and as the passage unfolds it becomes clear that the Spirit's role is to testify to the truth about Christ. In the second of the passages, 4:13-15, the connection between the assurance of abiding in him, the Spirit, and the orthodox confession is not explicit, but the context seems to point in that direction.

The striking thing about the bases of Christian assurance in 1 John is that they all appear to be related to objective rather than subjective criteria. Whether it be a matter of confidence on the day of judgement, confidence in prayer, or inner assurance that one knows God or abides in him, in every case the author notes that it is closely connected with right belief and right behaviour (especially loving acts for the benefit of others). Robert Law sums up what we have been saying in the following words:

> With St. John the grounds of assurance are ethical, not emotional; objective, not subjective; plain and tangible, not microscopic and elusive. They are three, or rather, they are a trinity: Belief, Righteousness, Love. By his belief in Christ, his keeping God's commandments, and his love to the brethren, a Christian man is recognized and recognizes himself as begotten of God.[240]

Pastorally this would seem to be of very great importance, not least in those circles where assurance is connected only to faith in God's promises or where assurance is connected to a person's experience of the Spirit. Of course, neither of these emphases is wrong in itself, and both find support elsewhere in the NT. However, when these things do not quell a person's fears and lack of assurance, the reasons may well be found in those matters which the author of 1 John stresses.

5:21 This final verse stands in contrast to 5:18-20, where the privileges of believers are described as being born of God, being the children of God, and especially knowing him that is true, that is, the true God. The exhortation, **Dear children, keep yourselves from idols**, enshrines the obligation of those who know the true God to have nothing to do with idols. What exactly the author had in mind in issuing this exhortation has puzzled interpreters. Is it to be taken literally as a warning against idolatry, and, if so, how should it then be related to the message of the letter as a whole? Or is it to be taken metaphorically and, if so, with what meaning? Not surprisingly many interpretations have been offered.

Among those who interpret idols here literally is Edwards, who ar-

---

240. Robert Law, *The Tests of Life: A Study of the First Epistle of St. John* (Grand Rapids: Baker, 1968 [reprinted from 3rd ed., Edinburgh: T. & T. Clark, 1913]) 207. Cf. the discussion in B. A. du Toit, 'The Role and Meaning of Statements of "Certainty" in the Structural Composition of 1 John', *Neot* 13 (1979) 84-100.

gues that the author's exhortation should be understood against the background of persecution, as when pagans demanded of Christians that they offer sacrifice to idols. Those who deny that Jesus is the Christ in this letter (2:22-23; 4:3; cf. 2 John 7) are people who yield to these pagan demands so as to avoid martyrdom. The author's reference, then, to Jesus coming by blood, as well as by water (5:6), is a reminder that Jesus himself paid the price for his testimony, and so must those who follow him. The exhortation, 'Jesus Christ laid down his life for us. And we ought to lay down our lives for our brothers' (3:16), also makes sense against the background of persecution because the betrayal of Christ before idols involved the betrayal of fellow believers as well.[241] Stegemann adopts a similar interpretation, arguing that 5:21 is an exhortation to avoid apostasy, not heresy.[242] Hills also believes that the author's reference to idols must be taken literally, and supports the view by arguing that 1 John draws upon OT traditions, especially Deutero-Isaiah. There the theme of witness is explicitly connected to the critique of idolatry. Hills argues that the author of 1 John likewise connects the theme of witness (which features prominently in his letter) with the rejection of idolatry.[243] Strecker argues that the author's exhortation to keep oneself from idols is related to the matter of sin that leads to death treated in 5:16-17, and that apostasy, in particular worship of idols, is an example of such a sin.[244]

Among those who interpret idols metaphorically is Sugit, who suggests that the word 'idol' (eidōlon) should be understood to mean 'phantom'. He bases his case on the meaning of eidōlon in classical Greek (phantom, ghost, mental image, falseness, fancy, unreality) and on its association with the unreality of idols in places in the LXX as well as the NT, where Paul asks, 'Do I mean then that a sacrifice offered to an idol is anything, or that an idol is anything?' (1 Cor 10:19). All this suggests that while the common meaning of eidōlon was 'idol', its original meaning of 'phantom' was never altogether forgotten. The injunction of 5:21 can then be understood as 'keep yourself from phantoms', meaning the 'imaginations of Docetics and those who deny the reality of the human life and the risen body of Jesus Christ'.[245] Schnackenburg also gives idols here a nonliteral meaning. He cites W. Nauck's view with approval, namely,

241. Edwards, 'Martyrdom and the First Epistle of John', 166-70.

242. Ekkehard Stegemann, ' "Kindlein, hütet vor den Götterbildern!" Erwägungen zum Schluss des 1. Johannesbriefes', TZ 41 (1985) 289.

243. Julian Hills, ' "Little Children, Keep Yourselves from Idols": 1 John 5:21 Reconsidered', CBQ 51 (1989) 301-2, 304-7.

244. Strecker, The Johannine Letters, 214.

245. J. N. Sugit, 'I John 5:21: ΤΕΚΝΙΑ, ΦΥΛΑΞΑΤΕ ΕΑΥΤΑ ΑΠΟ ΤΩΝ ΕΙΔΩΛΩΝ', JTS 36 (1985) 386-90.

that the word 'idols' here really stands for 'sin as a satanic power', and the exhortation to keep oneself from idols is but a warning to keep oneself from sin.[246] Brown lists ten possible explanations of idols here, both literal and nonliteral, but argues that it is best understood as a reference to the secession: 'In speaking of joining the secession and accepting its theology as "going after idols", the author would have been intelligible to a Christian community whose language and thought had Jewish parallels — a background we have found in both the Gospel of John and 1 John'.[247]

Many of these suggestions have merit, and it is hard to be decisive one way or another in the light of such scholarly variety. What does seem clear is that in the immediate context keeping oneself from idols is the necessary concomitant of knowing the true God through Jesus Christ. But in the context of the letter as a whole it is not the pagans who do not know the true God, but the secessionists (cf. 1:6; 2:4). For this reason, Brown's suggestion that the author's exhortation relates to the secessionists is probably the best, that is, it is an exhortation not to accept the false teaching of the secessionists.

---

246. Schnackenburg, *The Johannine Epistles*, 263-64.
247. Brown, *The Epistles of John*, 627-28.

Commentary on 2 John

This brief letter was written primarily to warn the readers about certain itinerant deceivers, and of the dire consequences of welcoming such people and thereby sharing in their 'wicked work'. It has a secondary and related purpose of reminding the readers of the command to love one another which they received 'at the beginning', and so ensuring that both writer and readers persist in their relationship of mutual love. In this way the writer seeks to make sure that the deceivers do not succeed in alienating the readers from fellowship with him. The paraenetic nature of the letter, comprising both encouragement and dissuasion, suggests that the writer is on friendly terms with the readers and that they regard him as a 'friendly superior'.[1] (See the Introduction, pp. 36-40, for a fuller discussion of the provenance of this letter.)

1-3 OPENING GREETINGS

v. 1   Unlike 1 John, this letter *does* begin with the usual A to B greeting formula, and the author *does* identify himself, but not as clearly as we, the modern readers, might like. He introduces himself simply as **the elder**. His self-references in the rest of the letter are entirely in the first person (unlike 1 John, where the author uses the first person plural in some places to associate himself with other eyewitnesses of the incarnate Christ). The term 'elder' may not denote an official position in the

---

1. Duane F. Watson, 'A Rhetorical Analysis of 2 John according to Greco-Roman Convention', *NTS* 35 (1989) 108.

church, for where office is indicated in the NT a plural form ('elders', *presbyteroi*) is always used, not the singular ('elder', *presbyteros*), as here. However, the fact that two such brief letters by the elder (2 John and 3 John) have been incorporated in the NT canon is strong evidence of the importance of the author and possibly indicates that he was 'the principal authority' in his circle, as Strecker suggests.[2] The term 'elder' itself does not necessarily indicate a person of advanced years. However, the paternal attitude the elder adopts towards his readers in this letter indicates that this was probably the case in this instance. See the Introduction, pp. 13-14, 36-37, for a discussion of the identity of 'the elder'.

The letter is addressed to **the chosen lady** *(eklektē kyria)* **and her children**. The expression *eklektē kyria* has been variously interpreted. Brown lists five possibilities: (i) 'the lady Electa', referring to a certain Babylonian woman called 'Electa'; (ii) 'the noble Kyria'; (iii) a term of courteous address to an individual woman: 'dear lady'; (iv) a term denoting the church at large; (v) part of a larger expression, 'the elect lady and her children', which is a metaphorical way of addressing a local church and its members.[3] This last alternative is the choice of most modern interpreters, and is supported by four considerations: (i) While the addressees are referred to as 'the chosen lady and her children' in verse 1 and the elder says 'it has given me great joy to find some of your [singular] children walking in the truth' in verse 4, in the rest of the letter (vv. 6, 8, 10, 12) he addresses all his readers in the second person plural ('you'), suggesting that 'the chosen lady and her children' is another way of addressing all members of a local church. (ii) In the OT and the Apocrypha Israel is referred to as a wife, bride, mother, and daughter,[4] indicating that there would have been some precedent for a Christian community to be addressed in similar terms. (iii) In 1 Pet 5:13 the church in Rome is described as 'she who is in Babylon', indicating that NT Christians could speak of a Christian community as a woman. (iv) The letter closes with the words 'the children of your chosen sister send their greetings' (v. 13), which ap-

---

2. Georg Strecker, *The Johannine Letters* (Hermeneia, Philadelphia: Fortress, 1996) 219.

3. Raymond E. Brown, *The Epistles of John* (AB 30, New York: Doubleday, 1982) 652-54.

4. Hans-Josef Klauck, '*Kyria ekklēsia* in Bauers Wörterbuch und die Exegese des zweiten Johannesbriefes', *ZNW* 81 (1990) 135-38, points out that BAG is misleading when it cites Hellenistic sources (which include references to *kyria ekklēsia*) in support of an interpretation of *eklektē kyria* as lady congregation. The references cited refer to an Athenian assembly and provide no support for a metaphorical interpretation of the *kyria ekklēsia*. However, Klauck agrees with most modern commentators, nevertheless, that *eklektē kyria* does refer to the congregation, and finds support for this in the many references in the OT and Apocrypha to Israel as wife, bride, mother, daughter, etc.

pears to be a way of conveying the greetings of the elder's Christian community to his readers. If this is the case, then the letter opens and closes with references to Christian communities: the one to which this letter is sent ('the chosen lady and her children'), and the one to which the elder belongs ('the children of your chosen sister').

The elder describes members of the Christian community to whom he writes as those **whom I love in the truth** *(en alētheia)*. The expression *en alētheia* can be construed in two ways: (i) 'in the truth' (as in the NIV); or (ii) 'truly'. In the first case, the elder would be saying that he loves the readers, who, like him, are 'in the truth', that is, those who continue faithful to the truth concerning Jesus Christ as it was heard at the beginning. In the second case the elder would be simply saying that he 'truly' loves his readers. The first option probably reflects what the elder intended, for he adds that it is **not I only, but also all who know the truth** who love the readers. Taken together, what he is emphasising is the community of love that exists among those who 'know the truth'; those who are 'in the truth'. The affirmation in the opening greeting of the letter that his readers are 'in the truth' would serve to silence doubts that may have arisen in their minds as a result of the teaching of the secessionists.

v. 2 Here the elder explains that this community of love exists among those who know the truth: **because of the truth, which lives in us and will be with us forever**. On the surface, the text appears to indicate that the truth of the message has been internalised by believers so that it 'lives in' them and this is what creates the community of love. The text may also be alluding to Christ, as the embodiment of truth (cf. John 14:6), who lives in believers and who will be with them 'forever'.[5] In this case, the community of love is created not simply by believers internalising the truth of the gospel, but also by the indwelling of Christ, who is the embodiment of the gospel message, in each of them. Either way it boils down to much the same thing, for one cannot know the truth without knowing the person of Christ who first proclaimed it and also embodied it. If the elder is alluding to the presence of Christ within his readers and assuring them of Christ's presence with them forever, this would function as a further encouragement to people unsettled by the secessionists' teaching.

v. 3 The opening greeting concludes with the words, **Grace, mercy and peace from God the Father and from Jesus Christ, the Father's Son,**

5. In the Fourth Gospel, Jesus promises his disciples that he will not leave them 'orphaned' but that he will come to them and abide with them forever, something which was to be effected by the coming of the Holy Spirit (cf. John 14:18-20).

will be with us in truth and love. Most NT letters include an expression of the writer's desire that the readers experience the grace and peace that come from God (Rom 1:7; 1 Cor 1:3; 2 Cor 1:2; Gal 1:3; Eph 1:2; Phil 1:2; Col 1:2; 1 Thess 1:1; 2 Thess 1:2; 1 Tim 1:2; 2 Tim 1:2; Titus 1:4; Phlm 3; 1 Pet 1:2; 2 Pet 1:2; Jude 2; Rev 1:4). What is found here in 2 John differs from the norm in several ways: (i) Here it is not so much a wish as an affirmation that grace, mercy, and peace will be with the writer and readers. (ii) Emphasis is placed on the fact that these blessings will be with them by placing the words 'will be with us' *(estai meth' hēmōn)* at the beginning of the sentence in the original language. (iii) The affirmation relates to the experience of both writer and readers ('with us'), not just readers. (iv) To the name Jesus Christ is added the description, 'the Father's Son'. (v) Grace, mercy and peace, the text says, will be with them 'in truth and love'. Each of these variations from the norm reflects something of the elder's concerns as he writes this brief letter. He reassures his readers by emphasising that God's grace, mercy, and peace will be with them, despite what the secessionists might say. He includes himself with his readers as a recipient of these blessings to reinforce the sense of their community of love. He emphasises that these blessings come from God the Father and Jesus Christ, 'the Father's Son', reflecting the truth about Jesus which he defends against the secessionists' teaching. He adds that these blessings from God are experienced 'in truth and love', a rather imprecise expression, possibly meaning that the blessings are experienced by those who continue to hold to the truth and practise love among themselves;[6] something he believes he and his readers do, but the secessionists do not.

4-6 WALKING IN THE TRUTH

In this passage the elder expresses his joy at having found some of the members of the church to which he writes walking in the truth. He asks that he and they might continue in a relationship of mutual love, something which was under threat due to the influence of the secessionists.

Several difficulties face the interpreter of this passage. These relate to the relationship between walking in the truth (v. 4) and obeying the love command (v. 5); the distinction, if any, between the commandment

---

6. Rudolf Schnackenburg, *The Johannine Epistles* (Tunbridge Wells, Kent: Burns & Oates, 1992) 281, suggests that 'truth and love' here are to be understood as 'the effect the divine blessing has upon the believers'.

(singular, v. 5) and the commandments (plural, v. 6); and the meaning of walking 'in it' (v. 6).[7] These will be addressed as we come to them.

v. 4 In the opening greeting the elder stated that he loved his readers 'in the truth', as did all those who 'know the truth', 'because of the truth' that lived in them both. He also assured them that God's grace, mercy, and peace would be with them 'in truth and love'. Continuing now in similar vein, he adds: **It has given me great joy to find some of your children walking in the truth**. To walk in the truth means to live in accordance with the truth of the message of the gospel as it was received in the beginning. The elder rejoices greatly that 'some of your children' are walking in the truth. On the surface, this might imply that some were not, that some had already succumbed to the deceit of the secessionists (cf. vv. 7-9). But there is no indication elsewhere in the letter that this is the case, so it is best to regard the elder's statement as expressing joy over those he has heard are walking in the truth, without implying that others are not. The elder, speaking about those who were walking in the truth, says that they were doing so **just as the Father commanded us** (lit. 'just as we received commandment from the Father'). What was the command of the Father, and when was it received? There are three possibilities to consider: (i) It is an allusion to the voice from heaven at the time of Jesus' transfiguration which said to Peter, James, and John: 'This is my Son, whom I love. Listen to him!' (Mark 9:7/Matt 17:5). (ii) It is a recognition that the teaching of Jesus was teaching that the Father had commanded him to pass on (cf. Jesus' words in John 12:50: 'Whatever I say is just what the Father has told me to say'). (iii) It is an equating of the gospel message itself with the Father's command. This last option is probably the correct one, for in 1 John 3:23 we find: 'And this is his command: to believe in the name of his Son, Jesus Christ, and to love one another as he commanded us'. It would appear that the elder's purpose in this verse was to reinforce his readers' commitment to the truth by telling them how much joy their doing so brings to their 'friendly superior'.

v. 5 Having explained how much joy it brings him to find members of the church walking in the truth, the elder now comes to a specific request in this brief section of the letter: **And now, dear lady, I am not writing you a new command but one we have had from the beginning. I ask that we love one another.** The request is that the elder and 'the dear lady' (i.e., the church) persist in their mutual love for one another. By making this request he is not seeking to lay on members of the church any new obligation; he is calling on them to obey the command

7. Cf. Urban C. von Wahlde, 'The Theological Foundation of the Presbyter's Argument in 2 Jn (2 Jn 4-6)', *ZNW* 76 (1985) 209-10.

they both received 'at the beginning'. The elder is referring back to the time when they first heard the gospel message (see 'A Note on "From the Beginning" [*ap' archēs*]', p. 57). The message they heard included the command of the Lord Jesus that those who believe in him should 'love one another'. This is the last of six references to Jesus' command that his disciples should love one another found in the Letters of John (the others are contained in 1 John 3:11, 23; 4:7, 11, 12). They are probably all dependent on the account of the Last Supper discourses found in the Fourth Gospel (cf. John 13:34; 15:12, 17). There are other allusions to Jesus' command (though not dependent on the Fourth Gospel) in Rom 13:8, 1 Thess 4:9, and 1 Pet 1:22. The elder expresses Jesus' command using the present subjunctive form of the verb 'to love', indicating that he has in mind an ongoing love of fellow believers. His purpose in making this appeal is almost certainly to counteract the influence of the secessionists on his readers.

v. 6 Having urged his readers to persist in mutual love, the elder now defines that love: **And this is love: that we walk in obedience to his commands.** In the Fourth Gospel Jesus defines his disciples' love for himself in terms of their obedience to his commands in general (John 15:10, 14), and in the same context he interprets that general obedience in terms of obedience to his command that they love one another (John 15:12). A similar pattern is found here in verse 6. Having defined love as walking 'in obedience to his commands' (plural), the elder defines that obedience in terms of a single command: **As you have heard from the beginning, his command is that you walk in love** (lit. 'that you walk in it', *hina en autē peripatēte*). The NIV translation interprets walking 'in it' to mean walking 'in love', a rendering which has much to commend it: (i) *autē* ('it') is a feminine pronoun and could therefore have *agapē* ('love'), a feminine noun, as its antecedent; (ii) love for one another is the primary focus of vv. 5-6 which form the immediate context of the words 'that you walk in it'.[8] An alternative approach would be to interpret 'in it' to mean 'in the truth'. In favour of this interpretation one should note that: (i) the feminine pronoun *autē* ('it') could also have as its antecedent the feminine noun *alētheia* ('truth'); (ii) the expression 'walking in the truth' appears in v. 4, and to 'walk in it' in v. 6 could be a parallel statement concluding the section vv. 4-6 on the same note with which it began.[9] Another approach to the interpretation of 'in it' is to regard *en autē* in v. 6 as an example of semantic density, that is, at this point the author deliberately intends the reader to understand that the antecedents of *autē* ('it') are *alētheia* ('truth'),

---

8. So Schnackenburg, *The Johannine Epistles*, 281.
9. So von Wahlde, 'The Theological Foundation of the Presbyter's Argument', 221.

entolē ('commandment'), and *agapē* ('love'). To walk in 'it', then, would be to walk in truth and love.[10]

One of the latter approaches which relate walking 'in it' to walking 'in the truth' is preferable because v. 7 which follows (and is logically connected with v. 6 by the conjunction *hoti* ['because'], which is left untranslated in the NIV) indicates why it is so important to walk in this way: '[because] many deceivers . . . have gone out into the world'.

7-9 DENIAL OF THE TRUTH

v. 7 A conjunction, 'because' *(hoti)*, left untranslated in the NIV, links the previous verse with this one and enables us to see why the elder regarded it so important for his readers to walk in the truth: **[because] many deceivers, who do not acknowledge Jesus Christ as coming in the flesh, have gone out into the world**. The way to avoid being taken in by deceivers is to continue walking in the truth. The deceivers mentioned here are people who 'have gone out into the world'. This is one of three texts found in the Letters of John that refer to people 'going out' (the others are 1 John 2:19: 'They went out from us, but they did not really belong to us. For if they had belonged to us, they would have remained with us; but their going showed that none of them belonged to us'; and 1 John 4:1: 'Dear friends, do not believe every spirit, but test the spirits to see whether they are from God, because many false prophets have gone out into the world'). As we argued in the Introduction (pp. 2, 15-16), each of these texts refers to the secessionists. It was these erstwhile members of the Christian community who were seeking to deceive those who remained in it (cf. 1 John 2:26; 3:7).

The elder states the nature of the secessionists' doctrinal aberration with which they were seeking to deceive his readers: they 'do not acknowledge Jesus Christ as coming in the flesh'. Based on a study of 1 John (see the commentary on 1 John 4:2-3a), we may say that what the secessionists denied, when stated fully, was that Jesus was the Christ, the Son of God come in the flesh, and the reality of his atoning death. The author of 1 John could signal this whole complex of ideas by referring to just one or another aspect of it (cf. 1 John 2:22; 4:2, 3; 4:15; 5:1, 5, 6), and it is probably best to read the present verse in the same way. The aspect of the false teaching picked up here is the reality of Jesus Christ's humanity (his

10. E. R. Wendland, 'What Is Truth? Semantic Density and the Language of the Johannine Epistles (with special reference to 2 John)', *Neot* 24 (1990) 310-11.

'coming in the flesh'), but this cannot be divorced from the purpose of his coming in the flesh, that is, to give himself as the atoning sacrifice for our sins (cf. 1 John 1:7; 2:2; 3:5; 4:10).

It is worth noting that, whereas in 1 John 4:2 the author used a perfect form of the verb 'to come' when speaking of Jesus' having come in the flesh, here the elder uses a present form of the verb. The former focuses upon Christ's status as one who came in the flesh, while the latter focuses upon the process of his coming in flesh. Some have suggested that the elder's use of the present form of the verb here points to Jesus Christ's future coming, his *parousia*.[11] Such an interpretation would have the secessionists denying the 'in the flesh' nature of both the first and second comings of Jesus Christ. The problem with this interpretation is that there are no hints elsewhere in the Johannine letters that the secessionists denied the 'in the flesh' nature of Jesus' coming *parousia*.

Any such person is the deceiver and the antichrist (lit. 'this is the deceiver and the antichrist'). Like the author of 1 John, who twice warns his readers against those who would deceive them (1 John 2:26; 3:7), the elder wants his readers to recognise those who deny 'Jesus Christ as coming in the flesh' for what they are: deceivers. By using the singular forms ('deceiver', 'antichrist') the elder may be implying that while 'many deceivers' (v. 1) have gone out into the world, what they are doing is the work of 'the deceiver', 'the antichrist'. In 1 John 2:18, 22; 4:3 the author indicates a connection between the secessionists, whom he describes as 'antichrists' (plural) who have already come, and the coming of 'the antichrist' (singular) towards the end of the age.

A full discussion of the expression 'antichrist' and its significance is included in the commentary on 1 John 2:18. Here it is sufficient to include a summary of the main points: First, the general concept of a powerful end-time figure opposed to God is found in Jewish apocalyptic writings, and it is probably in these writings that the background to the antichrist concept of 1 and 2 John is to be found. Second, it is clear that the coming of a powerful antichrist figure was part of early Christian teaching. Third, in early Christian teaching a distinction was made between the great antichrist figure who will appear near the very end, and lesser antichrist figures whose influence is already being felt. Fourth, it was widely recognised that the function of both the antichrist figure and those who precede him is to deceive people. Fifth, in NT sources apart from 1 and 2 John, the antichrist figures attack the church from without, and sometimes the portrayal of these figures has clear political overtones (Matthew/Mark, Revelation). Sixth, only in 1 and 2 John are antichrist figures

11. So Brown, *The Epistles of John*, 670, but less clearly on 686.

identified as former members of a Christian community. Seventh, while human beings certainly can function as antichrist figures (plural), the depiction of 'the antichrist' (singular) in both Jewish apocalyptic and NT writings involves characteristics which suggest a superhuman being in opposition to God and his purposes.

v. 8 Because of the threat of the deceivers, the elder warns his readers: **Watch out that you do not lose what you have worked for, but that you may be rewarded fully.** At this point in the text there are significant textual variants.[12] Most significant is the fact that some manuscripts read 'what *we* have worked for' (adopted in the NRSV) instead of 'what *you* have worked for' (found in the NIV).

If we adopt the NIV reading, what the readers must avoid losing is something for which *they* have worked. The 'work' of the readers would be their faith in Christ, and what they have worked for is eternal life. In John 6:27 Jesus says: 'Do not work for food that spoils, but for food that endures to eternal life, which the Son of Man will give you.' A verse or two later, when asked what is involved in doing the work of God, Jesus replies: 'The work of God is this: to believe in the one he has sent.'[13]

If we adopt the NRSV reading, the readers are urged to take care lest they lose something the elder and his associates[14] have worked to

12. A small number of inferior manuscripts have 'we do not lose . . . we may be rewarded' instead of 'you do not lose . . . you may be rewarded', and it is clear that the latter is the original because it is congruent with the second person plural 'watch out'. The more significant set of variants is that which offers either 'what we have worked for' and 'what you have worked for'. There is more external evidence for the latter, but the former is more intrinsically probable, as a scribe would be more likely to change 'we have worked for' to 'you have worked for' to put all the verbs in this verse into the second person plural, so that we then would have: '[*you*] watch out that *you* do not lose what *you* have worked for', rather than '[*you*] watch out that *you* do not lose what *we* have worked for'.

13. Another approach to understanding the work of the readers would be to study the use of the word group 'to work' *(ergazomai)* or 'work' *(ergon)*, in 1, 2, and 3 John. This would enable us to see the ways in which people's work is understood in these letters. In 1 John 3:12 Abel's works *(erga)* are described as righteous in contrast to Cain's, which were evil; in 1 John 3:18 the readers are exhorted to love with action *(ergō)* and in truth; in 2 John 11 the readers are urged not to provide hospitality for itinerant heretics lest they then share in their wicked works *(ergois)*; in 3 John 5 Gaius is commended for working *(ergasē)* to provide hospitality for the orthodox itinerants; and in 3 John 10 the elder threatens to expose the evil works *(erga)* of Diotrephes, who refuses to provide hospitality for the orthodox itinerants. In each case the works are what may be described as the 'good works' of the faithful. What the elder would then be warning the readers about is the loss of what *they* have worked for, the reward *(misthos)* that God will give them for their good works. However, such an approach ignores the way work and belief in Christ are interconnected in the Johannine writings.

14. There is another way of interpreting this second alternative: the 'we' means not just the elder and his associates, but the elder and his readers, i.e., the 'we' is inclusive,

provide for them. This again is best understood in terms of the readers' faith in Christ and the reward of eternal life which it brings. The elder has worked to make known the truth of Christ to them so that they might know God and have eternal life. In the very next verse the elder warns his readers against leaving behind the 'teaching of Christ', for that would result in their not 'having God' and therefore not having eternal life either.

v. 9 Here the elder makes plain what he fears: **Anyone who runs ahead and does not continue in the teaching of Christ does not have God.** Faced with the teaching of the secessionists, his readers were in danger of running ahead after new and spurious ideas instead of continuing in the teaching of Christ,[15] that is, in the gospel as they heard it from faithful witnesses in the beginning. It is tempting to speculate whether the expression 'running ahead' reflects the way the secessionists understood their teaching; new insights that ran beyond the old message and rendered the old message obsolete. Whether or not the secessionists saw it that way, the elder certainly did, and his letter stands as a warning against embracing avant-garde teaching simply because it is novel. For, as the elder claims, those who go ahead in this way, and do not continue in the teaching of Christ, do not have God. The secessionists, by running ahead and leaving behind the teaching of Christ, show that they do not have God.

However, it is also true that **whoever continues in the teaching[16] has both the Father and the Son**. The elder's purpose is, by stressing this, to encourage his readers to resist the pressure being applied by the secessionists, and to urge them to hold fast to the teaching of Christ; for in so doing they have 'both the Father and the Son'. In the letters of John, to have God is to know God and have eternal life, and this is possible only by having the Son (see the commentary on 1 John 5:12-13 and 'A Note on Eternal Life', pp. 184-87). But to have both the Father and the Son should perhaps be understood in the light of John 14:23, where Jesus says: 'If anyone loves me, he

---

not exclusive. However, the alternation between the 'you' and the 'we' would then be pointless.

15. Wendland, 'What Is Truth?' 310, notes that the 'teaching of Christ' *(didachē tou Christou)* could be construed as either an subjective genitive ('what Christ taught') or an objective genitive ('teaching about Christ'), but suggests that this is another example of what he calls semantic density, where the author intended both meanings to be picked up by the readers. That is, it was important not only to confess that Jesus Christ had come in the flesh (teaching about Christ), but also to acknowledge and obey Christ's teaching/command to love one another.

16. Some manuscripts read 'his teaching' *(tē didachē autou)* or 'the teaching of Christ' *(tē didachē tou Christou)* or even 'the righteousness of Christ' *(tē dikaiosynē tou Christou)* instead of simply 'the teaching' *(tē didachē)*. None of these alternatives is well attested, and all are clearly later scribal alterations.

will obey my teaching. My Father will love him, and we will come to him and make our home with him.' In this case 'having' the Father and the Son would involve not only knowing them but also the indwelling of the believer by the Father and the Son through the Spirit.

10-11 DO NOT RECEIVE THOSE
WHO DENY THE TRUTH

In these verses the elder advocates practical steps to be taken by his readers to limit the influence of the secessionists. In a word, he urges them not to provide hospitality to anyone who comes with a gospel different from the one they received. To appreciate the force of this exhortation it is necessary to understand the norms of hospitality operative at the time, which involved hosts in guaranteeing their guests as worthy individuals to the rest of the community (see 'A Note on Hospitality', pp. 215-16).

v. 10 The elder begins, **If anyone comes to you and does not bring this teaching. . . .** The teaching mentioned here is the 'teaching of Christ' referred to in the previous verse, that is, the message which the readers heard in the beginning. If anyone comes to them and does not bring this teaching, but brings instead a teaching that is at variance with it, the elder says, **do not take him into your house or welcome him** (lit. 'and do not say to him "greetings"').[17]

The expression, 'take him into your house *(oikian)*', could be understood in two ways. First it could be taken to mean receiving someone into one's home, that is, providing the person with hospitality. The provision of hospitality for itinerant Christians was very important in the early days of the church. There were inns, but these were of doubtful reputation, and most travellers preferred to find lodging with friends, relatives, acquaintances, or those to whom they bore letters of introduction and recommendation.[18] Those who welcomed and provided hospitality to travellers were providing them with patronage so that they would have the standing of protégé or guest in the community and so enjoy the protection afforded by the local laws. Otherwise they had no rights; 'no standing in law or custom'.[19]

17. Schnackenburg, *The Johannine Epistles,* 287, notes similar warnings given by Ignatius to his readers in Ign. *Eph.* 7:1; 8:1; 9:1; Ign. *Smyrn.* 4:1; 5:1; 7:2.

18. Abraham J. Malherbe, 'Hospitality and Inhospitality in the Church', in *Social Aspects of the Early Church* (2nd enl. ed., Philadelphia: Fortress, 1983) 94-96.

19. Bruce J. Malina, 'The Received View and What It Cannot Do: III John and Hospitality', *Semeia* 35 (1986) 181-83.

Second, it could be taken to mean receiving an itinerant preacher in the assembly of a house church. This letter is addressed to 'the chosen lady and her children' (v. 1), which we have taken to refer to a church and its members, not an individual and her children. This being the case, the elder could well be advising the members of the house church not to receive heretical teachers into the assembly of the church,[20] implying that they not be given opportunity to propagate their beliefs. These two alternatives are not mutually exclusive, for in the early days the church met in someone's home.

The elder not only counsels his readers against taking the purveyors of aberrant teaching into their houses, but even against saying 'welcome' (lit. 'greetings', *chairein*) to them. The word *chairein* was used as a rather bland greeting at the beginning of Greek letters. It is found in a number of places in the NT with this meaning (Acts 15:23; 23:26; Jas 1:1). However, in the NT greetings between believers usually carry a much stronger Christian content (cf., e.g., 1 Cor. 1:3: 'Grace and peace to you from God our Father and the Lord Jesus Christ'). Perhaps the elder's counsel to his readers not to greet the secessionists is to be understood in the light of the fact that Christian greetings generally carried a recognition of the Christian standing of those being greeted — a standing the elder believed the secessionist did not have any longer.

v. 11   Anyone who welcomes him (lit. 'he who says to him, "greetings"') **shares in his wicked work.** Because hosts acted as guarantors for their guests to the rest of the community, and because Christian greetings generally carried a recognition of the true Christian standing of those greeted (cf. v. 3) and invoked a blessing upon them (cf. Matt 10:13/Luke 10:6), the elder knew that it was not possible for his readers to 'greet' the secessionists without that greeting implying a recognition of the secessionists' Christian standing, and thus identifying themselves with their 'wicked work'. Their 'wicked work', of course, was propagating aberrant teaching. If his readers greeted these people or took them into their house(s), they would be associating themselves with the work the secessionists did.

When the elder maintains that anyone who welcomes or takes one of the secessionists into his house will share in his wicked work, he may be alluding to something more than sharing in their work by mere association. The word 'to share' *(koinōneō)* can carry connotations of a more for-

---

20. There are a number of references to the church that meets in so and so's house in the NT (Rom 16:5; 1 Cor 16:19; Col 4:15; 1 Tim 3:15; Phlm 2), though the word *oikos*, not *oikia*, is found in all these references. The word *oikia* is used in 1 Cor 16:15 and Phil 4:22 to refer to Stephanus's *household* and believers in Caesar's *household* respectively.

mal relationship. If there was in the elder's community a formal arrangement between missionaries who went out and Christian groups who received them, then the sharing the elder speaks about may have been a much more binding arrangement than that involved in simply providing hospitality for a traveller (see 'A Note on the Meaning of "Fellowship" (koinōnia)', pp. 59-61).

A Note on Hospitality

Malina provides a very helpful description of the nature of hospitality in the Mediterranean world. Hospitality 'might be defined as the process by means of which an outsider's status is changed from stranger to guest'.[21] Hospitality, then, is not something a person provides for family or friends but for strangers. They need such hospitality, for otherwise they will be treated as nonhuman because they are potentially a threat to the community. Strangers had no standing in law or custom, and therefore they needed a patron in the community they were visiting. There was no universal brotherhood in the ancient Mediterranean world.[22]

There were certain 'rules' to be observed by guests and hosts. Guests must not (i) insult their host or show any kind of hostility or rivalry; (ii) usurp the role of their host in any way, for example, by making themselves at home when not invited to do so, ordering the dependents of the host about, making demands of their host, etc.; (iii) refuse what is offered, especially food. Hosts must not (i) insult their guests or make any show of hostility or rivalry; (ii) neglect to protect their guests' honour; (iii) fail to show concern for the needs of their guests.[23]

Hospitality was not reciprocated between individuals (because once people became guests they were no longer strangers), but it was reciprocated between communities. And it was to the strangers' own community that they were obliged to sing the praises of their hosts if they had been treated well (cf. 3 John 5-8) and to which they would report adversely if they had not been welcomed properly (cf. 3 John 9-10). Communities would repay hospitality to strangers from another community if that community had treated their own people well.[24]

Letters of recommendation were important in the matter of hospitality. Their function was 'to help divest the stranger of his strangeness, to

21. Malina, 'The Received View and What It Cannot Do', 181.
22. Malina, 'The Received View and What It Cannot Do', 182-83.
23. Malina, 'The Received View and What It Cannot Do', 185.
24. Malina, 'The Received View and What It Cannot Do', 185-86.

make him at least only a partial stranger, if not an immediate guest'. To refuse to accept those recommended was to dishonour the one who commended them, and in the Mediterranean culture of the first century the one dishonoured had to seek satisfaction or bear the shame heaped upon him by the refusal of his commendation.[25]

12-13 FINAL GREETINGS

The elder brings this letter to a close with an expression of his desire to communicate with his readers in person, and by conveying the greetings of his own community.

v. 12   I have much to write to you, but I do not want to use paper and ink. Instead, I hope to visit you and talk with you face to face. The expression 'to talk face to face' (*stoma pros stoma lalēsai*, lit. 'to talk mouth to mouth') is found only in the writings of the elder within the NT.[26] The expression of a desire to be present with the person to whom one writes (rather than communicating by letter) is typical of the friendly letter tradition of the first-century Mediterranean world. Even though 2 John is not simply a friendly letter, the elder does make use of this typical expression here.[27]

This he says he wants to do **so that our[28] joy may be complete.** This is probably more than a traditional expression. In v. 4 the elder has already said, 'It has given me great joy to find some of your children walking in the truth', and in 3 John 4 he writes to Gaius: 'I have no greater joy than to hear that my children are walking in the truth'. The completion of the joy which the elder speaks of here in 2 John is then probably the joy he will experience when he sees all his readers walking in the truth. By speaking to them face to face, he will be able to say much more than he wants to put on paper now. And by doing so, the elder hopes to ensure

25. Malina, 'The Received View and What It Cannot Do', 187.

26. Paul uses the expression 'face to face' in 1 Cor 13:12 when he writes: 'Now we see but a poor reflection as in a mirror; then we shall see face to face', but the expression he uses there is *prosōpon pros prosōpon,* which does translate literally as 'face to face'.

27. Stanley K. Stowers, *Letter Writing in Greco-Roman Antiquity* (Philadelphia: Westminster, 1986) 60, notes that while there are no letters of friendship in the NT, 2 John 12 is an example of one of the commonplaces *(topoi)* of the friendly letter tradition which includes references to longing to be with the loved one.

28. Some manuscripts read 'your' *(hymōn)* instead of 'our' *(hēmōn)*, but the latter is to be preferred since the former appears to be a scribal assimilation to the second plurals *(hymin* and *hymas)* earlier in the verse.

that they continue walking in the truth, and that will make the great joy he already has (v. 4) complete.

v. 13   The children of your chosen sister send their greetings. This letter is addressed to 'the chosen lady and her children' (v. 1), a metaphorical expression denoting the local church and its members to which this letter is being sent. When the elder concludes the letter with greetings from 'the children of your chosen sister', he is conveying the greetings of the members of the local church of which he himself is a member.

Commentary on 3 John

This letter, unlike 2 John which is a letter written to a church, is a letter written to an individual, Gaius. The letter has little theological content, but it is nevertheless of significant interest because of the insight it provides concerning the life and tensions of an early Christian community. This letter, written by the elder to his friend Gaius, has essentially three functions: (i) to reinforce Gaius's commitment to the noble work of providing hospitality to travelling missionaries, something he was already doing (vv. 5-8),[1] (ii) to draw attention to the intolerable behaviour of Diotrephes and to foreshadow the steps he intends to take in response to it (vv. 9-10), and (iii) to commend Demetrius (v. 12).[2]

1 OPENING GREETINGS

v. 1 Like 2 John, this letter begins with the usual A to B greeting formula in which the author identifies himself as **the elder**. He writes in

1. Duane F. Watson, 'A Rhetorical Analysis of 3 John: A Study in Epistolary Rhetoric," *CBQ* 51 (1989) 500, argues that 'the Presbyter has chosen epideictic rhetoric in his letter to Gaius because Gaius does not need to be persuaded of the necessity of extending hospitality, but only to adhere more closely to that conviction'. Watson says the letter contains an *exordium* (vv. 2-4), *narratio* (vv. 5-6), *probatio* (vv. 7-12), and *peroratio* (vv. 13-14), the *praescriptio* (v. 1) and postscript (v. 15) functioning as *exordium* and *peroratio,* respectively.

2. Stanley K. Stowers, *Letter Writing in Greco-Roman Antiquity* (Philadelphia: Westminster, 1986) 156, says that 3 John has typical features of letters of recommendation but displays freedom in composition in comparison with the papyri. It is a letter of recommendation on behalf of travelling brethren (vv. 8, 10) that also contains a short invective *(psegein)* in vv. 9-10 and exhortation in vv. 11-12.

his own name (indicated by his use of the first person singular forms in vv. 1, 2, 3, 4, 9, 10, 13, 14), but in some places he associates himself with others from his community in what he writes (indicated by first person plural forms used exclusively in vv. 9, 10, and 12), and in other places he includes Gaius with himself in statements which reinforce values they hold in common (indicated by first person plural forms used inclusively in vv. 8 and 14). See the Introduction (p. 42) for a discussion of the identity of 'the elder'.

The elder addresses his letter **to my dear friend Gaius**. The name Gaius is found in four other places in the NT, and in each case the one bearing this name is associated with the apostle Paul. In Acts 19:29 a Gaius is one of Paul's travelling companions, and it is the probably the same Gaius who is mentioned as one of Paul's travelling companions in Acts 20:4 and described as 'Gaius from Derbe'. In 1 Cor 1:14 Paul speaks of a Gaius as one of the few people he himself baptised in Corinth, and it is probably the same Gaius Paul mentions in Romans 16:23 as his host in Corinth. It appears, then, that at least two different men called Gaius were numbered among Paul's associates. However, there are no indications that either of these men is to be identified with the Gaius to whom 3 John is addressed.

Gaius is addressed as 'my dear friend' *(tō agapētō)*, a term which reflects the affectionate regard in which the elder held this fellow believer. Gaius appears to be a significant person in a circle of Christian 'friends' (cf. v. 15), though there is no indication that he is the head of a house church or holds any position of authority in the church, as Diotrephes apparently did (cf. vv. 11-12).

The elder describes Gaius as one **whom I love in the truth** *(en alētheia)*. The expression *en alētheia* can be construed in two ways: (i) 'in the truth' (as in the NIV); or (ii) 'truly'. In the first case, the elder would be saying that he loves Gaius, who, like him, is 'in the truth', that is, is one who continues faithful to the truth concerning Jesus Christ as it was heard at the beginning. In the second case the elder would be simply saying that he 'truly' loves Gaius. The first option almost certainly reflects what the elder intended, for in v. 3 he mentions reports he has heard from others of how Gaius continues 'to walk in the truth'.

2-4 REJOICING THAT GAIUS WALKS IN THE TRUTH

Following the opening greetings in Greco-Roman letters there often followed an *exordium* in which the writer established rapport with his readers. Very often this included a prayer or wishes for the good health of the recipients,[3] and positive statements about their character and behaviour. This letter follows that model.

v. 2 The elder begins his *exordium* with the words: **Dear friend, I pray that you may enjoy good health and that all may go well with you**. Addressing Gaius again as his 'dear friend' *(agapēte)*, the elder underlines the affectionate regard he has for Gaius. His prayer that Gaius would 'enjoy good health and that all may go well with you' is typical of the good wishes found in many ancient letters.[4] To the prayerful good wish 'that all may go well with you', the elder adds, **even as your soul** *(psychē)* **is getting along well**. Normally the Greek word *psychē* is used in the Johannine writings to mean simply one's natural life (so, e.g., John 10:11, 15, 17; 12:25; 13:37, 38; 15:13; 1 John 3:16). However, on some occasions it refers to one's inner life as distinct from one's body (John 10:24, 27). This verse, then, appears to be a wish that all may go well with Gaius's whole person, as indeed it goes well with his soul. What the elder means by saying that things are going well with his soul is spelled out in the next two verses.

vv. 3-4 In this verse we find out why the elder can say that he knows that Gaius's soul 'is getting along well'. He tells his reader, **It gave me great joy[5] to have some brothers come and tell about your faithfulness to the truth** [lit. 'your truth'] **and how you continue to walk in the truth.** The evidence that Gaius's soul 'is getting along well' is that he remains faithful to the truth and continues to walk in the truth. The elder seems to be emphasising here that Gaius's faithfulness involves not only holding to correct doctrine, but also persisting in correct action. In the context of this letter that correct action is thought of primarily in terms of providing hospitality to those itinerant preachers who deserve support. In all three letters of John the author's joy is said to be complete when the readers maintain fellowship with him and walk in the truth (1 John 1:4; 2 John 4; 3 John 3-4).[6]

---

3. Stowers, *Letter Writing in Greco-Roman Antiquity*, 73, notes that the wishes for well-being or prayer (like that found in v. 2) occur in about one third of the papyrus family letters (as distinct from friendship letters).

4. His prayer for good health is expressed using the verbs *hygiainō* and *euodoō*. The verb *euodoō* can carry either the literal sense of being of sound health (as here and in Luke 5:31; 7:10; 15:27) or the metaphorical sense of being sound in thought or doctrine (as in 1 Tim 1:10; 6:3; 2 Tim 1:13; 4:3; Titus 2:1, 2). Clearly, the former is appropriate here. The verb *euodoō* is found frequently in the LXX (68x) with the meaning 'to prosper' or 'to be successful'. The word *euodoō* is also found in Rom 1:10 and 1 Cor 16:2, where it means 'to succeed' or 'to prosper'.

5. Some manuscripts have 'grace' *(charin)* instead of 'joy' *(charan)*, but the latter has much better support and is consistent with the elder's sentiments elsewhere (cf. 2 John 12).

6. This is one piece of evidence which suggests that one person wrote all three letters.

The elder evidently had received news from people who had visited Gaius, concerning Gaius's faithfulness to the truth (v. 3). Given the overall context of the three letters of John, Gaius's faithfulness to the truth is to be understood as steadfast commitment to the message of the gospel as it was heard at the beginning, and his rejection of the new teaching being spread abroad by the secessionists. However, the news that came to the elder was not only that Gaius held on to the teachings, but that he continued 'to walk in the truth', that is, he continued to order his life in accordance with the truth.

The elder completes the *exordium* (vv. 2-4) by saying to Gaius, **I have no greater joy than to hear that my children are walking in the truth**. His 'child' in this case is Gaius himself, and Gaius's faithfulness in walking in the truth is the source of the elder's greatest joy.

5-8 GAIUS COMMENDED FOR HIS HOSPITALITY

Following the *exordium*, the elder now addresses himself to the first of his concerns in this letter. He praises Gaius for his faithfulness in showing hospitality to travelling preachers and underlines the importance of this ministry. It may be, as Brown suggests, that these travellers had turned to Gaius for hospitality because they had been refused it by Diotrephes (cf. vv. 11-12).[7]

When one reads 3 John alongside 2 John, it becomes apparent that two groups of missionaries were moving around among the churches. There were those who were spreading heretical teaching, about whom the elder warns his readers lest they aid and abet their 'wicked work' by providing hospitality for them (2 John 7-11). There were also those who had gone out 'for the sake of the Name' and who deserved to be given hospitality (3 John 5-8).

v. 5 For the third time the elder addresses Gaius as his **dear friend** *(agapēte)*, and then compliments him for providing hospitality to the travelling preachers: **you are faithful in what you are doing for the brothers, even though they are strangers to you**. At this point in the letter, the elder's purpose is not to exhort but to reinforce. Missionaries ('brothers') from the elder's community who were unknown to Gaius ('strangers') had arrived in the city where Gaius lived, and Gaius had welcomed them into his house. In Gaius's world this involved more

7. Raymond E. Brown, *The Epistles of John* (AB 30, New York: Doubleday, 1982) 740-41.

than providing food and a place to sleep; it also meant being guarantor of their *bona fides* to the rest of the community (see 'A Note on Hospitality', pp. 215-16).

v. 6   When strangers received hospitality, it was incumbent upon them to report positively about their hosts to their own community when they returned from their travels. In order to encourage Gaius to continue this good work of his, the elder informs him that those to whom he gave hospitality have given a good report: **They have told the church about your love.** (Of course, if hospitality was denied, that, too, would be reported, and the loss of face experienced would need to be dealt with; cf. vv. 9-10.) This is the first of three references to the 'church' *(ekklēsia)* in this letter (vv. 6, 9, 10), the only places the word is found in the Johannine writings. Here it most likely refers to the Christian community to which the elder himself belongs, and in verses 9-10 it refers to the community in which Diotrephes exercised authority. The word 'church' *(ekklēsia)*, then, clearly denotes a local community of Christians.[8]

The elder then encourages Gaius to continue what he is doing for such people by adding: **You will do well to send them on their way in a manner worthy of God.** The expression 'to send them on their way' translates a form of the verb *propempō*, which functioned as a technical term for missionary support in the early church (cf. Acts 15:3; 20:38; 21:5; Rom 15:24; 1 Cor 16:6, 11; 2 Cor 1:16; Tit 3:13), and this is also its function here.[9] These people were preachers of the truth as it was heard at the beginning, and so it was appropriate to send them on their way as faithful missionaries 'in a manner worthy of God'.[10] This probably means to send them on their way in a manner befitting those who serve the living God.

vv. 7-8   These verses provide three reasons why it is appropriate for Gaius to send the preachers on their way 'in a manner worthy of God': The first reason is stated in v. 7a: **It was for the sake of the Name that they went out**. These people had gone out 'for the sake of the Name', that is, for the sake of Jesus Christ. The expression 'go out' *(exerchomai)* is

---

8. This indicates, as Brown, *The Epistles of John*, 709, notes, that the Johannine writings are not anti-church, as some have suggested.

9. Brown, *The Epistles of John*, 711, notes that 'Polycarp, *Philip*. 1:1, sees the action described by this verb as a manifestation of love: "I rejoice greatly with you in the Lord Jesus Christ that you have followed the pattern of true love and have sent forward on their way *(propempsasin)* those who were bound in chains"'.

10. There is only one other place in the NT where the expression 'worthy of God' *(axiōs tou theou)* is found, and that is 1 Thess 2:12, where the apostle Paul reminds his readers that when he was with them he urged them to behave in a way that was 'worthy of God' who called them into his kingdom.

found four times altogether in the Johannine letters, and in the other three places it is used in reference to the secessionists. Only here is it used of faithful missionaries who had gone out 'for the sake of the Name'. The words 'for the sake of the Name' *(hyper tou onomatos)* are found in five other places in the NT, most often in contexts where people suffer persecution on account of their witness to Christ (Acts 5:41; 9:16; 15:26; 21:13). In the one other place it is used by Paul when speaking of the grace he received to bring about the obedience of faith among the Gentiles 'for the sake of his name' (Rom 1:5). It is this last usage which most closely parallels that found here. The itinerant preachers had gone out 'for the sake of the Name', that is, to proclaim the gospel and to bring people to faith. They were not like the secessionists, who were seeking to deceive people with a new teaching which denied Jesus Christ 'as coming in the flesh' (cf. 2 John 7). They were faithful proclaimers of the Name; they proclaimed Jesus Christ 'as coming in the flesh'.

The second reason why these missionaries deserved to be sent on their way in a manner worthy of God is stated in v. 7b. It is because they went out **receiving no help from the pagans**. As they travelled from place to place they were dependent on the Christian community for hospitality, for they received none from the pagans.

The third reason why Christians should help the faithful missionaries is stated in v. 8: **We ought therefore to show hospitality to such men so that we may work together for the truth.** In 2 John 11 the elder warned his readers against providing hospitality to a secessionist preacher, for to do so would make them sharers 'in his wicked work'. But in respect of the faithful missionaries he counsels Gaius to do the opposite. He encourages him to provide hospitality to those who proclaim the original message, for in doing that, he says, we 'work together for the truth' (lit. 'we may become fellow workers for the truth'). To provide hospitality is to further the cause of the truth, and those who do so may be described as 'fellow workers for the truth'.

9-10 DIOTREPHES' OPPOSITION TO THE ELDER

In this passage the elder tells Gaius about the reprehensible behaviour of one Diotrephes, who had spoken maliciously about him and his friends. Diotrephes had refused hospitality to those whom the elder had recommended to the church as people who had gone out 'for the sake of the Name', even threatening to excommunicate any who did offer them hospitality.

In the commentary on vv. 9-10 which follows, we have adopted the position that the conflict between the elder and Diotrephes is related to the problem created by the secessionist teaching but was precipitated by Diotrephes' refusal to provide hospitality to the itinerant missionaries commended by the elder. The scenario is that the secessionists, having 'gone out' from the community in which the elder was a leader, began spreading their teaching among other churches. 1 John was written as a circular letter to warn these churches not to be deceived by the secessionists. 2 John also warns about these people, and advocates the denial of hospitality to them, lest those who provide it become participants in their 'wicked work'. 3 John reflects the denial of hospitality to itinerants, but in this case it is the denial of hospitality, not to the secessionists, but to the *bona fide* missionaries who have gone out from the elder's community 'for the sake of the Name'. This denial of hospitality is advocated by Diotrephes, and it appears to be motivated by some animosity between himself and the elder. It is difficult to say what the basis of this animosity is; whether it is personal, doctrinal, ecclesiastical, or whether it is because Diotrephes has sided with the secessionists and is treating the orthodox missionaries in the same way the elder contends the secessionist missionaries should be treated. (For a discussion of the relationship between the elder and Diotrephes and the various opinions that have been put forward concerning this, see the Introduction, pp. 44-47).

It has been suggested that the reference to Diotrephes and his actions in vv. 9-10 functions as a negative example. It shows what Gaius should *not* do in respect to the faithful itinerant missionaries, including Demetrius (cf. v. 12).[11] However, in the light of the conventions of hospitality which operated in the first century (see 'A Note on Hospitality', pp. 215-16), it is unlikely that the author's purpose was restricted to this. Diotrephes may provide a negative example, but the elder's purpose is far more pointed than this. He is responding to the shame heaped upon him by Diotrephes' refusal to accept those whom he recommended. This passage is the elder's culturally required attempt to secure satisfaction. If he did nothing in the face of Diotrephes' actions he would sacrifice his honour, something which would be a serious matter in a culture of shame.[12]

v. 9 In this verse the elder tells Gaius that he wrote formerly to Diotrephes, who, it appears, had some sort of leadership role in the

11. Birger Olssen, 'Structural Analyses in Handbooks for Translators', *BT* 37 (1, 1986) 126-27.
12. Cf. Bruce J. Malina, 'The Received View and What It Cannot Do: III John and Hospitality', *Semeia* 35 (1986) 171-89.

Christian community in the city where Gaius lived. The elder says: **I wrote**[13] **to the church, but Diotrephes, who loves to be first, will have nothing to do with us**. The elder's reference to a previous letter has been identified by some as 2 John,[14] but this is unlikely because there is no request for hospitality in that letter. The letter referred to here is probably now lost. The elder probably refers to it to highlight the recalcitrance of Diotrephes.[15]

It is clear from this verse that there did exist some animosity between the elder and Diotrephes. The elder describes Diotrephes as one 'who loves to be first'. While the verb 'to love to be first' (*philoprōteuō*) is not found elsewhere in the NT,[16] the cognate word *prōtos* is used in many places to refer to leading persons.[17] When the elder says that Diotrephes 'loves to be first', he is probably implying that he loves to be the leader and to exercise authority. It is clear from later statements that Diotrephes not only loved to be first, but had actually succeeded in being recognised as such (v. 10b). This led Harnack to regard Diotrephes as the prototype of the monarchical bishop in the early church.[18] However, this goes beyond what the evidence of 3 John allows. It is best to see the elder's reference to Diotrephes' desire to be first in terms of his refusal to accede to the elder's written request that he provide hospitality to those whom the elder recommended (see v. 10). It is to this that the elder refers when he says that Diotrephes 'will have nothing to do with us' (lit. 'does not receive us', *ouk epidechetai hēmas*). The elder uses the same verb (*epidechomai*) in the next verse when referring to Diotrephes' refusal to 'welcome the brothers', meaning to provide them with hospitality. The use of

13. Some manuscripts have 'I wrote something' (*egrapsa ti*), adopted by the NRSV, rather than 'I wrote' (*egrapsa*), the reading adopted by the NIV. It is possible that the 'something' (*ti*) was dropped by later scribes because it was thought to downgrade apostolic authority or raise speculation about a lost letter (see Bruce M. Metzger, *A Textual Commentary on the Greek New Testament* [2nd ed., Stuttgart: German Bible Society, 1994] *ad loc.*).

14. So Georg Strecker, *The Johannine Letters* (Hermeneia, Philadelphia: Fortress, 1996) 253-54.

15. Cf. Rudolf Schnackenburg, *The Johannine Epistles* (Tunbridge Wells, Kent: Burns & Oates, 1992) 297.

16. *Philoprōteuō* is not found in the LXX either. MM list only 3 John 9 as an example of this word. *Philoprōteuō* is not listed in the first eight volumes of *New Documents Illustrating Early Christianity*. MM cite *philoponeō* ('I love labor') as a corresponding word (for which there are examples), which provides some support for interpreting *philoprōteuō* as 'I love the first place'.

17. Cf. Matt 20:27; 22:38; Mark 6:21; 9:35; 10:31, 44; 12:28-29; Luke 13:30; 19:47; Acts 16:12; 17:4; 25:2, 8, 17; 1 Cor 15:3; 1 Tim 1:15-16.

18. A. Harnack, 'Über den 3.Johannesbrief', TU XV/3b (1987), 16ff. Cited by Jens-W. Taeger, 'Der konservative Rebell: Zum Widerstand des Diotrephes gegen den Presbyter', ZNW 78 (1987) 268.

the verb here in v. 9 is metaphorical: Diotrephes did not welcome the elder in that he did not accede to the request made by the elder in his letter.[19] To reject the 'brothers' recommended by the elder was the same as rejecting the elder himself. This way of thinking is common in the Fourth Gospel, where to receive the ones sent is the same as receiving the one who sent them (cf. John 5:23; 12:44-45; 13:20; 14:24). The elder's reference to 'us' in the expression, he 'will have nothing to do with us', probably refers to the elder and those in his community who with him remain faithful to the message as it came down to them at the beginning.[20]

v. 10 In this verse the elder spells out in some detail exactly what he believes Diotrephes was doing. Diotrephes' misbehaviour consists of four elements as far as the elder is concerned: (i) malicious gossip about the elder and his community; (ii) refusal to welcome the orthodox missionaries; (iii) preventing others from doing so; and (iv) putting out of the church those who defied him in this matter.

First he says, **So if I come, I will call attention to what he is doing, gossiping maliciously about us.** The verb *(phlyareō)* 'to gossip' is found only here in the NT, but the cognate adjective 'gossipy' *(phlyaros)* is found in 1 Tim 5:13, where people are warned against being idlers, gossips, and busybodies. The text here in v. 10 translates literally as 'gossiping evil words against us', indicating that the elder thought Diotrephes was speaking slanderously about him and his associates.[21] The elder evidently intended to make a visit to the city where Gaius and Diotrephes lived, and threatens that when he comes he 'will call attention to what he [Diotrephes] is doing'. Such action, a form of public rebuke, would be required of the elder in the culture of the first-century Mediterranean world to restore the honour he had lost when Diotrephes spoke evil of him.

However, Diotrephes' actions were not restricted to 'bad mouthing' the elder and his associates. The elder adds: **Not satisfied with that, he refuses to welcome the brothers.** In v. 9 the elder said that Diotrephes refused to welcome him (meaning he refused to heed the re-

19. Cf. Margaret M. Mitchell, '"Diotrephes does not receive us": The Lexicographical and Social Context of 3 John 9-10', *JBL* 117 (1998) 316-17, who points out that the verb *epidechomai* is found commonly in first-century texts referring to 'hospitable reception' in both private homes and in formal diplomatic relationships. She argues correctly that there are no good reasons why *epidechomai* should be translated one way in v. 9 and another way in v. 10.

20. Brown, *The Epistles of John*, 717, argues that the elder is speaking here as a member of the 'Johannine School'.

21. Brown, *The Epistles of John*, 745, suggests that Diotrephes might have acted in this way because he thought that the elder (and the secessionists) were acting in an arrogant and presumptuous way when they sent their missionaries to other communities.

quest he made in his letter), and here he says that Diotrephes 'refuses to welcome *(epidechetai)* the brothers' (lit. 'he did not receive the brothers'), that is, he refused to provide them with hospitality. By the 'brothers' here he means people like those mentioned in vv. 5-8, those whom Gaius had shown hospitality, people who had gone out 'for the sake of the Name'. It was these orthodox missionaries from the elder's community who had been refused hospitality by Diotrephes, even though they came with a letter of recommendation from the elder. This was another reason why the elder would have to 'call attention to what he is doing' when he came. Diotrephes had shamed him by rejecting those whom he had recommended. To reject those recommended was the same as rejecting the one who recommended them. The elder was obliged to act publicly to overcome the shame he had experienced as a result of Diotrephes' refusal.

Diotrephes' rejection of the elder's recommendation did not stop with his own refusal of hospitality, for the elder adds: **He also stops those who want to do so and puts them out of the church.** This man who loved to be first enforced his will upon others who would have heeded the elder's recommendation.[22] He was not content to deny hospitality himself to the travelling missionaries from the elder's community; he also stopped others from doing so. If anyone went against him in this matter, he put them out of the church.[23] It is not clear whether this constituted an official act of excommunication or not. In doing what he did, however, Diotrephes must have had the tacit approval of the majority of the members of the church; otherwise this action would have failed. Such action represents an abuse of leadership responsibility. It was a disturbing example of desiring to be first, and one which the elder could not allow to persist, not only because of the loss of honour he himself experienced when his letter of recommendation was rejected, but also because the overbearing behaviour of Diotrephes itself was quite unacceptable in the Christian community. Even the elder, who in 2 John 10-11 had urged his readers not to provide hospitality for the secessionists, had not threatened with excommunication any who did so.

22. By the way, this indicates that the elder's letter to Diotrephes was not a private letter but one whose contents were known to others as well, hence the need for the elder to respond publicly to Diotrephes' refusal to fulfil the request it contained.

23. The elder uses the word *ekballō* ('to put out'), a word used in John 9:34, 35 in reference to the Pharisees throwing the blind man whom Jesus healed out of the synagogue.

A Note on Love and Hate in the Christian Community

One of the puzzling features of the Letters of John is the strong emphasis on the command that believers love one another on the one hand, and the strong polemic statements made about the secessionists on the other. It raises the question whether the writer of these letters practises what he preaches.

The verb 'to love', *agapaō,* occurs 31 times in 1, 2, and 3 John. The greatest proportion (14x) of the 31 occurrences is used in descriptive contexts (1 John 2:10; 3:10, 14 [2x]; 4:7, 8, 12, 20 [3x]; 5:1 [2x], 2 [2x]) where the author distinguishes between:

> those who live/do not live in the light;
> those who are the children of God and the children of the devil;
> those who have/have not passed from death to life;
> those who have/have not been born of God;
> those who know/do not know God;
> those in whom God lives/does not live;
> those who love/do not love God;
> those who love/do not love the children of God

Then there are the uses of *agapaō* (7x) that occur in contexts where reference is made to the commandment believers had from the beginning to love one another, or where readers are in other ways exhorted to practise mutual love (1 John 3:11, 18, 23; 4:7, 21 [2x]; 2 John 5). After this come those occurrences of *agapaō* (6x) where God's love for believers is given as the basis of an exhortation for them to love one another (2x in each of the following verses: 1 John 4:10, 11, 19). Next come those occurrences of *agapaō* where the author describes the 'elect lady' (2 John 1) and Gaius (3 John 1) as those whom he loves, and finally those occurrences of *agapaō* in exhortations to his readers not to love the world (1 John 2:15 [2x]). The greatest proportion of the uses of *agapaō* relate to criteria to be used in exposing what the author believes are the false claims of the secessionists, suggesting that even the teaching about love has been laid under tribute for polemics.

There are a total of 21 occurrences of the noun 'love', *agapē,* in 1, 2, and 3 John. The greatest proportion of these (9x) is used to denote the fact that God is love (1 John 4:8, 16), that love is from God (1 John 4:7), that to abide in love is to abide in God (1 John 4:16), and that God (1 John 3:1; 4:9, 10, 16) or Christ (1 John 3:16) loves us. Next, three occurrences of *agapē* are used in connection with believers' love for God (1 John 2:5, 15; 5:3), two further occurrences denote God's love through believers for others (1 John 3:17; 4:12), and another four occurrences are found in contexts which emphasise love as the basis of the believers' confidence before God (1 John 4:17, 18 [3x]). There are two uses of *agapē* to show how particular individuals have fulfilled their love obligations to itinerant missionaries (2 John 6; 3 John 6). Finally, there is one occurrence in a greeting formula (2 John 3: 'grace mercy, and peace . . . in love and truth'). The greatest proportion of the occurrences of *agapē* relate to the fact that God is love, and that to abide in God is to abide in love, and this only highlights what the author believes are shortcomings in the behaviour of the secessionists. *Agapē*, too, plays a part in the author's polemics.[24]

The verb 'to hate', *miseō*, is found five times in 1 John, but not at all in 2 or 3 John. Four of the uses are in contexts where the author highlights the falsity of the claims of the secessionists. Their hatred of other believers (probably those associated with the author) shows that despite their claims they walk in darkness (2:9, 11), are 'murderers' (3:15), and are liars when they claim that they love God (4:20). The one other use of *miseō* is to remind the readers not to be astonished if the world hates them (3:13). It goes without need of comment that *miseō* is also used as part of the author's polemic vocabulary.

The polemical attitude of the author of 1, 2, and 3 John is found throughout these letters. In 1 John the 'if we say' formulae of 1:6, 8, 10 with which the author introduces the spurious claims of the secessionists pave the way for him to characterise them as liars (1:6), as those who deceive themselves and in whom the truth is not found (1:8), and as those who, by their statements, make God a liar, and in whom God's word is not found (1:10). The 'whoever says' formulae of 2:4, 9, 11, with which the author introduces other claims and certain behavioural characteristics of the secessionists, pave the way for him to depict them again as liars in whom the truth does not exist (2:4), and as those who are still in darkness (2:9, 11). In 2:19 the author informs his readers that it became clear that the secessionists were not really true members of the Christian community when they withdrew. In this context he calls them antichrists (2:18-19), liars (2:22), and deceivers (2:26). In 1 John 3 the author seems to have the secessionists in mind when he speaks of those who do not love their brothers and sisters as children of the devil (3:10) and murderers (3:15). In 1 John 4 the author refers to the secessionists as false prophets (4:1), those who are moved, not by the Spirit of God but by the spirit of antichrist (4:3) and the spirit of error (4:6). Later in the same chapter the secessionists who claim to know God but do not love their brothers and sisters are called liars (4:20). In 1 John 5:16-17 the author probably has the secession-

24. See Brown, *The Epistles of John*, 254-57, for a detailed discussion of *agapē*.

ists in mind when he speaks of those whose sin is mortal and suggests that his readers should not pray for such people. Finally, the author may be implying that for his readers to adopt the teaching of the secessionists would be tantamount to idolatry (5:21). In 2 John the elder refers to the secessionists as deceivers who have gone out into the world, and as antichrists (7). In 3 John the elder criticises Diotrephes as one 'who likes to put himself first' (9).

This polemical attitude finds practical expression in 2 John 10, where the elder exhorts his readers not to provide hospitality to itinerant preachers who do not confess that Jesus Christ has come in the flesh. To do this, he says, would be to participate in their evil deeds. In 3 John we see this strategy turned back on those whom the elder has commended when Diotrephes refuses hospitality, and even excommunicates any who go against his wishes in this matter (9-10)

It is possible, as Lieu suggests, that the shock of the schism that we find in the Letters of John led to the strong emphasis on love for fellow believers at the expense of those outside.[25] Brown suggests that by taking the stern measures he did against the secessionists, the elder was responsible for fuelling the fire of intolerance and providing a precedent for 'those Christians of all times who feel justified in hating other Christians for the love of God'.[26] But this criticism is probably unjustified because what was at stake was a true understanding of God. To adopt the secessionist view was to be alienated from God and to lose hold on eternal life. As Whitacre observes, it is one thing to acknowledge diversity within early Christianity, but that is not to say there are no boundaries at all, and the strength of the author's feeling 'reflects the importance of the issue at stake, which is the very life of God'.[27]

11-12 THE ELDER'S COMMENDATION OF DEMETRIUS

v. 11   Addressing Gaius once more as **dear friend** *(agapēte)*, the elder urges him: **do not imitate what is evil but what is good**. At first glance this might appear to be just an exhortation along the general lines

25. Judith Lieu, *The Theology of the Johannine Epistles* (Cambridge: Cambridge University Press, 1991) 68-69. Cf. Martin Rese, 'Das Gebot der Bruderliebe in den Johannesbriefen', *TZ* 41 (1985) 44-58.

26. Raymond E. Brown, *The Community of the Beloved Disciple* (New York: Paulist, 1979) 135.

27. Rodney A. Whitacre, *Johannine Polemic: The Role of Tradition and Theology* (SBLDS 67, Chico, CA: Scholars Press, 1982) 183-84.

of the teaching found in 1 John, where doing what is right is the mark of those who are from God (cf. 1 John 3:7-10). But here it is a matter, not of doing 'what is right' *(dikaiosynē)* but imitating what is 'good' *(agathon)*. And this is reinforced by what follows: **Anyone who does what is good** *(agathopoiōn)* **is from God**. Both the adjective 'good' *(agathos)* and the verb 'to do good' *(agathopoieō)* are found only here in the Johannine letters.[28] This raises, then, the question whether in fact to do 'good' is equivalent to doing what is 'right'. In 1 John doing what is 'right' stands in contrast to sinning, especially the sin of lawlessness *(anomia)*, or rebellion. But doing what is 'good' in 3 John comes in a context of providing or withholding hospitality. Therefore, doing what is 'good' should probably be understood in terms of providing hospitality to the travelling missionaries.[29] Gaius, of course, had been doing good in this sense, and the elder wants him to do so also in the case of Demetrius (cf. v. 12). The corresponding statement, **Anyone who does what is evil has not seen God**, then, would mean refusing to provide hospitality to the travelling missionaries. This is what Diotrephes had been doing, and this was not an example which the elder wanted Gaius to follow.

v. 12   In this verse the elder comes to his commendation of Demetrius. What seems to be implied in the commendation is that Gaius should provide Demetrius with hospitality. This would especially be the case if Demetrius himself was the bearer of the letter (and therefore present when Gaius read it), and even more so if he was one of the travelling missionaries who had gone out from the elder's community. Concerning this man the elder comments: **Demetrius is well spoken of by everyone — and even by the truth itself**. The only other reference to a Demetrius in the NT is to Demetrius the silversmith of Ephesus (Acts 19:24, 38), and attractive as it might be to conjecture that this Demetrius became a convert to Christianity and was the one whom the elder commended to Gaius, there is no evidence to support it. Also quite conjectural and without supporting evidence is the suggestion that the name 'Demas' is a short-

28. Elsewhere in the NT the verb *agathopoieō* is found only in Luke 6:9, 33, 35 and 1 Pet 2:15, 20; 3:6, 17. In Luke it is used in relation to doing good to others (acts of kindness). In 1 Peter it is used in contexts where believers are urged to do good (act faithfully whatever their situation) even though they may suffer as Christians.

29. Cf. Tibor Horvath, '3 Jn 11b: An Early Ecumenical Creed?', *ExpTim* 85 (1973-74) 339-40, who also notes that 'doing good' here means 'works of charity'. However, his suggestions that those who do these include both believers and unbelievers, that 'whoever helps his fellowmen is from God and shares in faith', that 'this does not necessarily imply the explicit knowledge of Christ and the hearing of the word of the apostles', and that 'the children of the light and the children of the darkness are separated not so much by their reception or rejection of Christ, but more fundamentally by their acts of charity', go well beyond what the text of 3 John 11 allows.

ened form of 'Demetrius', and that this Demetrius may be identified with
Paul's failed colleague (Col 4:14; 2 Tim 4:10; Phlm 24).

The first part of this commendation needs no particular clarifica-
tion. It means what it says, Demetrius 'is well spoken of *(memartyrētai)* by
everyone', an expression found in several places in the NT (Acts 6:3;
10:22; 16:2; 22:12; 1 Tim 5:10; Heb 11:2, 4, 5, 39). The second part of the
commendation needs some explanation. What does it mean that Demetrius is well spoken of 'even by the truth itself'? When the elder speaks
of the 'truth' *(alētheia)* elsewhere in this letter, it refers to the truth of the
gospel, and therefore this statement must mean something like 'even his
commitment to the truth speaks well of him'. The nature of Demetrius's
commitment to the truth, Brown suggests, involved his having appropriated it through faith and expressed it in his behaviour and love for others.[30]

Adding to the widespread testimony of others, and even the testimony of Demetrius's commitment to the truth, the elder now gives his
own personal commendation: **We also speak well of him,** reminding
Gaius that his commendation may be trusted: **and you know that our
testimony is true.** When the elder says 'we' also speak well of him, he is
probably speaking on behalf of the community to which he belongs, as
well as on his own behalf.[31] On the basis of all this the elder expects that
Gaius will provide the necessary hospitality to Demetrius (who, as has
been suggested, was probably the bearer of this brief letter).

13-14 FINAL GREETINGS

vv. 13-14a The elder's final sentiments here are identical with
those with which he concluded his earlier letter (2 John 12): **I have much
to write you, but I do not want to do so with pen and ink. I hope to see
you soon, and we will talk face to face.** The expression 'to talk face to
face' *(stoma pros stoma lalēsai,* lit. 'to talk mouth to mouth') is unique to the
elder within the writings of the NT.[32] The expression of a desire to com-

---

30. Brown, *The Epistles of John,* 724. Judith Lieu, *The Second and Third Epistles of John:
History and Background* (Edinburgh: T. & T. Clark, 1986) 119, asserts that 'Demetrius' approval is upheld by the very spirit and norm of Johannine Christianity'.

31. Brown, *The Epistles of John,* 724, thinks that he is speaking here as a member of
the 'Johannine School'.

32. Paul uses the expression 'face to face' in 1 Cor 13:12 when he writes: 'Now we
see but a poor reflection as in a mirror; then we shall see face to face', but the expression
he uses there is *prosōpon pros prosōpon,* which does translate literally as 'face to face'.

municate face to face rather than by letter is typical of the friendly letter tradition of the first-century Mediterranean world. Even though 3 John is not simply a friendly letter, the elder does make use of this typical expression here.[33]

v. 14b   The letter concludes with the typical greeting, **Peace to you**. To this the elder appends greetings from the believers in his community to Gaius: **The friends here send their greetings**, followed by the elder's request that his greetings be conveyed to the believers in Gaius's household (or the wider Christian community to which Gaius belonged): **Greet the friends there by name.** The expression 'friends' *(philoi)* is an unusual one to be used for believers, and it is used in this way only here among the letters of the NT. It may have derived from Jesus' description of his disciples as his 'friends' in John 15:13-15. There Jesus says that no one has greater love than that a person lay down his life for his friends, and adds that the disciples are his 'friends' because they do what he commands, and because he treats them as such by informing them of 'everything' he has learned from the Father. It probably reflects the way early believers spoke of themselves, as 'the friends'.

33. Stowers, *Letter Writing in Greco-Roman Antiquity*, 60, notes that while there are no letters of friendship in the NT, 2 John 12 and 3 John 13-14 are examples of one of the commonplaces *(topoi)* of the friendly letter tradition which includes references to longing to be with the loved one.

Appendix: Biblical and Extrabiblical References to Cain

Genesis 4:1-25 (NIV)

Adam lay with his wife Eve, and she became pregnant and gave birth to Cain. She said, "With the help of the LORD I have brought forth a man." Later she gave birth to his brother Abel.

Now Abel kept flocks, and Cain worked the soil. In the course of time Cain brought some of the fruits of the soil as an offering to the LORD. But Abel brought fat portions from some of the firstborn of his flock. The LORD looked with favour on Abel and his offering, but on Cain and his offering he did not look with favour. So Cain was very angry, and his face was downcast.

Then the LORD said to Cain, "Why are you angry? Why is your face downcast? If you do what is right, will you not be accepted? But if you do not do what is right, sin is crouching at your door; it desires to have you, but you must master it."

Now Cain said to his brother Abel, "Let's go out to the field." And while they were in the field, Cain attacked his brother Abel and killed him.

Then the LORD said to Cain, "Where is your brother Abel?"

"I don't know," he replied. "Am I my brother's keeper?"

The LORD said, "What have you done? Listen! Your brother's blood cries out to me from the ground. Now you are under a curse and driven from the ground, which opened its mouth to receive your brother's blood from your hand. When you work the ground, it will no longer yield its crops for you. You will be a restless wanderer on the earth."

Cain said to the LORD, "My punishment is more than I can bear. To-day you are driving me from the land, and I will be hidden from your presence; I will be a restless wanderer on the earth, and whoever finds me will kill me."

But the LORD said to him, "Not so; if anyone kills Cain, he will suffer vengeance seven times over." Then the LORD put a mark on Cain so that no one who found him would kill him. So Cain went out from the LORD's presence and lived in the land of Nod, east of Eden.

Cain lay with his wife, and she became pregnant and gave birth to Enoch. Cain was then building a city, and he named it after his son Enoch. To Enoch was born Irad, and Irad was the father of Mehujael, and Mehujael was the father of Methushael, and Methushael was the father of Lamech.

Lamech married two women, one named Adah and the other Zillah. Adah gave birth to Jabal; he was the father of those who live in tents and raise livestock. His brother's name was Jubal; he was the father of all who play the harp and flute. Zillah also had a son, Tubal-cain, who forged all kinds of tools out of bronze and iron. Tubal-cain's sister was Naamah.

Lamech said to his wives, "Adah and Zillah, listen to me; wives of Lamech, hear my words. I have killed a man for wounding me, a young man for injuring me. If Cain is avenged seven times, then Lamech seventy-seven times."

Adam lay with his wife again, and she gave birth to a son and named him Seth, saying, "God has granted me another child in place of Abel, since Cain killed him."

Apocalypse of Abraham 24:3-5 (*OTP* 1:701)

The original document was probably written in Hebrew in the first-second century A.D. The extant work is an Old Slavonic translation. The original was most likely composed in Palestine. It analyses the causes of the destruction of Jerusalem (the infidelity of Israel toward the covenant with God and the opportunistic politics of some leaders).

"Look now at everything in the picture." And I looked and saw there the creatures that had come into being before me. And I saw, as it were, Adam, and Eve who was with him, and with them the crafty adversary and Cain, who had been led by the adversary to break the law, and (I saw) the murdered Abel (and) the perdition brought on him and given through the lawless one.

1 (Ethiopic Apocalypse of) Enoch 22:5-7 (OTP 1:24-25)

Written in second century B.C.–first century A.D., this document reflects the historical events immediately before and after the Maccabean revolt. It originated in Judea and was in use at Qumran before the beginning of the Christian era. There is debate over the original language, whether it was Hebrew or Aramaic or a combination of the two. The book was well known to the Essenes and early Christians (notably the author of Jude). It was used by the authors of *Barnabas, Apocalypse of Peter,* and a number of apologetic works. Many Church Fathers, including Justin Martyr, Irenaeus, Origen, and Clement of Alexandria, either knew *1 Enoch* or were inspired by it.

> I saw the spirits of the children of the people who were dead, and their voices were reaching unto heaven until this very moment. I asked Rufael, the angel who was with me, and said to him, "This spirit, the voice of which is reaching (into heaven) like this and is making suit, whose (spirit) is it?" And he answered me, saying, "This is the spirit which had left Abel, whom Cain, his brother, had killed; it (continues to) sue him until all of (Cain's) seed is exterminated from the face of the earth, and his seed has disintegrated from among the seed of the people."

Hellenistic Synagogal Prayers 12:53-54 (OTP 2:693)

These prayers are found scattered among Christian liturgy in Books 7 and 8 of the *Apostolic Constitutions.* Sixteen of these prayers appear to be remnants of Jewish synagogue prayers. The Jewish authorship of at least some of the prayers is recognised. The earliest date at which the prayers could have been composed is the middle of the second century A.D., and they could be as early as A.D. 150 or as late as A.D. 300.

> And while indeed from Abel, as from a devout man, you favorably received a sacrifice; and from the brother-murderer Cain, you turned aside the offering as from an accursed person.

Life of Adam and Eve (OTP 2:266-267)

Original Hebrew compositions were made between 100 B.C. and A.D. 200, probably in Palestine, and reflect Pharisaic theology. The Greek and Latin texts were produced between that time and A.D. 400. *Vita* = Latin text; *ApocMos* = Greek text.

Vita 23:1-5:
For Eve later conceived and bore a son, whose name was Abel. And Cain and Abel used to stay together. And Eve said to Adam, "My lord, while I was sleeping I saw a vision — as if the blood of our son Abel was in the hand of Cain (who was) gulping it down in his mouth. That is why I am sad." And Adam said, "God forbid that Cain would kill Abel! But let us separate them from each other and make separate places for them." And they made Cain a farmer and Abel a shepherd, that in this way they might be separated from each other. After this Cain murdered Abel, at which time Adam was 130 years old, while Abel when he was murdered was 122.

Vita 24:1-2:
And after this Adam knew his wife and she bore a son and called his name Seth. And Adam said to Eve, "See, I have sired a son in place of Abel, whom Cain struck down."

ApocMos 2:1-4:
After these things [the birth of Cain and Abel] Adam and Eve were together and when they were lying down to sleep, Eve said to her lord Adam, "My lord, I saw in a dream this night the blood of my son Amilabes, called Abel, being thrust into the mouth of Cain his brother, and he drank it mercilessly. He begged him to allow him a little of it, but he did not listen to him but swallowed all of it. And it did not stay in his stomach but came out of his mouth." And Adam said to Eve, "Let us rise and go to see what has happened to them. Perhaps the enemy is warring against them."

ApocMos 3:1-3:
And when they both had gone out they found Abel killed by the hand of Cain, his brother. And God said to Michael the archangel, "Say to Adam, 'The mystery which you know do not report to your son Cain, for he is a son of wrath. But do not mourn, for I will give you another son in his place; this one shall reveal to you all that you shall do; but you tell him nothing!" These things God said to his angel, and Adam kept the word in his heart, with him and Eve, grieving over Abel their son.

ApocMos **4:1-2:**

After these things Adam knew his wife and she conceived and bore Seth. And Adam said to Eve, "See, we have begotten a son in place of Abel, whom Cain killed; let us give glory and sacrifice to God."

4 Maccabees 18:6-19 (*OTP* 2:563)

This document was written in the first century A.D., emanating from either Alexandria or (more likely) Antioch in Syria. As the title of the work suggests, it reflects the period of the Maccabean struggle for independence.

> The mother of the seven sons also addressed these righteous sayings to her children. . . . "Through all the days of my prime I stayed with my husband. When these sons were grown up, their father died. Happy was he, for the life he lived was blessed with children, and he knew not the pain of the time when they were taken away. He, while he was still with you, taught you the Law and the Prophets. He read to you of Abel, slain by Cain, of Isaac, offered as a burnt offering, and of Joseph in prison. He spoke to you of the zeal of Phineas, and taught you about Hananiah, Azariah, and Mishael in the fire. He sang the praises of Daniel in the lions' den and called him blessed. He reminded you of the scripture of Isaiah which says, *Even though you walk through the fire, the flame shall not burn you.* He sang to you the psalm of David which says, *Many are the afflictions of the righteous.* He recited the proverb of Solomon which says, *He is a tree of life to those who do his will.* He affirmed the word of Ezekiel, *Shall these dry bones live?* Nor did he forget the song that Moses taught which says, *I kill and I make alive,* for this is your life and the length of your days."

Pseudo-Philo (*OTP* 2:305, 323-24)

This document was written in the first century A.D., and it seems to reflect 'the milieu of the Palestinian synagogues at the turn of the common era'. It is a witness to the understanding of the Bible in the Palestinian synagogues prior to A.D. 70.

2:1-4:

Now Cain dwelt in the land trembling, as God had appointed for him after he had killed Abel his brother. And the name of his wife was Themech. *And Cain knew* Themech *his wife, and she conceived and bore Enoch.* Now

Cain was fifteen years old when he did these things, and from that time he began to *build cities* until he had founded seven cities. . . . And after he became the father of Enoch, Cain lived 715 years and became the father of three sons and two daughters. And these are the names of this sons: Olad, Lizaf, Fosal; and of his daughters: Citha and Maac. And all the days of Cain were 730 years, and he died.

16:1-3a:
In that time he commanded that man about the tassels. And then Korah and two hundred men with him rebelled and said, "Why is an unbearable law imposed upon us?"

And God was angry and said, "I commanded the earth, and it gave me man; and to him two sons were born first of all, and the older rose up and killed the younger, and the earth quickly swallowed up his blood. But I drove Cain out and cursed the earth and spoke to the parched land, saying, 'You will swallow up blood no more.' And now the thoughts of men are very corrupt; behold I command the earth, and it will swallow up body and soul together. And their dwelling place will be in darkness and the place of destruction; and they will not die but melt away until I remember the world and renew the earth."

Jubilees (OTP 2:61, 64)

This document, which recounts the things revealed to Moses during the forty days he spent on Mount Sinai, was produced in the second century B.C. (between 161 and 140 B.C.), and was written by a Palestinian Jew, probably from a priestly family.

4:1-6:
And in the third week in the second jubilee, she bore Cain. And in the fourth she bore Abel. And in the fifth she bore 'Awan, his daughter. And at the beginning of the third jubilee, Cain killed Abel because the sacrifice of Abel was accepted, but the offering of Cain was not accepted. And he killed him in the field, and his blood cried out from the earth to heaven, making accusation because he killed him. And the LORD rebuked Cain on account of Abel because he killed him. And he made him a fugitive on the earth because of the blood of his brother. And he cursed him upon the earth. And therefore it is written in the heavenly tablets, "Cursed is one who strikes his fellow with malice. And all who have seen and heard shall say 'so be it.' And the man who saw and did not report (it) shall be cursed like him." Therefore when we come before the LORD our God we will make known all the sins

which occur in heaven and earth and which are in the light or in the darkness or in any (place).

4:31-32:

At the end of that jubilee Cain was killed one year after him [Adam]. And his house fell upon him, and he died in the midst of his house. And he was killed by its stones because he killed Abel with a stone, and with a stone he was killed by righteous judgment. Therefore it is ordained in the heavenly tablets:

> "With the weapons with which a man kills his fellow
> he shall be killed;
> just as he wounded him,
> thus shall they do to him."

Testament of Benjamin 7:1-5 (*OTP* 1:827)

The *Testaments of the Twelve Patriarchs*, of which the *Testament of Benjamin* is a part, was written by a Hellenised Jew, possibly in Syria sometime after 250 B.C. The *Testaments of the Twelve Patriarchs* purport to be the final utterances of the twelve sons of Jacob.

> "So I tell you, my children, flee from the evil of Beliar, because he offers a sword to those who obey him. And the sword is the mother of the seven evils; it receives them through Beliar: The first is moral corruption, the second is destruction, the third is oppression, the fourth is captivity, the fifth is want, the sixth is turmoil, the seventh is desolation. It is for this reason that Cain was handed over by God for seven punishments, for in every hundredth year the Lord brought upon him one plague. When he was two hundred years old suffering began and in his nine hundredth year he was deprived of life. For he was condemned on account of Abel his brother as a result of all his evil deeds, but Lamech was condemned by seventy times seven. Until eternity those who are like Cain in their moral corruption and hatred of brother shall be punished with a similar judgment.

Heb 11:4 (NIV)

> By faith Abel offered God a better sacrifice than Cain did. By faith he was commended as a righteous man, when God spoke well of his offerings. And by faith he still speaks, even though he is dead.

Jude 11 (NIV)

Woe to them! They have taken the way of Cain; they have rushed for profit into Balaam's error; they have been destroyed in Korah's rebellion.

1 John 3:11-12 (NIV)

This is the message you heard from the beginning: We should love one another. Do not be like Cain, who belonged to the evil one and murdered his brother. And why did he murder him? Because his own actions were evil and his brother's were righteous.

Index of Modern Authors

Index of Biblical and Extrabiblical Literature